Herron's
Price Guide to Dolls
and Paper Dolls

R. Lane Herron

Library of Congress
Catalog Number 81-50508

ISBN 0-87069-364-6

10 9 8 7 6 5 4 3 2 1

Cover photograph by Perry Struse, West Des Moines,
Iowa. German-made Queen Louise, #287, 23" tall,
courtesy of Yvonne's Doll Spa, Ankeny, Iowa.

Published by

Wallace-Homestead Book Company
1912 Grand Avenue
Des Moines, Iowa 50305

To my brother

Joseph Samuel Herron,

with affection,

for his enthusiasm in

my work and collections.

Contents

Key to Abbreviations 6
Acknowledgments 7
Preface 8
1 French Dolls 11
2 German Bisque Socket and Shoulder Heads 32
3 German Babies and Toddlers 59
4 Miniature Dolls—the Tinies 78
5 China Head Dolls 100
6 Parians .`. 121
7 Wax Dolls 129
8 Wax-Over Dolls 133
9 Old Papier-Mache and Composition Heads 139
10 Wooden Dolls 149
11 Fabric Dolls 156
12 Odd-Material Dolls 167
13 Popular 20th Century Dolls 183
14 The Shirley Temples 213
15 Effanbee Dolls 217
16 The Effanbee Patsy Line 223
17 Paper Dolls 226
Meet the Author 240

Key to Abbreviations

BJ	Ball-jointed	mld	Molded
c	Circa	OCM	Open-closed mouth
cir	Circumference	OM	Open mouth
CM	Closed mouth	pc	Piece
compo	Composition	PE	Pierced ears
HHW	Human hair wig	PI	Pierced-in ears
jtd	Jointed	PN	Pierced nostrils
lt	Light	ptd	Painted
mache	Papier-mache	PW	Paperweight

Acknowledgments

The author wishes to express a debt of gratitude to the following collectors for the use of their precious doll photographs in this book: Mrs. D. Kay Crow, Mrs. Sheila Scheetz, Mrs. Mildred Seeley, Mrs. D. Van Baaren (Sunny Lupton), and Mrs. Elva Weems. A special thanks to my friends R, E, and M, who sent photographs and wished to remain anonymous.

I also wish to extend a special thanks to Mrs. Lita Wilson of NIADA who introduced me to the collections of Mrs. Crow, Mrs. Scheetz, and Mrs. Van Baaren, and to my editors Ginger Van Blaricom and Liz Fletcher for their laborious tasks.

Mrs. Scheetz's dolls were photographed by Edward A. Ekis. Phil Spittler photographed those belonging to Elva Weems. The remainder of the dolls pictured were photographed by their owners, with the exception of those owned by the author.

Preface

Nowadays, when I visit even the most ordinary doll and toy shop, I am immediately taken aback—even outraged—at the prices of the cheaply made toys on display. For dolls *are* toys, or once were, despite their present untouchable status. I suddenly get the peculiar impression that these high-priced items made of vinyl, plastic, fabric, and porcelain are no longer made for children. Who in their right mind would pay fifty dollars or more for a doll to be used as a mere "plaything"?

Needless to say, doll and toy manufacturers are cashing in on the lucrative doll collecting market. Their dolls are instant collectibles in competition with the mind-boggling prices of old dolls. This contrived trend has turned the hobby of collecting dolls completely upside down and opened the door to profiteers and speculators—people who can afford to gamble their money on dolls and related collectibles. The doll hobby is no longer a collectors' market. But there isn't an ill wind that doesn't blow *some* good. Collecting dolls has become a good investment, as dolls sell faster than any other collectible. And people will always collect dolls.

I can well remember a time when a collector hesitated to spend $200 on a popular Bru. The year? 1960. Today, at an auction, a collector might pay as much as $20,000 for a Bru without batting an eyelash. Such is the faith collectors have in their chosen field of investment. In the 1940s, Eleanor St. George, one of the most prominent doll historians and authorities, lamented the high price of dolls. She was afraid then that the high prices would eventually destroy the hobby. Now, over thirty years later, the hobby hasn't been destroyed, but it has definitely separated the rich from the poor. Price-forcing has placed French dolls and the rare German character dolls completely out of the market for 99 percent of the people who truly enjoy doll collecting, forcing them to collect dolls they wouldn't have collected twenty years ago!

Inflation alone decrees a 10 to 20 percent increase almost every year. Dolls, like everything else, should be restricted to the normal inflationary amount and not be price-forced as much as double or triple in one year! We know what happens to castles built on a foundation of sand. One of the most respected dealers in the field states, "We feel collectors should remember that this is truly a hobby not a business or investment program, and get to the old philosophy of enjoying the dolls themselves for their beauty and their antiquity and the interesting stories which revolve around them." I wholeheartedly agree. Nonetheless, dolls have now reached a certain level of "value," and they do sell at these prices. Nothing short of a complete collapse of the world money market will upset this applecart, at least not for a while.

This book is based on a great deal of research into the present pricing field. I've been interested in old dolls since the age of five, when I was taken from antiques shop to antiques shop and auction house to auction house by an enthusiastic father who loved antiques and enjoyed being around dealers and auctioneers. I can still vividly recall a barrel of antique dolls and toys which my father purchased at an auction. He gave them to me for play. My doll research began during my junior high school days and has continued to this day. There isn't a doll type I haven't handled, inspected, and loved dearly. Hence, doing research on this book, though time-consuming, was highly interesting.

Doll prices will vary. And pricing a doll at a heady amount doesn't always mean one will get that price. It's easier to go down in price than it is to go up, most sellers reason. Auction prices are not stable, as they are built on competition, hysteria, and greed. People love to outdo each other. Still, auctions often bring the highest prices. Collectors will often sell dolls for less, as do some antiques shop owners. Show prices are usually higher due to the high overhead, travel, and other expenses. Consequently, doll prices fluctuate.

The prices given here are high and low averages, possibly even the true worth of your doll at the present. But, again, your doll might bring less or considerably more on the open market. Value is always in the eye of the beholder. Many unseasoned collectors are paying French prices for run-of-the-mill doll types, such as Armand Marseille. Before a novice collector buys any doll, he or she should study the market first. At a recent flea market, I saw a neophyte pay an outlandish price for a beautifully frocked Toni doll by Ideal, simply because the seller said the doll was porcelain and antique!

For over a decade I have declined offers to write a price book, fearing I would price myself and my friends out of a hobby. Well, I didn't have to worry about that. An avalanche of doll price books *did* price us out of the market! And how! Since that time I have become a *free,* walking price guide. I can't make a public appearance at a flea market, antiques show, or friend's house without being asked to price a doll. Most appraisers quote a fee. But how does a walking price guide do this without losing a friend? Some people even use my name, after I have appraised a doll, for selling purposes. If R. Lane Herron said a doll was worth such and such, well then, it must be worth that much—or more! Thus, when my publisher Don Brown suggested a doll price book, I finally acquiesced. The task was a difficult one. There seemed to be no end to the dolls that needed evaluating. And it seems I have only scratched the surface.

Clothing should never affect the price of a doll, as dolls should *always* be dressed— especially since the prices being asked are usually "top." Original or old clothes are usually worn and faded, so how can they add much to a doll's true value? What *is* of interest to the collector paying the ultimate dollar are condition, degree of originality, and good markings. Only *mint* speciments merit top dollar. That means (since the most expensive dolls are china or bisque) no cracks, no chips, no repaired or overhauled bodies, and no replaced parts. A tiny chip the size of a pinhead at the corner of an eye, or a missing bisque finger or two, does not devaluate the doll. Nor does a flawless (and minor) mending job where dolls have been expertly refired. A large chunk out of a doll's face is something else again.

Expensive dolls should always have the original wig or a quality human hair replacement. A bald head, however, cannot devaluate a doll. Do *not* be conned into paying thousands of dollars for just a head. A head without the original body or limbs cannot command the price of a complete doll. Again, do not expect an ancient Queen Anne wooden doll, a Montanari wax doll, a rubber doll, an old papier-mache, composition, celluloid, or rawhide doll to be in mint condition. These dolls do have their scuffs and flaws, and this must be taken into consideration. What you are buying is antiquity. Again, top price means an original old body and limbs, flawed though they may be. Remember, too, dolls in great-grandmother's day were toys. That means they were played with.

Paper dolls are next to dolls in desirability, though fortunately they are not as overpriced. Paper doll collectors, unlike doll collectors, have tried to keep prices down by trading and buying among themselves. However, a number of reproductions are selling for prices almost as high as the prices for the bona fide product. If this practice continues, dealers will eventually price themselves out of business.

To demand top dollar, paper dolls must be mint and uncut. The next best thing is the cut doll, mint, with her complete mint wardrobe. Dolls with missing limbs and incomplete wardrobes are sold for whatever the seller can get. Remember, value is always in the eye of the beholder. No one is ever forced into buying anything.

For years we have been brainwashed into believing that French dolls are best, a closed mouth is better, and that character, googly, black, portrait, and rare hairdo dolls should be collected by any means. So what happened to the ordinary dolls, the homely dolls, the so-called "perishable" dolls, and the unwanteds? Well, while the popular damsels disappeared from the market, the less popular dolls such as the common chinas, parians, papier-mache, composition, fabric, wax, celluloid, rawhide, and other odd-material dolls, leveled in price and remained in a steady bracket. In some cases, they even dropped somewhat in price. Which proves a point: popularity, not age or rarity, governs doll prices. In another generation, however, this trend may reverse itself, and those who collected these charming playthings will be happy they did.

1
French Dolls

Though not always manufactured in France, the French doll has become the most coveted, high-priced doll in toy history. Most of the early French dolls were actually made in Germany and given French characteristics. The only French connections are the costume, the accessories, and the labeled box. Later French dolls were custom-made, while the German dolls were mass-produced. Hence, more detail was given to marketing and wardrobe. French dolls were also later made in New York.

There was a rather tenuous period between 1900 and World War I when Germany once again began to manufacture dolls for the French export market. It was not until after the war that the French regained their weak hold on the doll market. Their product, in many instances, was even gaudier. (But, we can find closed-mouth "French" dolls conceived in the 1920s that can stand alongside one made in the 1880s and almost fool an expert.)

Unfortunately, any high-quality unmarked doll is instantly denoted French, and any poor quality doll is considered German, often erroneously. The French made their share of assembly-line mediocre dolls. As a rule, the Germans were the best modelers, with their dolls looking more like real children. The French dolls, even those of the finest quality, look overly decorated.

The list of French dolls which follows includes the types most often found in collections, in shops, and at auctions. They are all in good condition and, for the most part, original in every way. Lesser examples cannot command these prices.

6¾", Belton Child. Solid-dome head with two holes, CM, brown glass eyes, skin wig, flange neck, early wooden body........ **$500-600**

7½", Jumeau Child. Blue glass eyes, OM, mohair wig, BJ body, original Arabic costume. Tag on costume reads: "Bebe Jumeau—Paris Exposition" ...**$1,200-1,500**

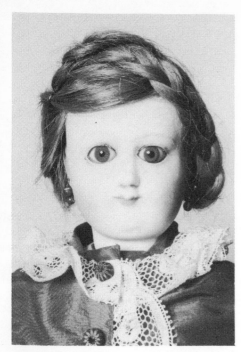

An Unmarked French Fashion with a most unusual smirking expression, 18", kid body, parian bisque quality, $1,200.

A Closed-Mouth Jumeau, 16", $2,100.

8½", Maker Unknown, French Fashion. Rare mld cafe au lait hair, early 1800s hairstyle, CM, ptd blue eyes, lt brown lid lines, red nose dots, beautifully sewn miniature kid fashion body, kid arms, long drawers and old clothes, very rare type and size **$2,000-2,500**

9", Gaultier Boy. Mohair wig, CM, PW eyes, BJ body **$895-995**

9", Steiner Child. Mohair wig, CM, PW eyes, BJ body, original clothes, cloisonne watch. Mark: "Flae A-4" **$1,200-1,300**

10", Bru Jne 0. Incised on shoulders, bisque shoulder head and lower arms, CM, PW eyes, HHW, gusseted kid body **$1,750-1,850**

10", Emile Jumeau Child. Mohair wig, CM, PW eyes, BJ body, straight wrists (this is the rare size) **$1,500-2,000**

10", Gaultier Child. Blue-gray eyes, CM, PE, HHW, BJ body, straight wrists. Bisque socket head incised: "F2G" **$1,950-2,200**

10", Gaultier Child. Straight legs, CM, PW eyes, unpierced ears, compo BJ body with straight wrists, HHW. Incised: "F.G." (in scroll) and "1" (back of head) **$675-795**

10", Gaultier Child. Size 1, BJ body, CM, PW eyes and also Jumeau stamped HHW **$1,400-1,500**

10", Maker Unknown, French Fashion. Mohair wig, CM, PW eyes, kid body and kid arms **$695-795**

10½", E. Denamur Belgian Milk Girl. Pupil-less glass eyes, OM with four teeth, HHW, crude body, straight wrists, original outfit, including costume, wooden shoes, sabots, and milk cans **$795-895**

11", Belton Child. Three holes, CM, PW eyes, HHW, pale smooth bisque, BJ body, straight wrists **$600-700**

11", Jumeau Portrait Type. Bisque socket head, CM, brown PW eyes, mohair wig, BJ body **$1,500-1,800**

11", Steiner Child. Skin wig, CM, PE, PW eyes, BJ body. Incised: 'STA" **$1,300-1,400**

11½", Unmarked Gaultier French Fashion. Bisque swivel head on bisque shoulder plate, CM, PE, PW eyes, mohair wig, kid fashion body and arms **$725-825**

11¾", Maker Unknown, Child Fashion. Swivel head, CM, bisque lower arms, PW eyes, skin wig, fashion body **$795-895**

12", Belton Child. Socket head with a flat solid top and two small holes (some Beltons have three holes), CM, PW eyes, HHW, BJ body, ptd shoes and socks, straight wrists......................... **$700-800**

12", Bru Jne 1. Bisque head, bisque lower arms, CM, PW eyes, HHW, gusseted kid body **$1,900-2,000**

12", Jumeau Child. Blue PW eyes, CM, mohair wig, unmarked head on marked BJ body **$1,400-1,500**

12", Maker Unknown, French Fashion. Incised "O" on each shoulder, CM, blue PW eyes, mohair wig, cork pate, kid body and arms **$850-950**

A Talking Jumeau, 22", bellows activated by pulling cords, "10" incised on back of head, French markings on body, OM, PE, dressed by owner, $2,000.

12", Maker Unknown, French Fashion Bride. Bisque shoulder head, CM, PW eyes, mohair wig, kid body and arms, PE, original bridal gown, veil, and bouquet **$875-975**

12", Negro Bru. Circle and dot mark, "Bru" incised on shoulder plate, bisque lower arms, dark kid body, wooden lower legs, PE, PW eyes, black mohair wig, CM ... **$5,000-6,000**

12", Rabery & Delphieu Child. CM, PW eyes, HHW, BJ body, rare size **$1,250-1,400**

12", Schmitt & Fils Child. Mohair wig with cork pate, CM, PW eyes, PE, straight wrists, BJ body. Mark: shield with crossed hammers and "SCH".................. **$2,500-3,000**

12", Tete Jumeau. Signed, CM, brown glass eyes, mohair wig, BJ body. Mark: "Depose Tete Jumeau Bte SGDG 6".... **$1,400-1,600**

12½", Gaultier Child. Mohair wig, CM, PW eyes, BJ body. Incised: "F4G" **$1,000-1,200**

12½", Jumeau French Fashion. Kid body,

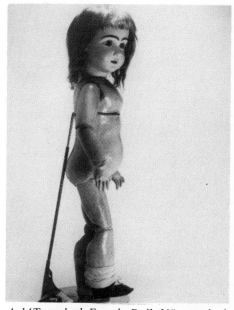

A 14T-marked French Doll, 28", rare body construction, blue PW eyes, Mil Seeley collection, $18,000.

E. Barrois French Fashion, 16", kid body, CM, Jim and Sheila Olah Scheetz collection, $2,500.

CM, PW eyes, PE, HHW. Body mark: "JUMEAU".................. **$900-1,000**

12½", S.F.B.J. 252. Pouty, CM, PW eyes, HHW, BJ body............. **$1,800-2,000**

13", Bru Jne 2. Bisque head and lower arms, CM, PW eyes, skin wig and gusseted kid body **$2,000-2,500**

13", Early Bru Child. Circle and dot mark, CM, PW eyes, 2-pc head and shoulder plate, mld bust, bisque lower arms, gusseted kid body **$2,500-3,000**

13", S.F.B.J. 215. Googly, bisque head, round glass eyes, smiling mouth, with BJ body **$3,000-3,500**

13", S.F.B.J. 235. Smiling OCM with two teeth, PW eyes, flocked hair, BJ body with original sticker.............. **$1,000-1,200**

13", S.F.B.J. 239. Poulbot character, CM, fixed brown PW eyes, original red wig, 5 pc wood and compo body, old clothes and old cap........................ **$6,000-8,000**

13", Three-Faced Bru. Bisque head, face revolves into papier-mache cap, sweet face-cry face-serene sleeping face, tears mld on cheek for cry face, PW eyes, metal knob turns head, cloth-over-mache body, compo jtd arms and legs, marked "CB" (a similar doll, c. 1867, with two faces (sleep-wake) is worked by a lever on the shoulder) **$15,000-18,000**

13½", Jumeau Negro 1907. Brown glass eyes, OM, PE, wears a mohair wig, BJ black body, signed **$1,000-1,200**

13½", Jumeau Pouty Type. Brown PW eyes, HHW, BJ body, CM. Mark: "F3 made by Jumeau Co".................. **$950-1,200**

13½", Steiner Child. Straight wrists, CM, PW eyes, PE, HHW, BJ body. Head incised: "Steiner Paris A-5".......... **$1,450-1,600**

14", E. Barrois French Fashion. Swivel neck, CM, PE, PW eyes, mohair wig, bisque lower arms, kid body **$1,700-1,800**

14", Belton Child. Three holes, CM, PW eyes, skin wig, BJ body, straight wrists........................ **$895-995**

14

14", Bisque-Hip Steiner. Bisque swivel head on bisque shoulder plate, PW eyes, CM, skin wig, dome head, cloth joins legs, arms, and torso, squeeze box **$5,000-6,000**

14", Brevete Bru. Mohair wig, CM, lt blue PW eyes, cork pate, bisque socket head on bisque shoulder plate, lower bisque arms, gusseted kid body. Mark: "Bebe Brevete SGDG, Paris." (Although the face of this doll resembles the Bru, the true origin remains a mystery. It's possibly a Bru socket head on another French or German body. The bisque hands are not Bru, and the straight edges around the shoulder plate do not have the familiar Bru scalloped edges) .. **$2,500-3,000**

14", Jumeau Negro 1907. Black HHW, OM, PE, brown glass eyes, BJ black compo body, marked **$1,000-1,200**

14", Jumeau Portrait Type. Bisque socket head, CM, inset PW eyes, mohair wig with cork pate, BJ body **$1,750-1,850**

14", Maker Unknown, French Fashion. Shoulder head, CM, PW eyes, HHW, bisque lower arms, kid body, kid-covered wooden upper arms, well-dressed **$950-1,100**

14", Schmitt & Fils Child. CM, PE, PW eyes, HHW, BJ body, body marked with hammers and a shield. Incised on head: "Bte SGDG..................... **$2,900-3,250**

14", S.F.B.J. 3. Googly, large round flirty eyes, HHW, BJ body **$6,000-7,000**

14", S.F.B.J. 60. Brown glass sleep eyes, OM, HHW, BJ body **$395-495**

14", Tete Jumeau. Deep PW eyes, OM, PE, cork pate, HHW, BJ body **$1,500-1,600**

14", Tete Jumeau. CM, PW eyes, HHW, BJ body, body and head marked .. **$1,500-1,600**

15", Emile Jumeau Male French Fashion. Rare bisque shoulder head, CM, PW eyes, HHW, pink kid body, dressed in original Audubon Mardi Gras costume (red silk turban, red silk pants, blue lace over - blouse gold jacket and original belt)..................... **$4,000-5,000**

Gaultier Automaton on Music Box, wind key, CM, all-original, c. 1860, Jim and Sheila Olah Scheetz collection, $2,000.

Gaultier French Fashion, 17", kid body, CM, D. Kay Crow collection, $1,500.

15

French Fashion, 16½", Steiner mark, CM, all-original, old clothes, D. Kay Crow collection, $1,800.

Clara Maid 1267, 20", bisque reproduction of French Steiner, all-original, marked, D. Kay Crow collection, $3,000.

15", Gaultier Child. Straight wrists, OM with teeth, PW eyes, HHW, BJ body $1,500-2,000

15", Jumeau Child. Blue PW eyes, HHW, BJ body, OM, unmarked $350-500

15", Maker Unknown, French Fashion. Unpierced ears, CM, PW eyes, fine pale bisque, mohair wig, kid arms $895-995

15", Mechanical Belton. Squeeze tummy and he clasps his cymbals, original costume and wig, OCM, PW eyes.......... $1,200-1,500

15", Portrait Jumeau. Signed body, CM, violet-blue glass eyes, blond curly mohair wig, BJ body, unjointed wrists $1,800-2,000

15", Rabery & Delphieu Child. Pale bisque, CM, PW eyes, HHW, BJ body $1,400-1,500

15", S.F.B.J. 237. Boy, OM with teeth, blue jewel eyes, flocked hair, BJ body $1,300-1,400

15", S.F.B.J. 238. Mechanical torso, PW eyes, OCM with mld teeth $3,000-3,500

15", Steiner Child. CM, PW eyes, HHW, BJ body, signed................. $1,600-1,700

15", Steiner Walker. Bisque head, OM with upper and lower teeth, fixed PW eyes, kid upper body and upper arms, bisque lower arms, lower body cone-shaped and dressed, inside cone is the mechanism that walks the doll, "Steiner" mark on bellows. Mark: "J. Steiner, Bte. SGDG, Paris." This doll rolls across the floor, raises her arm, and cries "mama" $2,000-2,500

15½", Gaultier Child. Tip of tongue sculpted between lips, PW eyes, skin wig, stockinet body with wire frame. Head incised: "F4G." Body marked: "Gesland"...... $2,800-3,000

15½", Nursing Bru. Blue glass sleep eyes, OM, HHW, BJ compo body $4,000-4,500

15½", S.F.B.J. 227. Character boy, OCM, blue sleep eyes, BJ body $950-1,100

16", Bru Circle & Dot. Bisque lower arms, OCM with mld teeth, PE, PW eyes, skin wig, mld bosom with tinted nipples, pink kid-gusseted body **$4,500-5,000**

16", Bru Jne R. OM, PW eyes, PE, HHW, BJ body **$1,500-1,600**

16", E. Denamur Negro Girl. Black mohair wig, CM, PW eyes, PE, black BJ Jumeau body (since most E. Denamur's are found on Jumeau bodies, the Denamur dolls may have Jumeau connections) **$1,800-2,000**

16", Gaultier Child. Bisque shoulder head, CM, PW eyes, mohair wig, bisque lower arms, kid-gusseted body with stitched toes **$1,400-1,500**

16", Gaultier French Fashion. Mohair wig, kid body, kid arms, CM, PW eyes, "3" incised on head. Mark on shoulder plate: "FG" **$1,450-1,600**

16", Gaultier Negro French Fashion. Black wig, CM, PW eyes, brown kid body, brown kid arms, dressed as a very fashionable lady with hat, fancy underclothes, shoes, stockings, incised head **$2,000-3,000**

Jumeau, 13", "V" mark on head, CM, pale bisque quality, straight wrists, D. Kay Crow collection, $2,000.

16", Gaultier Negro French Fashion. Black fuzzy wig, CM, PW eyes, kid body, kid arms, dressed as a fancy gentleman, original costume, incised head **$2,500-3,500**

16", Jumeau Child. Blue glass sleep eyes, OM, straight wrists, blond HHW, BJ body. Signed on head: "S.F.B.J." **$500-700**

16" Maker Unknown, Dome-Head Fashion. Cobalt-blue eyes, CM, wears a mohair wig, kid body **$1,350-1,500**

16", Maker Unknown, Early French Fashion. Shoulder head, gray PW eyes, CM, skin wig, kid body and arms **$975-1,200**

16", Maker Unknown, French Fashion. Smiling CM, PW eyes, HHW, kid body and arms. Shoulder head incised: "E" **$895-995**

16", S.F.B.J. 235. Character boy with OCM, mld blond hair, blue jewel eyes and a toddler BJ body **$1,275-1,375**

16½", E. Denamur Child. OM, PW eyes, HHW, BJ body **$650-750**

Long-Faced Jumeau, 18", marked "8" on back of neck, CM, old clothes, D. Kay Crow collection, $3,000-4,000.

Jumeau, 21", marked "Jumeau" in red, CM, body marked ".TRNY. BEBE," modern clothes, D. Kay Crow collection, $2,300.

Jumeau, 17", body mark only, CM, $2,100.

16½", S.F.B.J. 233. Screaming boy, solid dome, mld blond hair, blue jewel eyes, OCM with mld teeth, BJ body **$2,000-2,500**

16½", Steiner Child. Marked body and head, CM, PW eyes, mohair wig, PE, BJ body, straight wrists **$1,700-1,800**

17", E. Barrois French Fashion. Swivel neck, PW eyes, PE, CM, mohair wig, kid body, bisque lower arms, early French bisque. Marked on front shoulder plate: "E. Depose B" **$2,000-2,500**

17", Bru Jne 5. Negro, dark brown bisque socket head on shoulder plate, dark bisque lower arms, Bru hands, brown kid jtd body, brown wooden lower legs, CM, PW eyes, PE, wears gold earrings, black lamb's wool wig. Small cross incised on back of head. Paper sticker on chest reads: "Bebe Bru Bte SGDG. Tout contrefacteur sera saisy et pour suivi conformament a la Loi" **$7,000-8,000**

17", E. Denamur Child. OM, PW eyes, HHW, BJ body, c. 1857 (initials are also on dolls made by E. Dumont and others)........................**$850-950**

17", E. Denamur 10. Large brown PW eyes, CM, pug nose, thick brows, PE, HHW, BJ body, Jumeau-signed **$1,200-1,500**

17", Fleischmann & Blodel Eden Bebe. Mohair wig, PW eyes, PE, BJ body, OM. Head mark: "Eden Bebe Paris" ...**$750-850**

17", Gaultier Child. Papier-mache swivel head on pressed wood plate, OCM, PW eyes, mohair wig, stockinet body stamped "Gesland," rare **$3,000-4,000**

17", Lady Jumeau. Very rare, bisque swivel head on bisque shoulder plate, fully modeled bosom, bisque lower arms, beautiful hands, bisque lower legs (very shapely, with rare molded-on high-heeled shoes covered with original fabric), kid body with small waist and protruding buttocks, HHW, fixed PW eyes, CM, PE, dressed to type. Mark: "Jumeau-Medaille D'Or—Paris".......**$5,000-7,000**

17", Maker Unknown, French Fashion. Swivel head on bisque shoulder plate, CM, PW eyes, PE, kid body, HHW (this is the rare type with the long bisque arms and the kid-

over-wood upper arms—with a swivel
socket) **$1,400-1,500**

17", Rabery & Delphieu Child. CM, PW eyes,
PE, HHW. Mark: "R.O.D." ... **$1,650-1,750**

17", Schmitt & Fils Child. Mohair wig, CM,
PW eyes, BJ body with the familiar
protruding buttocks. Mark: hammers and
shield **$3,200-3,500**

17", Steiner Child. Wears a mohair wig, CM,
PW eyes, BJ body. Incised: "Steiner FC 12
Paris" **$1,750-2,000**

17", Steiner Kicker. Semi-mechanical, bisque
head **$1,350-1,500**

17½", Bebe Phenix Steiner. Mohair wig, OM,
PW eyes, fine bisque quality, BJ body. Head
incised: "Star 90" **$795-895**

17½", Jumeau-Marked French Fashion.
Bisque shoulder head with mld bosom, CM,
PW eyes, PE, mohair wig, bisque lower arms,
kid body **$2,700-3,000**

*Jumeau, 21", marked "TETE JUMEAU" on
head in red ink, OM with teeth, wears old
handmade silk and lace dress and underwear,
D. Kay Crow collection, $900.*

17½", Steiner Child. Wears a mohair wig,
CM, PW eyes, BJ body, straight wrists. Mark:
"Ste A" **$1,750-1,850**

18", E. Barrois French Fashion. Bisque swivel
head on shoulder plate, CM, PW eyes, skin
wig, bisque lower arms, wooden upper
arms covered with gesso, rare twill body,
wooden lower legs covered with
gesso **$2,450-3,000**

18", Belton Child. Two holes, CM, PW
eyes, HHW, BJ body, straight
wrists...................... **$1,300-1,400**

18", Bru Jne 6. Skin wig and cork pate, CM,
PW eyes, bisque lower arms, wooden lower
legs, gusseted kid body **$5,850-6,000**

18", Fleischmann & Blodel Eden Bebe. Early
BJ body, unjointed wrists, CM, PW eyes,
PE, HHW. Head mark: "Eden
Bebe" **$1,200-1,300**

18", Gaultier Child. Tip of tongue sculpted in
a Bru-type mouth, rare green PW eyes, PE,
HHW, pale bisque, stockinet body, CM.
Incised: "F6G".............. **$3,500-4,000**

*Jumeau, 17", red "V" mark, square teeth,
OM, stationary eyes, kid body, old white
muslin embroidered dress, D. Kay Crow
collection, $795.*

Unmarked French Fashion, kid body, CM, old clothes, D. Kay Crow collection, $750.

Unmarked French Fashion with a Bru look, 18", stationary eyes, CM, PE, new clothes, D. Kay Crow collection, $2,000.

18", Gaultier & Fils French Fashion. Child with fully articulated wooden body, swivel waist, CM, PW eyes, skin wig, "F.G." incised on back of head **$3,500-4,000**

18", Jumeau French Fashion. Swivel neck, CM, rare body construction, kid-over-wood upper arms, jtd bisque lower arms, jtd wood over kid lower and upper legs, kid-over-wood body, blue PW eyes, bisque shoulder head, signed **$2,200-2,700**

18", Lazarski Mascotte. Incised head and marked body, CM, PE, bulgy blue glass eyes, HHW, BJ body, jtd wrists **$2,000-2,500**

18", Maker Unknown, French Fashion. Swivel-head shoulder plate, CM, kid-over-wood articulated body, bisque lower arms and legs, PW eyes, mohair wig **$2,500-3,000**

18", Nursing Bru. Dark blue PW eyes, OM, PE, HHW, kid body, kid-over-wood upper arms, jtd bisque lower arms, bisque tone more florid than most. Head incised on back: "Bru Jne 8" **$6,000-7,000**

18", Rabery & Delphieu Child. PW eyes, OM, PE, HHW, BJ body, c. 1856. Mark on body: "R.4D **$495-595**

18", S.F.B.J. Laughing Jumeau 236. Blue sleep eyes, eyelashes, mohair wig, BJ toddler body, OCM **$800-1,000**

18", S.F.B.J. 247. Blue sleep eyes, OCM, mohair wig, BJ toddler body **$2,000-2,500**

18", S.F.B.J. 301. Adult, OM with teeth, blue sleep eyes, HHW, BJ body **$495-595**

18", Steiner Child. Large blue PW eyes, OM with teeth, HHW, BJ body **$900-1,000**

18", Tete Jumeau. Flirty glass eyes, OM, HHW, BJ body. This late 1938 signed Jumeau has a rather open, modern face quite unlike earlier dolls **$450-650**

18", Two-Faced Jumeau. Smile-cry faces, hood, PW eyes, bisque head, mohair wig, BJ body, rare, signed **$3,000-4,000**

18½", Gaultier French Fashion. Kid-covered wooden body, kid arms, stitched fingers, CM,

PW eyes, HHW, head and shoulder plate signed **$1,795-1,900**

18½", Negro Bru. Circle and dot mark, dark bisque shoulder head and lower arms. CM, PW eyes, kid body **$9,000-10,000**

18½", Schmitt & Fils Child. Head incised with hammers and shield, CM, PW eyes, HHW, BJ body, straight wrists **$3,500-4,000**

19", Depose Tete Jumeau Bte SGDG. Early type, pale fine bisque quality, blue PW eyes, CM, mohair wig, BJ body **$2,000-2,500**

19", Gaultier Child. Attached to a music box, OM, PW eyes, mohair wig, dressed as music instructor with high, pointed cap and long coat, music questions written in French on skirt **$1,200-1,500**

19", Gaultier Child. Mohair wig, CM, PW eyes, BJ body, straight wrists .. **$1,900-2,000**

19", Jumeau Child. Blue PW eyes, PE, HHW, BJ body, CM, marked **$2,200-2,500**

19", Jumeau Child. Marked, OM, blue glass flirty eyes, mohair wig, BJ body **$950-1,100**

19", Jumeau Child. Sleep eyes, OM, PE, HHW, BJ body. Mark: "Dep 8".......................... **$750-900**

19", Jumeau Child. Ball head with string holes through the top (holds head to body), CM, compo head, blue PW eyes, HHW, BJ body. Head inscribed in ink: "2nd Modelle Jumeau 1877"..................... **$1,500-2,000**

19", Jumeau Marie Antoinette. French-fashion lady type, large blue glass fixed eyes, swivel neck, shoulder plate, CM, PE, original white mohair wig, kid body, leather arms, stitched fingers, elaborate original court costume. Mark: "JUMEAU-Medaille D'Or Paris" **$2,000-3,000**

19", Jumeau-Marked French Fashion. Bisque swivel head on shoulder plate, no bosom modeling, PW eyes, CM, HHW, leather arms, stitched fingers, kid body **$3,000-3,500**

19", Long-Faced Cody Jumeau. Pale smooth

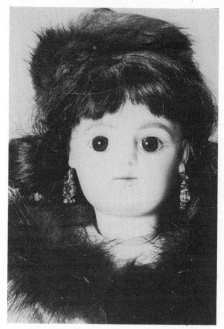

Gaultier Brown-Eyed French Fashion, 17½", kid body, $1,600.

Bisque Head of Man in Scottish Costume, 11", marked "JE Masson Lorraine A.L. & C. Limoges," OCM, glass eyes, $425.

French Bisque Socket Head, 22", marked "Depose Fabrication Francaise Favorite No. 6 Ed Tasson Alec 10 Limoges," typical French face, $795.

S.F.B.J. 60 PARIS 0, 16", bisque head, OM, brown glass eyes, BJ compo body, Jim and Sheila Olah Scheetz collection, $575.

bisque, CM, large blue PW eyes, blond curly mohair wig, applied ears with deep canals, early Jumeau-signed BJ body, straight wrists, original clothes (including signed Jumeau shoes), rare size **$3,000-4,000**

19", Maker Unknown, French Fashion. Bisque head and limbs, CM, wood-articulated body, PW eyes, mohair wig . . . **$2,500-3,000**

19", Princess Elizabeth Jumeau. Flirty glass eyes, mohair wig, BJ body, CM. Mark: "UNIS FRANCE 71-149 306 JUMEAU 1938 PARIS" **$795-1,000**

19", Steiner Child. Mohair wig, BJ body, straight wrists, OM, PW eyes, PE. Mark on head reads: "A-13 Paris, Le Parisien" **$950-1,100**

20", Bru French Fashion. Shoulder mark only, mld eyelids, PW eyes, CM, faint smile on lips, lamb's wool wig, kid body and arms, stitched fingers **$1,750-1,850**

20", Jumeau Child. Brown PW eyes, OM, mohair wig, BJ body, unmarked head. Body mark: "Bebe Jumeau" **$825-925**

20", Maker Unknown, Portrait Fashion. A true portrait with fine detail, CM, PW eyes, HHW, kid body and arms **$2,000-3,000**

20", Portrait Lady Bru. The face of this rare doll resembles a human being, and is often called Marie Antoinette. Shoulder-head type with fairly long neck, inset blue glass eyes, CM, bisque lower arms, gusseted kid body (fashion type), original white mohair wig, original court costume. Incised on shoulder plate: "M. Bru" **$15,000-17,000**

20", Rabery & Delphieu Child. CM, PW eyes, HHW, BJ body **$1,800-2,000**

20", Schmitt & Fils Child. Unmarked, CM, PW eyes, wears a mohair wig, BJ body (don't confuse these dolls with the early Kestners) **$1,500-2,000**

20", Surprise Bru. Bisque shoulder head, CM, lt blue fixed PW eyes, HHW with cork pate, fully articulated wooden body, hollow upper torso contains multi-disk music box which does not work, unmistakable Bru facial

22

modeling, old clothes. Right foot marked: "191-09" **$10,000-12,000**

20", Tete Jumeau. Blue PW eyes, CM, HHW, early body, rare straight legs, unjointed straight wrists, signed **$1,500-2,000**

20½", Kissing Bru. Blue glass sleep eyes, OM, PE, HHW, BJ compo body. When string is pulled, the hand moves to the mouth and throws a kiss. Doll cries with leg movement. Mark: "Bru Jne R 9" **$1,850-2,000**

20½", Oriental Bru. Usual Bru socket head and shoulder plate designed to represent an Oriental, CM, brown glass eyes, black mohair wig, kid body, bisque lower arms, wooden lower legs, original costume, "Bru Jne" incised on head and shoulder....... **$10,000-12,000**

20½", Signed Jumeau. Rare compo head, OM, blue glass eyes, HHW....... **$725-900**

21", Jumeau Child. Brown PW eyes, CM, PE, HHW, BJ body. Mark: "Medaille D'Or" and "D" **$3,000-3,500**

21", Late Jumeau Child. Large blue glass eyes, OM, PE, HHW. Mark: "Dep" **$800-900**

21", Maker Unknown, French Fashion. Wardrobe trunk and original trousseau, CM, PW eyes, curly skin wig, early kid body, arms with stitched fingers, old trunk filled with everything imaginable (clothes, hats, corset, nightgown, wedding gown and dozens of tiny accessories)................. **$3,000-4,000**

21", Maker Unknown, French Fashion Fortune-Telling Doll. Mohair wig, CM, PW eyes, kid body and arms, skirt has 340 fortunes written in French............ **$3,000-4,000**

21", Negro Steiner. Brown PW eyes, OM, mohair wig, BJ body. Head incised: "A-13 Paris" and "Le Parisien Bte SGDG 13." Body mark: "Bebe Le Parisien" **$1,250-1,500**

21", Negro Steiner. Brown PW eyes, CM, African wig, BJ body. Head incised: "A-13 Paris." Body stamped with the words "Bebe Le Parisien"................ **$1,950-2,500**

21", Phenix Steiner. Bulbous blue glass eyes, CM, fat cheeks, high-quality bisque, HHW, BJ body, straight wrists, large

French Bisque Head, 19", OM, mld bisque teeth, unmarked head with body marked "Brevette-France," Jim and Sheila Olah Scheetz collection, $1,000.

R1D, 20", CM, BJ compo body, Jim and Sheila Olah Scheetz collection, $1,350.

23

French Belton, 14", straight wrists, OCM, three holes in top of head, Jim and Sheila Olah Scheetz collection, $800.

French Fashion, 17", CM, kid body, individually stitched fingers, Jim and Sheila Olah Scheetz collection, $950.

hands with long, slender fingers, c. 1899 ....$2,000-2,500

21", S.F.B.J. 252. Pouty, CM, blue glass sleep eyes, HHW, round fat face, BJ toddler body, signed, 12" head cir $2,500-3,000

22", Bebe Petite Pas Bru. Walks and talks, bisque socket head, OM, PW eyes, HHW, BJ body, clockwork, c. 1891.....$2,500-3,000

22", E. Denamur Child. Blue PW eyes, OM, HHW, fine quality bisque, Jumeau-marked, BJ body $895-995

22", Emile Jumeau E-10 J. Bisque shoulder head, CM, applied ears, brown PW eyes, BJ body, unjointed wrists, HHW. Body stamped in red: "L Dep".............$2,500-3,000

22", Fleischmann & Blodel Eden Bebe. Walking compo body, OM, PW eyes, PE, HHW $895-995

22", Gaultier Child. Mohair wig, OM, PW eyes, BJ body $695-795

22", Maker Unknown, Male Parisian Fashion. Rare pink bisque swivel head on pink bisque shoulder plate, black glazed mld hair with fine brush marks around hairline and temples, dip waves in center of forehead, inset PW eyes, PE, CM, mld and ptd mustache, upper and lower lashes, one-stroke brows, kid body, handsome face, dressed in original costume and hat (Rajput Court), all original $4,000-5,000

22", S.F.B.J. Paris. Blue sleep eyes, OM, mld teeth, PE, HHW, BJ body, very fine bisque quality........................$650-750

22", Steiner La Petite Parisienne. Signed BJ body, CM, PW eyes, HHW ...$2,200-2,500

22", Tete Jumeau. Wire-eyed (lever operates from back of head), workable mama-papa strings, cobalt-blue PW eyes, BJ body, OM with teeth, signed $2,200-2,500

22", Walking Jumeau. Brown PW eyes, OM, HHW, BJ body. Mark on body reads: "Dep" $1,000-1,200

22½", S.F.B.J. Walker. Blue glass sleep eyes,

24

OM, HHW, BJ body, throws a big kiss when she walks, straight legs.......... **$650-750**

23", Emile Jumeau Child. Applied ears, CM, PW eyes, skin wig, peaches and cream bisque, BJ body **$2,600-3,000**

23", Lazarski Mascotte. Has blue PW eyes, CM, HHW with a signed BJ body c. 1925 .... **$2,700-3,000**

23", Tete Jumeau. Blond curly mohair wig, CM, PW eyes, PE, BJ body, unjointed wrists, head and body signed **$2,500-3,000**

24", Bru Jne R 10. Mohair wig, CM, PW eyes, gusseted kid body, bisque lower arms and hands **$7,500-8,000**

24", Bru Jne 9. Fine kid body, CM, PW eyes, HHW, bisque lower arms, hand-carved wooden legs. Chest label: "Bebe Bru Bte SGDG." Incised on shoulder plate: "Bru Jne 9"......................... **$8,500-9,000**

24", Gaultier Child. Applied ears, PW eyes, wears a mohair wig, CM, "FG9" incised on head. "Bebe Gesland" stamped on stockinet body **$3,700-4,000**

24", Jumeau Phonograph Doll. Blue Jumeau stamp, winding key, OM, PW eyes, PE, mohair wig, BJ compo body with open stomach which houses phonograph. Incised: "Jumeau 230—Paris" **$1,600-1,800**

24", S.F.B.J. 234. Character baby, smiling mouth, very rare **$3,500-4,500**

24", Steiner Child. Very pale bisque, CM, PW eyes, HHW, BJ body, head and body are marked **$3,000-4,000**

24", Steiner Walker. Semi - mechanical, bisque head, CM, PW eyes, skin wig........................ **$2,500-3,000**

25", Steiner Child. Steiner label on body, PW eyes, CM, PE, BJ body, straight wrists, "A-17" incised on head **$3,500-4,000**

26", E. Denamur Child. Large blue PW eyes, OM, PE, HHW, straight wrists, BJ Jumeau body, signed................ **$1,000-1,200**

26", Jumeau Child. Blue PW eyes, CM, skin

Portrait Jumeau, 16", marked "6," CM, straight wrists, eyeshadow, BJ body, Jim and Sheila Olah Scheetz collection, $2,000.

French Fashion, 8½", rare size and features, mld cafe au lait hair, CM, ptd eyes, exquisite kid fashion body, old clothes, Herron collection, $2,000.

25

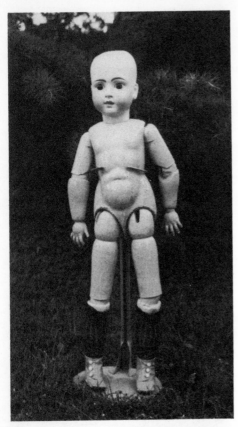

Belton, 28", all-wood, unusual body construction, long legs, CM, two holes, marked "137" and "6" (bottom of neck), Elva Weems collection, $1,600.

wig, BJ body, old clothes, signed Jumeau shoes. Head incised: "Depose Tete Jumeau Bte SGDG 12." Body stamped: "Medaille D'Or" **$2,700-3,000**

26", Unmarked Jumeau Child. Blue PW eyes, OM, old mohair wig, BJ body **$900-1,000**

27", Emile Jumeau Toddler. Large bisque socket head, fat cheeks, pouting CM, fixed PW eyes, applied ears, old mohair wig over cork pate, rare, BJ body. Mark: "Medaille D'Or" **$3,500-4,000**

27", Jumeau Mama-Papa Doll. Sleep glass eyes, OM, pull string, BJ body. Mark: "Diplome d'Honneur" **$1,200-1,500**

27", S.F.B.J. 236. Clown, white ptd bisque head, red ptd face patches, white mohair wig, blue fixed glass eyes, OM with two teeth, BJ compo body, original outfit and hat **$1,300-1,400**

28" Bru Child. Bisque shoulder head, CM, PW eyes, red mohair wig, kid-over-wood upper arms and upper legs, wooden lower arms, exquisite carved hands, wooden lower legs, exquisite toe detail. Label on chest reads: "Bebe Bru Bte SGDG. Tout Contrefacteur sera saisi et pour suivi confirmement a la Loi"..................... **$12,000-13,000**

28", Gutta-Percha Bru. Brown fixed glass eyes, CM, HHW, BJ body, wooden limbs, some facial mars. This is the well-known rubber Bru. Mark on body reads: "Bru 12 Bebe Bru 12" **$2,000-3,000**

28", S.F.B.J. 301. Brown glass sleep eyes, OM, mohair wig, BJ body **$925-1,100**

29", Adult Jumeau. Adult body construction, bisque shoulder head with high mld bosom, kid body with small waist, wide hips with protruding buttocks, OM with teeth, PE, HHW, PW eyes, signed **$2,500-3,500**

29", Bourgoin Steiner. CM, PW eyes, HHW, BJ body **$6,000-7,000**

29", Tete Jumeau. Brown sleep PW eyes, OM, HHW, BJ body.............. **$1,300-1,500**

30", S.F.B.J. Jumeau. Blue glass eyes, OM, mohair wig, BJ body **$1,200-1,400**

31", Long-Faced Cody Jumeau. Pale bisque quality, patrician nose, CM, blue PW eyes, applied ears, BJ body, HHW, cork pate, old clothes. Incised on head: "14" **$6,000-7,000**

34", Steiner Child. Wire-eyed type, CM, HHW, signed BJ body, straight wrists **$10,000-12,000**

43", Bru Boy Mannequin. Flange neck, CM, PW eyes, HHW cut in Dutch style with straight bangs, unpierced ears, four tie holes, mache mannequin body, wooden lower legs, undressed. Mark: "Bru Jne-716A" **$18,000-20,000**

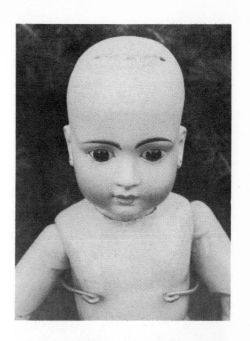

Miscellaneous French Dolls

11", Danel & Cie Bisque Paris. Socket head, OM, brown glass sleep eyes, HHW, BJ body. Incised: "PARIS" **$395-495**

11", Mon Cherie. Fine bisque quality, OM with teeth, PE, PW eyes, HHW, BJ body, possibly made by Lanternier. Back of head incised: "Mon Cherie Paris" **$475-575**

11½", S.F.B.J. Unis France 251. Character girl, OM, sleep eyes, mohair wig... **$350-450**

13", Lanternier & Cie Toddler. Bisque socket head, OM, sleep eyes, HHW, BJ toddler body, 8½" head cir, Limoges, France.... **$450-550**

15", Lanternier & Cie Character Child. Fixed glass eyes, OCM with mld teeth, HHW, BJ body, Limoges, France **$525-625**

15", J. Verlingue Bisque Child. Violet PW eyes, OM with four teeth, HHW, BJ body. Socket head incised: "Petite Francaise, France (anchor) 3/0 D LIANE" **$350-450**

16", Bisque Socket Head. CM, PW eyes, PE, HHW. Incised: "CF" over "E" **$1,000-1,200**

16", Huret Character. Bisque head, CM, PW eyes, original white mohair wig, bisque lower arms, metal jtd body **$9,000-10,000**

A 3T-marked French Bisque, 12½", another of the rarest French dolls in the world, Mil Seeley collection, $10,000.

16", Imhof's Walking Doll. Similar to the German model with permanently affixed shoes that have tiny "walking wheels." Mark on sole of shoes: "Brevete 305-269 SGDG." Celluloid-compo head, purplish eye brows, blond mohair wig, fixed glass eyes, OM, original chemise and nailed-on drawers **$2,500-3,000**

16", Lanternier Child. Bisque socket head, OM, PW eyes, mohair wig. Mark: "Fanricatio Francaise A. Lee Cherie" **$495-595**

16", Rohmer Child. Skin wig, CM, PW eyes, bisque head, hands, and feet, articulated wooden body, marked **$8,500-9,500**

16", Rohmer Child. Bisque socket head on shoulder plate, CM, PW eyes, round face with full cheeks and double chin, bisque lower arms, HHW, gusseted kid body. Oval Rohmer mark on body: "Mme Rohmer Brevete SGDG-Paris" **$7,000-8,500**

16", J. Verlingue Child. Kid body, OM, PW eyes, HHW, bisque lower arms . . . **$395-495**

16½", Danel & Cie Paris Bebe. Eiffel Tower mark, CM, PW eyes, PE, HHW, BJ body, marked, c. 1890 . . . . **$2,300-2,500**

17", Alexandre Celestin Tiburee Bebe Mothereau. Bisque socket head, CM, large blue PW eyes, HHW, BJ body. Body mark: "B.M." **$2,000-2,200**

17", Rohmer Child. Mohair wig, CM, PW eyes, bisque head with wood jtd shoulders, kid-gusseted body and bisque lower arms, Rohmer stamp **$7,800-8,800**

17", S.F.B.J. Unis 251. Sleep eyes, OM, HHW, BJ body, character baby **$425-525**

17", Tasson-Lanternier & Cie Lady. Blue fixed glass eyes, CM, upper and lower lashes, HHW, BJ body, inferior bisque quality. Mark: "Ed Tasson-ALE Cie-Limoges." Incised: "FAVORITE" **$495-595**

17¼", S.F.B.J. Unis France Girl. Unpierced ears, OM with mld upper teeth, sleep eyes, HHW, BJ body. Incised: "UNIS FRANCE" (in oval) and "30" (back of head) **$425-525**

17½", Masson Lady Doll. Bisque socket head, portrait face, OCM with mld teeth, blue glass eyes, mohair wig, poor bisque quality, BJ body. Head mark: "J. E. Masson, S. O. Lorraine No. O-A.L. et Cie Limoges" **$550-650**

18", Huret Child. Bisque shoulder head, CM, blue ptd eyes, skin wig, round fat face with double chin, bisque lower arms, gusseted kid body with familiar Huret stamp. These dolls resemble those of Mlle. Rohmer and are sometimes found on Rohmer bodies. The Rohmer doll is actually more rare, as Rohmer was in business only a short time. Perhaps when the company folded, Huret purchased Rohmer bodies. There is a definite connection between these firms, making one wonder whether the firm likewise designed heads and limbs for Rohmer .. **$6,000-8,000**

18", Jumeau Bebe Louvre. Brown fixed glass eyes, CM, PE, mohair wig, BJ body, c. 1922. Mark on head: "B7L." Jumeau made these dolls for the famous Louvre department store in Paris **$2,500-3,000**

18", Lanternier & Cie Child. Bisque shoulder head, OM, blue glass eyes, auburn mohair wig, kid body and arms. Incised on back of head: "Fabrication Francaise A.L. & Cie Limoges" **$650-750**

18", Lanternier & Cie Toto-Mialono. Deep dimple, OCM with two mld upper teeth, PW eyes, HHW (braided and coiled over each ear), fine bisque quality, BJ body **$650-750**

18", Tasson-Lanternier & Cie Child. Pink bisque head, OM with four teeth, highly colored cheeks, blue glass eyes, mohair wig, original Heinrich Handwerck body (this doll has a startled expression) **$695-795**

19", Benon & Cie Negro. Brown glass eyes, OM with four teeth, HHW, BJ body. Socket head incised: "S.T." Body mark: "DEP." Body label: "Aux Enfants Sages 13, 15 & 17 passage Gouffroy, Paris" **$795-895**

19", Petit & Dumontier Bebe. Blue PW eyes, CM, PE, HHW, BJ body **$2,000-2,500**

19½", Jullien Child. Cobalt-blue PW eyes, CM, HHW, BJ body **$2,000-3,000**

A marked Rohmer, 18", bisque head, hands and feet, kid body, CM, old gown, Mil Seeley collection, $3,000-5,000.

A. Marque, 22", rarest doll in the world and most expensive, all-original and mint, bisque arms to elbows, old clothes, marked, Mil Seeley collection, $32,000.

29

Steiner Twins, 8½", all-original and mint, BJ compo bodies, Mil Seeley collection, $3,000.

S.F.B.J. 301 Paris 10, 23", body mark "Bebe Jumeau Diplome d'Honneur," $650.

20", A. Marque Child. Bisque socket head, CM, large PW eyes, mohair wig, PE, BJ body, unusual upper eyelash painting (two rows of eyelashes with mld eyelids between), pointed chin, PE mld away from head, rare doll, c. 1916. Mark: "A. Marque" **$30,000-up**

20" B.F. Bebe. Looks Jumeau, possibly a Bebe Ferte or Bebe Francaise, may even be a Jumeau product made for Danel & Cie, CM, PW eyes, PE, HHW **$2,500-3,000**

20", S.F.B.J. Unis France 251. Sleep eyes, OM with wobbly tongue, BJ bent limb baby body, mohair wig **$550-650**

20", S.F.B.J. Unis France 301. Sleep eyes, OM, mohair wig, BJ body and wooden limbs **$495-595**

23", Danel & Cie Paris Bebe. Mohair wig, CM, PW eyes, cork pate, BJ body, body stamp only **$2,700-2,800**

23", Henri Rostal Mon Tresor. OM, PW eyes, PE, HHW, BJ body. Mark on back of head: "Mon Tresor, Germany 10" **$675-775**

23", S.F.B.J. Unis. Sleep eyes, OM with mld teeth, mohair wig, BJ body. Incised on back of head: "Unis France" (in oval) and "301" **$600-700**

25", Albert Levy Tanagra Paris. Sleep eyes and eyelashes, HHW, BJ body, OM with mld teeth **$765-865**

25", Lanternier & Cie Character Girl. Blue glass eyes, OCM with mld teeth, HHW, BJ body, Limoges, France **$795-895**

25", Maker Unknown, A12T. Possibly A. Thuillier, Paris, 1875-1890, bisque socket head, CM, PE, PW eyes, mohair wig, rare adult BJ body. Buttocks mark: "DEP PARIS" **$15,000-16,000**

25", F. Simonne Child. Straight wrists, CM, PW eyes, BJ body, HHW, Simonne sticker, rare type **$2,000-3,000**

26", Bisque Child. Possibly Lazarski, head marked "L" in red ink, CM, fixed PW eyes, applied ears, skin wig, BJ body, high - quality doll **$2,000-3,000**

30

30", F. Simonne French-Fashion Type. Pale early bisque, blue PW eyes, CM, PE with earrings, early fashion body, kid arms with stitched fingers, turquoise-blue stamp on chest, HHW, old clothes, stockings, high-button shoes with tiny heels ... **$7,000-8,000**

32", Muller Child. "Olympia" in script on back of bisque socket head, OM with teeth, PW eyes, HHW, BJ body **$795-895**

French Oddities

3¼", Maker Unknown, Spinning-Top Doll. Bisque head and arms, black ptd hair, ptd features, mint condition, c. late 1800s (the hands on most of these types are usually broken) **$295-395**

9", Maker Unknown, French Swimming Doll. Key wind, celluloid turtle-marked head, wood and metal limbs, cork body, all original **$795-895**

9", Maker Unknown, Ondine. Swimming doll, bisque head, CM, PW eyes, HHW, cork body, winding-key **$1,500-1,600**

12½", Maker Unknown, Marotte on a Stick. Brown glass eyes, OM with teeth, HHW, PE, card squeaker, red silk dress and high hat, two bells attached to ribbons on dress, tiny bells on hat. Bisque head marked: "Limoges 02 France" **$395-495**

12½", Maker Unknown, Marotte on a Stick. Standing on top of this silk-draped affair is a bisque-head doll with BJ body, PW eyes, CM, HHW, completely dressed, original shoes, activated by wrist movements **$495-595**

13", Maker Unknown, Old Man. Bisque shoulder head, deeply mld wrinkles and handlebar mustache, mld hair, mld sideburns, all gray-painted, swivel head, blue ptd eyes, CM, bisque hands with white ptd gloves, kid body, original costume (black satin top hat, black coat with tails, pinstripe trousers, red brocade vest, spats, cane). Appears to be a man

French Head, 16½", marked "7" on kid body, $1,500.

about town or an opera fancier (the author has come across several of these over the years, each similarly dressed) **$975-1,200**

15", Jester French Clapper. Plays cymbals when tummy is pressed, original .. **$395-495**

22", Maker Unknown, French Bisque. Swivel head, bust with mld bosom, CM, PW eyes, PE, HHW, cork pate **$3,500-4,000**

31

2
German Bisque Socket and Shoulder Heads

The dolls described in this category are types most often found in collections and sold by dealers. These dolls are in good condition, have wigs of old mohair, human hair, or skin, are dressed in either original, commercially made clothing or old clothing, and are priced accordingly. A doll's wig or costume does not necessarily add to the price, as all dolls should be dressed and have wigs, shoes, and socks.

(L. to R.) Doll marked "K H" on back of neck, 16", $300. Doll marked "Hh 6/0 H" (Heinrich Handwerck), 17½", $300. Both dolls from the Herron collection.

J. D. Kestner
Waltershausen, Thur
1805-1930s

11½", Kestner Character Boy. Mohair wig, CM, ptd eyes, plaster pate, BJ body, no body mark **$1,600-2,000**

12", Kestner Character Girl 178. Plaster pate, CM, ptd eyes, skin wig **$1,500-2,000**

12", Kestner Character Girl 220. Bisque socket head, OM, sleep glass eyes, mohair wig, BJ body, original peasant costume and wooden shoes **$395-495**

12", Kestner Twins 152. Bisque socket head, OM, sleep eyes, mohair wig, bent limb compo body, dressed in original diaper and shirt, sold as a pair **$625-725**

12", Kestner 143. Bisque socket head, OM, sleep eyes, HHW, BJ body, made from the 1880s through the 1930s **$225-325**

Kestner 171, 14", all-original, an early favorite doll, Herron collection, $325.

(L. to R.) 250 KH Walkure, 20", marked "0 ¾ Germany," all-original, $395. Kestner 154-DEP, 20", $395. Both dolls from the Herron collection.

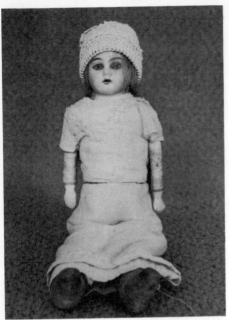

13", Kestner Googly Girl 221. Round glass eyes to the side, watermelon mouth, HHW, BJ body, separated fingers **$4,750-5,000**

13½, Early Unmarked Kestner Child. Pale, fine bisque shoulder head, PW eyes, mld teeth, mohair wig, bisque lower arms, kid body **$350-395**

15", Early Kestner Child. Cork-stuffed, bisque shoulder head, bisque lower arms, PW eyes, OM, mohair wig, kid body. Body sticker: "J.D.K. Germany ½" **$250-350**

15", Four-Head Kestner. Three heads with CM, one head with OM, PW eyes, skin wig, BJ body, rare. Mark: size number only **$5,000-6,000**

15", Kestner 143. Bisque socket head, OM, sleep eyes, HHW, BJ body **$295-395**

15", Kestner Gibson Girl 172. Sleep eyes, CM, HHW, bisque shoulder head, bisque lower arms, kid body, c. 1910 . . . . . . **$1,800-2,000**

Doll incised with a horseshoe mark and "1908," 13½", all-original except for one little hand replaced long ago, original old clothes, one of the author's earliest dolls, $225.

(L. to R.) Early Kestner, 18". Kestner 154-DEP 7, 20", $395. Both dolls from the Herron collection.

15½", Kestner Fashion Type. Turned head, CM, PW eyes, mohair wig, bisque shoulder head and bisque lower arms, kid and cloth body **$425-525**

16", Kestner Gibson Girl. Sleep eyes, OM, HHW, BJ body with rare mld bosom. Body label reads: "Made for G.A. Swartz, Phila. Made in Germany." Head incised: "B. Made in Germany 6-162 A" **$795-895**

16", Kestner 164. Bisque socket head, OM, sleep eyes, HHW, BJ body, dressed in original Oriental costume **$1,600-1,700**

17", Kestner Boy. Mohair wig, CM, PW eyes (eyes feel rough to the touch), BJ body, dressed as a boy with boy wig. Bisque socket head incised: "7½" **$795-895**

17", Kestner Googly 221. Watermelon mouth, glass eyes glancing to the side, mohair wig, Kestner pate, BJ body. Incised: "Made in Germany 12" **$6,000-6,500**

17½", Kestner 154. Sleep eyes, OM, HHW, kid body, bisque shoulder head, bisque lower arms. Mark: "Dep" **$265-365**

18", Early Kestner Child. Bisque shoulder head, bisque lower arms, CM, PW eyes, HHW, kid body has Kestner label. Marked and incised: "8" **$695-795**

18", Kestner Child. Pouty, CM, PW eyes, HHW, BJ body. Marked: "X" **$1,300-1,500**

18", Kestner Child. CM, PW eyes, HHW, BJ body. Marked: "XI" **$1,400-1,600**

18", Kestner 154. Bisque shoulder head, bisque lower arms, kid body, OM, sleep glass eyes, HHW **$265-365**

18½", Kestner Fashion Lady. Swivel neck on bisque shoulder plate, CM, PW eyes, mohair wig, bisque lower arms, kid body with original corset. Mark: "C" **$1,000-1,200**

19", Kestner Child. Bisque socket head, CM, sleep eyes, mohair wig, BJ body, straight wrists, c. 1880 .... **$825-925**

Turned-Head German Fashion, 20", faintly incised "Made in Germany" on rear shoulder plate, OCM, kid fashion body, old clothes, Herron collection, $650.

Kestner 9-154, 22", kid body, marked "9-154-DEP Made in Germany," Pat and Sunny Lupton collection, $415.

Bisque Shoulder Head, 12", marked "Germany 79/0", bisque forearms on old cloth body, OM, Pat and Sunny Lupton collection, $295.

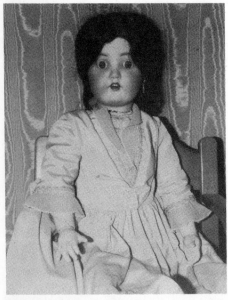

Bisque Socket Head, 30", incised "CALLERFELDEN PUPPENFABRIK 264/6 ½," BJ body, Pat and Sunny Lupton collection, $1,000.

19", Kestner 639. Early turned head, CM, PW eyes, mohair wig, kid body, bisque shoulder head, bisque lower arms **$795-895**

20", Kestner Fashion Lady. Sleep eyes, OM, mohair wig, BJ body. Mark: "H-Made in Germany 12" **$265-365**

20", Kestner 171. Sleep eyes, OM, HHW, BJ body (this doll was made from the late 1880s through the 1930s) **$375-475**

20½", Kestner Gibson Girl. Bisque shoulder head, bisque lower arms, CM, sleep eyes, HHW, kid body, c. 1910. Body mark: "Gibson Girl" **$3,000-3,500**

23", Kestner 167. Bisque socket head, OM, sleep eyes, mohair wig, BJ body .. **$325-425**

23", Kestner 171. Bisque socket head, OM, PW eyes, mohair wig, BJ body ... **$295-395**

24", Kestner 154. Bisque shoulder head, bisque lower arms, OM, sleep eyes, HHW, kid body **$325-425**

25", Kestner Girl. Sleep eyes, CM, HHW, pate, BJ body. Marked: "Made in Germany 15"........................ **$975-1,200**

27", Early Kestner Fashion Lady. Turned head, CM, deep bisque shoulder plate, PW eyes, mohair wig, kid body, kid arms, stitched fingers. Incised: "N" (this doll's face looks Jumeau) **$2,200-2,500**

27", Kestner Fashion Lady. Bisque shoulder head, bisque lower arms, CM, PW eyes, mohair wig, rare Goldsmith-type corset body. Incised: "11" **$2,200-2,500**

29", Kestner Shoulder Head. Sleep eyes, OM, HHW, BJ arms, kid body **$595-695**

29", Kestner 171. Bisque socket head, OM, PE, PW eyes, mohair wig **$695-795**

30", Kestner Child. Pale bisque shoulder head, CM, bisque lower arms, PW eyes, mohair wig, kid body **$1,800-2,000**

31", Kestner Fashion Lady. Bisque socket head, CM, PW eyes, HHW, BJ body, fine pale bisque quality. Mark: size number only **$1,995-2,500**

36

42", Kestner Child. Bisque socket head, OM, sleep eyes, HHW, BJ body **$1,500-1,600**

Simon & Halbig
Grafenhain near Ohrdruf
1870-1930s

10½", S & H Santa 1249. Sleep eyes, OM, HHW, BJ body, rare size **$225-325**

11½", Dressel-S & H Jutta 1349. OM, PW eyes, HHW, BJ body **$195-295**

13", S & H Oriental 1329. Yellow bisque socket head, OM, PW eyes, black wig, BJ body, original costume........ **$1,200-1,400**

13½", S & H 1159. Bisque socket head, OM, PW eyes, mohair wig, BJ body ... **$525-625**

14", S & H 929. Dome head with two holes, CM, PE, PW eyes, BJ body ... **$1,000-1,200**

14", S & H 949. Bisque socket head, OM with top and bottom teeth, PW eyes, HHW, BJ body **$325-425**

14", S & H Negro Character Girl 1368. Brown PW eyes, OM, black wig, French-type BJ body, rare..................... **$750-850**

14½", S & H-K Star R Character 151. Blue ptd eyes, OCM with mld teeth, HHW, BJ body **$2,500-3,000**

14½", S & H Oriental 1329. Quality yellow bisque, PW eyes, OM with teeth, black wig, BJ body **$1,200-1,500**

16", S & H 949. Sleep eyes, OM, PE, mohair wig, BJ body **$500-600**

16", S & H 1248. Mohair wig, OM, PW eyes, BJ body **$395-495**

16", S & H 1488. Sleep eyes, OM, mohair wig, compo toddler body......... **$1,650-1,750**

16", S & H Negro Girl 939. Early black BJ body, OM, PW eyes, black wig, straight wrists...................... **$950-1,200**

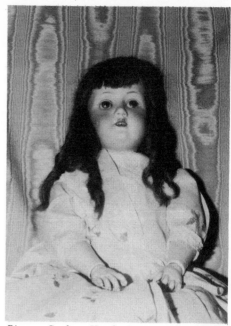

Bisque Socket Head, 27", incised "MOA Germany 200-0," Pat and Sunny Lupton collection, $450-500.

Bisque Socket Head, 24", incised "ARMAND MARSEILLE GERMANY 390n A6M," Pat and Sunny Lupton collection, $395.

German Socket Head, 27", incised "15 147 MADE IN GERMANY," cloth body with bisque forearms, Pat and Sunny Lupton collection, $595.

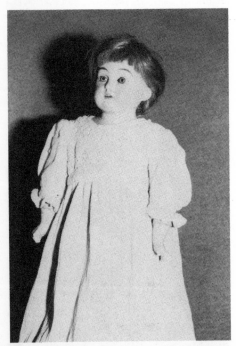

Bisque Shoulder Head, 14", kid body with bisque forearms, marked "3200 AM 4/0 DEP," Pat and Sunny Lupton collection, $250.

16", S & H Negro Girl 1009. Dark BJ body, OM, PW eyes. Incised: "S & H 1009 Dep" **$695-795**

17", S & H 117 (for Kammer & Reinhardt). Bisque socket head, CM, PW eyes, HHW, BJ body **$2,800-3,000**

17½", S & H 1079. Sleep eyes, OM. Mark: "DEP GERMANY"....... **$350-400**

17½", S & H 1249. Rare mark, OM, sleep eyes, HHW, BJ body. Incised: "DEP. GER. SANTA 7".................... **$425-525**

18", C.M. Bergmann-S & H Boy. Mohair wig, OM, PW eyes, BJ body.......... **$225-325**

18", S & H 1159. Sleep eyes, OM, HHW, dressed as a Gibson Girl, c. 1910 .. **$675-775**

19", S & H 738. Black wig, OM, PW eyes, lt brown bisque socket head on similarly colored BJ body, dressed in original Moroccan clothes (dark red caftan, white trousers and turban, red and white striped jacket).... **$975-1,500**

19", S & H Character Girl 1299. OM, PW eyes, HHW, BJ body **$395-495**

20", S & H 949. Black wig, CM, PW eyes, kid body signed on shoulder plate, bisque lower arms, Belton-type . :............. **$675-775**

20", S & H 1079. Sleep eyes, OM, mohair wig, bisque shoulder head, compo lower arms, pink kid body **$395-495**

21", S & H 1079. Green flirty eyes, OM, HHW, BJ body................. **$395-495**

22", S & H 550. Sleep eyes, OM, HHW, BJ body **$425-525**

22", S & H 1039. Flirty eyes, OM, mohair wig, mechanical body, throws kisses and cries, swivel neck................. **$1,000-1,200**

22", S & H Gabriel Benda. Sleep eyes, OM, HHW, BJ body, rare mark **$395-495**

23", C.M. Bergmann-S & H 4/0. Mohair wig, OM, PW eyes, BJ body.......... **$300-400**

24", S & H Lady Doll 1159. Blue sleep eyes,

OM, mohair wig, PE, BJ body, dressed as a
Gibson Girl **$1,000-1,200**

24", S & H Santa 1249. Sleep eyes, OM,
HHW, BJ body **$525-625**

25", S & H 1079. Sleep eyes, OM, mohair wig.
Marked "Jumeau" **$595-695**

25", S & H Lady Doll. OM, PW eyes,
HHW, BJ lady body. Stamped:
"Jumeau" **$1,200-1,500**

25", S & H Character Boy 1498. Solid dome,
OCM with protruding upper lip, PW
eyes, brushstrokes, BJ toddler
body **$2,000-2,500**

26", S & H 1250. Sleep eyes, OM, PE, mohair
wig, kid body, bisque shoulder head, bisque
lower arms, cloth lower legs **$475-575**

27", C.M. Bergmann-S & H Child. OM, PW
eyes, HHW, BJ body **$365-465**

27", S & H 1009. Sleep eyes, OM, mohair wig,
BJ body **$495-595**

28", S & H 1010. Bisque shoulder head, bisque
lower arms, OM, PW eyes, PE, mohair wig,
pink kid fashion body, cloth lower legs,
1889-1930s **$595-695**

29", S & H 949. Sleep eyes, OM, PE, mohair
wig, BJ body **$975-1,200**

30", S & H 1009. Sleep eyes, OM, PE, HHW,
BJ body **$600-700**

33", S & H 1010. Sleep eyes, OM, mohair wig,
BJ body **$650-750**

35", S & H 1079. Sleep eyes, OM, PE, HHW,
BJ body **$750-850**

Armand Marseille
Koppelsdorf, Thur
1865-1930s

9", Armand Marseille Just Me. Bisque socket
head, fixed blue glass eyes to the side, HHW,
CM, BJ body, quality bisque, c. 1925. Mark:

*German Twins, 12", incised "ARMAND
MARSEILLE GERMANY 390 A 6/0 M,"
Pat and Sunny Lupton collection, $400.*

*Kestner 10 DEP 154, 23", bisque shoulder
plate on kid body, bisque forearms, dressed by
Bess Fantl for her collection, $425.*

39

(L. to R.) Bisque Head, 10", incised "410/13/0," moving teeth and tongue, $425. Bisque Head, 8", marked "300-13/0," $350. Both dolls from the Fantl collection.

Armand Marseille Brown Bisque Head, 23", OM, original costume and wig, 5-pc compo body with mld/ptd shoes, Jim and Sheila Olah Scheetz collection, $500.

"JUST ME REGISTERED GERMANY A3/0/5/OM"................... **$825-925**

9", Armand Marseille Just Me. Bisque socket head, fixed blue glass eyes to the side, HHW, CM, BJ body, ptd bisque **$325-425**

9½", Armand Marseille Florodora. Sleep eyes, OM, mohair wig, compo body with shoulder and hip joints only, dressed in original rabbit-fur suit **$135-145**

10½", Armand Marseille Googly 323. Bisque head, blue glass eyes to the side, smiling CM, HHW, plump BJ body **$695-795**

11", Armand Marseille Character Girl 560A. Mohair wig, PW eyes, smiling mouth, crude 5-pc body **$350-450**

11¾", Armand Marseille Googly 353. Sleep eyes, OM, mohair wig, 5-pc compo body **$925-1,200**

12", Armand Marseille Character Boy 500. Blue ptd eyes, CM, blond mld hair, straight wrists, BJ body, c. 1910 .... **$695-795**

12", Armand Marseille Head on Marotte Base. Dress covers music box which is activated by swinging marotte attached to wooden stick, bisque head, OM with teeth, fixed PW eyes, clown hat and wig, flange neck....................... **$245-345**

12" Armand Marseille Mabel. Mohair wig, PW eyes, OM with seven teeth, gusset-jointed kid body, bisque lower arms. Incised: "Germany Mabel 7/0" **$185-285**

13", Armand Marseille Child. Sleep eyes, mohair wig, original clothes, similar to the 14" Armand Marseille Lady Doll. Mark: "401" **$625-725**

14", Armand Marseille Character Boy 500. Mohair wig, CM, PW eyes, BJ body, c. 1910......................... **$395-495**

14", Armand Marseille Florodora. Sleep eyes, OM, HHW, BJ body, c. 1901. Mark: "MADE IN GERMANY A/3/OM" **$150-200**

14", Armand Marseille Lady Doll. Orange ptd mouth, oval face, pointed chin, BJ flapper body, arched feet, original coat, blouse, skirt, undies, stockings, high-heeled slippers. Mark: "Germany 401 A 5/0 M"........ **$750-850**

15", Armand Marseille Witch. Gray straggly mohair wig, wrinkled face, pointed nose, CM, PW eyes, mld brown warts, bisque head, BJ body, original witch clothes and hat. Signed: "Hexe" **$925-1,200**

16", Armand Marseille Character Girl. Mohair wig, OM, PW eyes, straight wrists, c. 1890. Mark on body reads: "DEP A.M. 3600"......................... **$295-395**

16", Armand Marseille Character Girl. Blue intaglio eyes, CM, mld eyelids, one-stroke lt brown brows, pinkish facial tone with orange-pink lips, mohair wig, BJ body. Incised: "Made in Germany A3M"........ **$495-595**

16", Armand Marseille 370. Sleep eyes, OM, mohair wig, bisque shoulder head, bisque lower arms, kid body and upper legs, compo lower legs, c. 1890.............. **$195-295**

16", Armand Marseille 390. Bisque head on Imhof walking body. This doll wears permanent shoes with tiny wheels designed for walking when held and guided along the floor, original costume, mohair wig, OM, PW eyes **$795-1,000**

17", Armand Marseille 1894. Bisque shoulder head, bisque lower arms, kid body, OM, PW eyes, mohair wig **$265-365**

18", Armand Marseille Character Girl 400. Sleep eyes, CM, mohair wig, BJ body, c. 1910...................... **$1,400-1,500**

19", Armand Marseille 231. Sleep eyes, CM, mohair wig, BJ body, straight wrists. Mark: "Fany A7M 231" **$3,200-4,200**

20", Armand Marseille Child. Mohair wig, OM, PW eyes, BJ body, c. 1890. Mark: "AM 390DRGM 246-6-½" **$195-295**

20", Armand Marseille Queen Louise. Louis Wolf & Co. trademark, Armand Marseille bisque head often used, OM, sleep eyes, HHW, BJ body, c. 1910 .... **$195-295**

23", Armand Marseille Florodora. Sleep eyes, OM, HHW, BJ body **$245-275**

German Mechanical Automaton, 9", marked "44-15," bisque head, compo body, metal hands, glass eyes, original wig and costume. Horse is covered with real horsehair and has glass eyes and wind key. Horse gallops and doll moves up and down, $1,200.

K Star R Simon & Halbig 58, 23", OM, old clothes, Jim and Sheila Olah Scheetz collection, $425.

41

*Little Lamplighter Candy Container, 9",
marked "76-924 Germany," bisque head,
CM, wooden hands and feet. Doll comes
apart in middle for candy placement, all-
original, Jim and Sheila Olah Scheetz
collection, $350-450.*

*Bisque Head, 20", marked "Germany H,"
sleep eyes, OM, kid body, Jim and Sheila
Olah Scheetz collection, $395.*

23", Armand Marseille Girl. Mohair wig, OM,
PW eyes, BJ body, 1890-1930s. Mark: "Made
in Germany 390 A6M" **$225-325**

24", Armand Marseille Queen Louise. Louis
Wolf & Co. trademark, Armand Marseille
head often used, OM, sleep eyes, HHW, BJ
body, c. 1910 .... **$235-335**

29", Armand Marseille Columbia. Armand
Marseille bisque head, C.M. Bergmann body,
distributed by Louis Wolf & Co., sleep eyes,
OM with four teeth, bisque shoulder head,
bisque lower arms, HHW, early kid body,
1904-1915 .... **$395-495**

33", Armand Marseille 370. OM, PW eyes,
HHW, BJ body, c. 1890 .... **$495-595**

40", Armand Marseille 18. OM, PW eyes,
HHW, BJ body **$900-1,000**

Heinrich Handwerck
Gotha near Waltershausen
1876-1930s

17", Handwerck Negro Girl. Sleep eyes, OM,
black wig, black BJ body **$525-625**

18", Early Handwerck Child. Linen covering
on torso and thighs, PE, BJ body, straight
wrists, HHW, CM, PW eyes. Mark: "H" (on
back of bisque socket head) **$850-950**

21", Handwerck Child. Very pale bisque
socket head, OM, PE, sleep eyes, HHW, BJ
body. Mark: "109-11" **$550-650**

22", Handwerck Negro Child. Negro socket
head, OM, PW eyes, PE, black wig, BJ body.
Mark: "Handwerck 109-11" **$550-650**

23", Handwerck 69. Mohair wig, OM, PW
eyes, BJ body **$265-365**

28", Handwerck Child. Sleep eyes, OM,
HHW, PE. Mark: "119-13"....... **$425-525**

28", Handwerck-S & H Child. Sleep eyes,
OM, mohair wig, BJ body **$425-525**

30", Handwerck-S & H Child. OM, PW eyes,
HHW, BJ body................ **$495-595**

30", Handwerck-S & H 109. Sleep eyes, OM, mohair wig, BJ body. Incised: "DEP" **$495-595**

32", Handwerck Child. Sleep eyes, OM, PE, HHW. Head mark: "99 Dep H." Red mark on BJ body: "Handwerck" **$525-625**

40", Handwerck Child. Sleep eyes, OM, HHW, 19" head cir **$1,200-1,300**

Kammer & Reinhardt Waltershausen, Thur 1886-1930s

11", K Star R 101. Blue-gray ptd eyes, CM, mohair wig, BJ body **$1,400-1,500**

12", K Star R 114. CM, PW eyes, HHW, BJ body **$1,900-2,000**

13", K Star R 127. BJ toddler body, CM, PW eyes, mld blond hair, rare **$4,000-5,000**

13½", K Star R 109. Blue intaglio eyes, CM, HHW, BJ body **$3,500-3,700**

14", K Star R 122. Sleep eyes, OM, HHW, BJ bent limb body **$395-495**

16", K Star R 101 .... **$1,800-2,000**

16", K Star R 115. Mohair wig, CM, ptd eyes, BJ body **$1,900-2,200**

16", K Star R 116A **$1,700-2,000**

17", K Star R 117. Sleep eyes, CM, HHW, BJ body **$1,800-2,000**

18", K Star R 112 .... **$4,500-5,000**

18", K Star R 114. Mohair wig, CM, PW eyes, BJ body **$2,600-3,000**

19", K Star R Pouty Boy 101. Blue ptd eyes, CM, boy wig, BJ body **$2,000-2,500**

19", K Star R 117. Sleep eyes, CM, mohair wig, original BJ body **$2,000-2,500**

19", K Star R 126. Sleep eyes, OM, HHW, bent limb compo body **$415-515**

Kestner Turned Head, 28", CM, kid body, Jim and Sheila Olah Scheetz collection, $1,800.

Heubach Brat, 13", Heubach mark, mld hair, OCM, intaglio eyes, kid body, bisque head and hands, Jim and Sheila Olah Scheetz collection, $1,500.

43

*(L. to R.) Stone Bisque Bonnet Head, 15",
and Stone Bisque Bonnet Head, 16",
bisque limbs, cloth body, Jim and Sheila
Olah Scheetz collection, $350-395.*

*Simon & Halbig 949, 16", bisque head on
compo lady body, CM, $1,800-2,000.*

20", K Star R Character Girl 117N. Flirty
eyes, CM, HHW, BJ body **$825-925**

24", K Star R 103. Mohair wig, CM, PW eyes,
BJ body **$3,000-3,500**

Heubach-Koppelsdorf
Koppelsdorf, Thur
1887-1930s

13", Heubach-Koppelsdorf Brother and
Sister. Sleep eyes, OM, movable tongue,
mohair wig, bent limb compo body, original
clothes (boy wears white shirt, blue pants; girl
wears pink and white dress), sold as a pair.
Mark: "300/3/0" **$595-695**

17", Heubach-Koppelsdorf Character 342.
Sleep eyes, OM, mohair wig, bent limb compo
body, c. 1910 .... **$395-495**

18", Heubach-Koppelsdorf 250. Sleep eyes,
OM, mohair wig, c. 1887 .... **$195-295**

22", Heubach-Koppelsdorf 275. Bisque
shoulder head, bisque lower arms, OM, sleep
eyes, mohair wig, kid body, compo lower legs,
c. 1887 .... **$225-325**

30", Heubach-Koppelsdorf Breather 320.
Bent limb body, OM, PW eyes, HHW, c.
1910......................... **$795-895**

Gebruder Heubach
Lichte near Wallendorf, Thur
1863-1930s

13½", Gebruder Heubach Girl. Bisque hands,
kid body, mld bisque braids coiled over each
ear, OCM with four teeth **$1,200-1,300**

18", Gebruder Heubach Infant. Sleep eyes,
OM, HHW, BJ body **$475-575**

19", Gebruder Heubach Laughing Boy. Blue
intaglio eyes, mld hair,........ **$950-1,100**

Schoenau & Hoffmeister
Burggrub near Kronach
Bavaria
(Porzellanfabrik, Burggrub)
1901-1930s

12", Schoenau & Hoffmeister Oriental 4900. Yellow bisque socket head, OM, PW eyes, black wig, yellow 5-pc BJ body, original Japanese costume **$825-1,000**

14", Schoenau & Hoffmeister 5700. Bisque socket head, OM, sleep eyes **$235-335**

16", Schoenau & Hoffmeister Princess Elizabeth. Bisque socket head, OM with teeth, sleep eyes, mohair wig, 5-pc compo body, c. 1939 . . . . **$1,900-2,000**

17½", Schoenau & Hoffmeister 1906. OM, PW eyes, HHW, BJ body **$225-325**

24", Schoenau & Hoffmeister Hanna 749. Sleep eyes, OM, wears a mohair wig, bent limb body **$365-465**

Belton-Type Turned Shoulder-Head Doll, 24", original kid body, bisque forearms, CM, either German or French, antique gown, D. Kay Crow collection, $1,200.

24", Schoenau & Hoffmeister 5500. Kid body, OM, PW eyes, HHW, bisque shoulder head, bisque lower arms **$265-365**

Kley & Hahn
Ohrdruf, Thur
1895-1930s

13", Kley & Hahn Pouty 169. Fine bisque quality, CM, PW eyes, HHW . . . . : **$750-850**

15½", Kley & Hahn Crying Boy. Sleep eyes, OCM, wears a mohair wig, BJ bent limb body **$350-450**

18", Kley & Hahn Walkure Child 43. Sleep eyes, OM, mohair wig, BJ body . . . **$295-395**

18½", Kley & Hahn Character Boy. Blue ptd eyes, CM, boy wig, rare **$1,200-1,300**

23", Kley & Hahn Walkure. Sleep eyes, OM, PE, mohair wig, BJ body **$295-395**

Kestner Child, 32", head incised "P 5 Made in Germany," OM, sleep eyes, kid body, D. Kay Crow collection, $850.

Bisque Socket Head, 22", incised "S & H 1079," OM, D. Kay Crow collection, $515.

German Bisque Shoulder Head, 20", incised with Cuno and Otto Dressel mark, sleep eyes, OM, from the D. Kay Crow collection, $295-315.

26½", Kley & Hahn Walkure. Sleep eyes, OM, HHW, BJ body............... **$400-500**

32", Kley & Hahn Child. Sleep eyes, OM, HHW, BJ body............... **$525-625**

34", Kley & Hahn Walkure. OM, PW eyes, PE, HHW, BJ body, c. 1902 ..... **$695-795**

Miscellaneous German Dolls

7", Maker Unknown, Floating Bisque Bath Doll. This baby has mld cap, mld hair around hairline, and is sculpted all in one, one arm separate from body, legs apart, mld and ptd swimsuit, c. 1890. These dolls were designed for baby's bathtub **$195-295**

8", Maker Unknown, Half Doll. Bisque head, ptd blue eyes, skin wig, delicate hands with long slender fingers, CM, original pincushion bottom, dressed as a fortune-teller, completely original, c. 1850................. **$350-450**

9", Otto Dressel Admiral Dewey. Bisque socket head, CM, mld gray mustache, mld gray hair, mld gray goatee, PW eyes, 5-pc mache body, original old uniform, c. 1898 .... **$395-495**

9½", Cuno & Otto Dressel Grandpa. Bald head with gray sideburns, mld eyeglasses, ptd eyes, bisque head and hands, cloth body and legs, dressed **$625-725**

10", Maker Unknown, Bisque Head Monkey. Old and all-original, squeeze toy........................... **$225-325**

10", Maker Unknown, Bisque Socket Head. OM, PW eyes, HHW, BJ body. Head incised: "XXX" **$195-295**

11", Maker Unknown, Old Man. Bisque socket head, mld mustache, BJ body, skin wig, CM, PW eyes, dressed **$495-595**

11½", Maker Unknown, Candy Box with 9" Doll. Bisque legs, mache arms, cloth body, mohair wig, ptd features, original costume. Head incised: "925-78" **$350-450**

11½", Maker Unknown, Pouty. Sleep eyes, CM, character face, HHW, BJ body, possibly an early Kestner. Mark on body: "128-2-Germany" **$2,000-2,500**

46

12", Gebruder Ohlhaver Revalo Character. Coquette, bisque socket head, mld hair, blue ptd eyes, OCM, BJ body **$675-775**

12", Kestner Googly Boy. Buster Brown wig, watermelon mouth, round glass eyes, original sailor suit. Mark: "Ges. Gesch. Germany, J.D.K." **$3,700-4,000**

12", Kestner Googly 165. Watermelon mouth, PW eyes, HHW, toddler body, original clothes **$3,500-4,000**

12", Maker Unknown, Lady Doll. Bisque turned head, OCM, PW eyes, HHW styled in high Gibson Girl pompadour, well-sculpted adult features and ears, long neck, mld bosom, nice slope to shoulders, no sew holes, shoulder plate glued to cloth body, compo limbs, mld shoes and stockings, dressed in 1910 style **$695-795**

12¾", Maker Unknown, Bonnet Bisque. Bisque limbs, CM, ptd features, wears a wide-brimmed bonnet (straw melon type), wide blue ribbon tied into large bow beneath chin, long hair mld onto shoulders, bangs, c. 1890 . . . . **$225-325**

German Bisque, 20", marked "125," OM, sleep eyes, kid body, fur eyebrows, D. Kay Crow collection, $295-315.

13", Maker Unknown, Bisque Flapper. Dressed as Pierrette, blue ptd flirty eyes, blond mohair wig, white satin cap with black pompon, satin suit, cigarette in mouth, cloth body and limbs, c. 1920 . . . . **$125-175**

13", Maker Unknown, Flapper. Bisque socket head, OM, sleep eyes, bobbed mohair wig, slender limbs and knee joints, all-bisque, old original clothes and high heels. Incised: "1 4/OM" **$395-495**

13", Maker Unknown, Three-Faced Doll. Bisque head, smile-sleep-cry faces, ring under hair and hood moves head, strings at waist for voice box, compo limbs, arms jtd at shoulders, body covered with old calico, original clothes. Body mark: "Geschutzt" **$1,500-1,600**

13", Maker Unknown, Two-Faced Bisque Child. Cry and smile faces, blue PW eyes, compo jtd body with hood, hair, and old clothing **$1,250-1,350**

13", Maker Unknown, Uncle Sam. Bisque

K Star R Simon & Halbig, 21", OM, sleep eyes, PE, c. 1890, D. Kay Crow collection, $350-400.

47

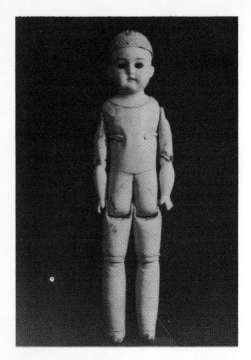

Armand Marseille DRGM 20101, 19", rare eye-movement mechanism, D. Kay Crow collection, $750-850.

socket head, CM, PW eyes, BJ body, original wig and costume. Mark on body: "S1 Germany" **$1,200-1,500**

13½", Borgfeldt Alma. "Alma" incised on bisque socket head and bisque shoulder plate, OM, PW eyes, mohair wig, kid body with bisque lower arms, c. 1900 . . . . **$195-295**

13½", Maker Unknown, Three-Faced Doll. Little Red Riding Hood, Grandma, and the Wolf, bisque head, PW eyes, wig, BJ body, original outfit **$1,200-1,500**

13½", Spanish Type. Dark bisque, OM, black wig, PW eyes, BJ body, original Spanish costume. Incised: "LC" (in anchor) and "D 8/0" **$395-495**

14", Helen Jensen Bisque-Head Gladdie (for Borgfeldt). Blue glass sleep eyes, compo limbs, cloth body, rare **$1,000-1,200**

14", Heubach & Einco Googly. Eyes move by wire lever, bisque head, mohair wig, CM, 5-pc toddler body, dressed. Mark: "Heubach" with "Einco" above **$2,000-3,000**

14", Maker Unknown, Bonnet Bisque. Blue ptd eyes to the side, OM, wears an elaborate mld bonnet with plume, mld blond curly hair, leather arms, cloth body with ptd corset, leather boots on cloth legs, dressed to period, c. 1890 . . . . **$285-385**

14", Maker Unknown, Two-Faced Toddler. Bisque head, large blue glass eyes on one face, tiny squinting eyes on the opposite face, blond mohair wig, hand-turned type head, compo jtd body at shoulders and hips, looks French (both mouths are open and show teeth, one mouth is pleasant, the other cries), old clothes **$1,300-1,500**

14½", Cuno & Otto Dressel Lady Golfer. Bisque head, CM, sleep eyes, HHW, jtd lady body, original costume (pleated skirt, knit sweater and tam, high-heeled slippers and silk stockings, golf bag and club) . . . **$965-1,200**

15", Maker Unknown, Mammy. Brown bisque shoulder head, brown bisque lower limbs, brown glass fixed eyes, large red lips, OM with tongue and five upper and lower teeth, black and gray wig styled in bun at back, cloth body, original mammy clothes and red kerchief on head **$595-695**

15", Maker Unknown, Two-Faced Baby. Crying face and pleasant face with CM, compo limbs, cloth body, HHW, original bonnet and dress **$1,000-1,200**

15½", Maker Unknown, Tommy Tucker Type. Bisque socket head, solid dome, CM, sleep eyes, BJ body. Head mark: Roman numeral 11 and 154 .... **$1,000-1,500**

16", Cuno & Otto Dressel Child. Mohair wig, OM, blue-gray glass eyes, BJ body, straight wrists **$295-395**

16", Gebruder Krauss. Eisfeld, 1863-1921, CM, PW eyes, solid dome with tiny wig hole, mohair wig, Mark: "GbrK".... **$1,000-1,200**

16", Maker Unknown, Bisque Shoulder Head. Kid body, OM, PW eyes, HHW, bisque lower arms. Incised: "N184" **$295-395**

16", Maker Unknown, Two-Faced Child. Fine quality bisque doll with mld blouse on shoulder plate, compo hands and legs, kid body, blond mohair wig **$1,600-1,700**

17", Maker Unknown, Bisque Shoulder Head. Four-leaf clovers mld on blond hair, hair has bangs and long curls spilling onto shoulders, two green clovers with long stems decorate front shoulder plate, four sew holes, bisque limbs, cloth body, c. 1890 .... **$395-495**

17", Maker Unknown, Lady Doll. Bisque socket head on bisque shoulder plate, human hair inserted into wax crown, CM, PW eyes, kid-covered body, rare type. Doll looks more German than French **$1,500-2,000**

18", B.J. & Co. My Sweetheart 101. Sleep eyes, OM, HHW, c. 1902 .... **$275-375**

18", Gebruder Ohlhaver Revalo Child. Blue sleep eyes, OM, HHW, BJ body. Head mark: "Revalo 3" **$265-365**

18", Maker Unknown, Bisque Bathing Beauty. Diving position, finely detailed, quality bisque, delicately tinted, blond mld hair piled high on dainty head, red bathing suit, mint. c. WW I **$225-300**

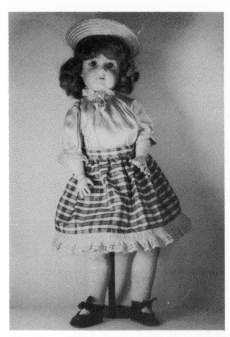

Floradora, 22", incised "A-7 ½-M, Armand Marseille Made In Germany," $310.

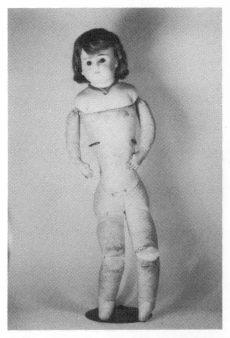

German Fashion, 20", OM, applied ears, marked "Germany N 7 DEP," $700.

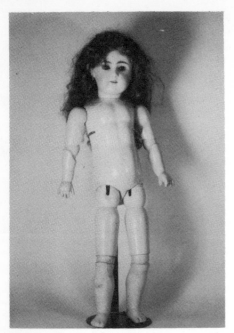

German Child, 19", marked "201 DEP Made in Germany 10," OM, $395.

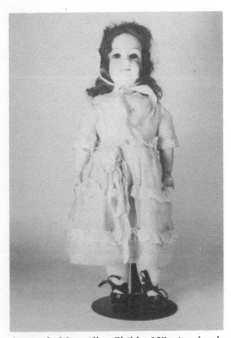

Armand Marseille Child, 15", is clearly marked "370-AM-5-0-DEP, Made in Germany," $225-250.

18", Maker Unknown, Bisque Socket Head. Mohair wig, OM, PW eyes, "D" and "K" over "3 DEP" incised on head **$385-485**

18½", R.B. 118. Kid body with bisque lower arms, OM, PW eyes, HHW. Bisque shoulder head incised: "R.B. 118" **$285-385**

19", Maker Unknown, Bisque Shoulder Head. Blue ptd eyes, CM, mohair wig, bisque lower limbs, cloth body. Incised: "J." (This doll has a French look. Some early Jumeaus were signed "J," but as there is no definite proof that this doll is a Jumeau, it is classified here as German) **$925-1,100**

19", Maker Unknown, Fashion Shoulder Head. Wears a mohair wig, CM, PW eyes, bisque lower arms, kid fashion body, pale bisque quality, size number denotes Kestner make. Incised on both head and shoulder: "6" **$1,000-1,200**

19", Maker Unknown, German Child Fashion. Bisque shoulder head, OM, bisque lower arms, PW eyes, HHW, ... **$495-595**

19", Maker Unknown, German Fashion. Bisque swivel head on bisque shoulder plate, bisque lower arms, kid fashion body, CM, HHW, PW eyes **$695-795**

19", Maker Unknown, Mobcap Bisque. Possibly early Kestner, CM, PW eyes, blue mld mobcap with blue ribbons and bows, leather arms, hair-stuffed cloth body, cloth legs with sewed-on red leather boots, dressed. Incised on shoulder: "10545" **$595-695**

19", Maker Unknown, Two-Faced Baby Girl. Unmarked, looks French, bisque head, PW eyes, PE (four holes), curly skin wig, pretty smiling face, ugly fretful face, OM with tongue mld to the side, jtd toddler body, wears old costume **$1,600-2,000**

20", Alt, Beck & Gottschalck Child. Sleep eyes, OM, mohair wig, c. 1893 . . . . **$265-365**

20", Bahr & Proschild Character. Doll has a plump face and double chin, OCM with two mld upper teeth, sleep eyes, HHW, BJ body, 1871-1930s **$495-595**

20", Cuno and Otto Dressel Jutta. Flirty glass eyes, OM, mohair wig, BJ body, PE. Mold mark: "1348" **$275-375**

20", Kestner Turned Shoulder Head. Sleep eyes, OM, mohair wig, bisque lower arms, cloth body. Incised: "J" **$395-495**

21", Felix Arena and Michel Lafond Mignon Child. OM, PW eyes, HHW, BJ body, c. 1920 . . . . **$385-485**

21", Gebruder Heubach Dolly Dimple. Character girl, OM with teeth, PW eyes, mohair wig, BJ body, original blue snowsuit with matching hat, original blue shoes and socks. Incised: "Dep-Dolly Dimple-H-Germany-8" **$1,500-2,000**

21", Gebruder Krauss 165. Sleep eyes, OM, mohair wig, BJ body, c. 1907 . . . **$275-375**

21", Maker Unknown, Blond Stone Bisque. Blue ptd eyes, mld hair parted down center and waved in a high pompadour, red lines, bisque limbs, ptd and mld shoes with tiny heels, cloth body **$185-285**

21", Paul Schmidt Character. Bisque socket head, OM, PW eyes, HHW, BJ body, 1921-1925 . . . . **$265-365**

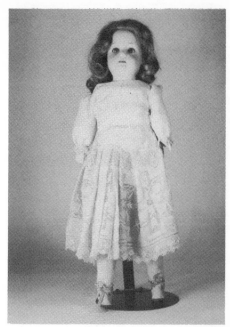

Bisque Shoulder Head, 15", hands on cloth body, OM, marked "Germany 370 A 7/0 M," $225-250.

22", Kestner Bisque Socket Head. Pouty expression, CM, sleep eyes, mohair wig, straight wrists. Incised: "4" . . **$1,000-1,200**

23", Maker Unknown, Bisque Socket Head. OM, PW eyes, HHW, BJ body. Head incised: "13619 Germany" **$295-395**

23", Otto Dressel Turned Shoulder Head. Bisque head, OM, PW eyes, HHW, bisque lower arms, kid body **$295-395**

23", S & H Walker. Flirty eyes, OM, HHW, BJ body, unmarked **$595-695**

23½", Maker Unknown, Bisque Socket Head. Sleep eyes, OM, mohair wig, BJ body. Head incised: "B5 Germany" **$295-395**

24", Borgfeldt Bisque Socket Head. Sleep eyes, OM, HHW, BJ body. Body incised: "G.B." **$325-425**

24", Borgfeldt Bisque Socket Head. Sleep eyes, OM, HHW, BJ body. Body incised: "Pansy 11, Borgfeldt-US & Germany 1910-22" **$365-465**

Bisque Socket Head, 17", jtd wooden body, marked "Germany Handwerck," $350.

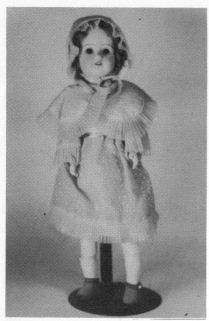

24", Guttmann & Schiffnie Child 8. Sleep eyes, OM, HHW, 1897-1920s **$325-425**

24", Maker Unknown, Special. Bisque socket head, OM, sleep eyes, HHW, BJ body. Dolls marked this way were made by Adolf Wislizenus, Dolly Princess, and C.M. Bergmann **$385-485**

25", Adolf Wislizenus Special. Incised bisque socket head, OM, PW eyes, HHW, BJ body **$295-395**

25", Bruno Schmidt Bisque Socket Head. Tommy Tucker type, OM, PW eyes, mld blond hair, BJ body, c. 1900. Incised: "BSW" (in heart) "2048-5½" **$925-1,200**

Bisque Socket Head, 14", marked "R/A DEP 1-1610," mache body and arms, jtd wooden legs, c. 1907, $300.

Bisque Socket Head, 13", jtd wooden body, marked "Armand Marseille 3/0 DEP," c. 1894, $225.

Armand Marseille Head, 17", stamped Handwerck body, marked "390-A 0½ M," $250-300.

25½", Borgfeldt Alma. Bisque socket head on bisque shoulder plate, OM, PW eyes, bisque lower arms, wears a mohair wig, kid body, c. 1900 ....,............... **$245-345**

26", Gebruder Ohlhaver Revalo Child. Sleep eyes, OM, HHW, BJ body (bisque has a matt finish), c. 1921 .... **$385-485**

29", Recknagel of Alexandrinenthal Child. Sleep eyes, OM, HHW, bisque head has stringing holes near crown, BJ body, 1886-1910 .... **$485-585**

34", E.U. Steiner Majestic. Bisque socket bald head, OM, PW sleep eyes, BJ body, dressed in original nun's outfit **$695-795**

Bisque-Head Boy, 9", cloth body, marked "Made in Germany GES 216-GESCH 15/0," $200.

Mother Superior Marie Immaculate of the Franciscan Sisters, 12", Quebec, Canada, marked "17/0 SH DED," $250.

Reproduction Butterfly Bonnet Doll, 12", brunch souvenir doll for Region 12 of the Western Reserve Doll Club, $75.

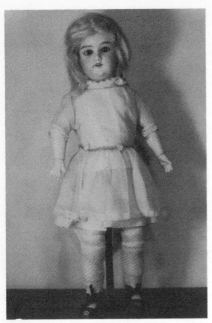

Armand Marseille Child, 20½", marked "390 A5M 1909," $225.

E.U. Steiner Bisque Head, 14", kid body, c. 1893, marked "E.U. St.," $295.

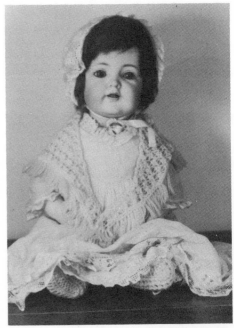

Heubach-Koppelsdorf, 17", marked "Germany 302 4/0," $225.

K Star R-Simon & Halbig-128/36, 15", movable tongue, $500.

Heinrich Handwerck Bisque Head, 30", compo body, OM, sleep eyes, PE, Elva Weems collection, **$495-595.**

Kestner Shoulder Head, 30", cloth swing-jointed body, fur eyebrows, crown sticker on back of shoulder, Elva Weems collection, **$750.**

German Socket Head, 40", BJ compo body, sleep eyes, Elva Weems collection, **$1,000.**

Simon & Halbig 1248, 32", sleep eyes, PE, Elva Weems collection, **$700.**

Kestner 360 Germany 27, 12½", rare character face with four teeth in slightly open lips, soft blond mohair wig, BJ toddler body, $395-425.

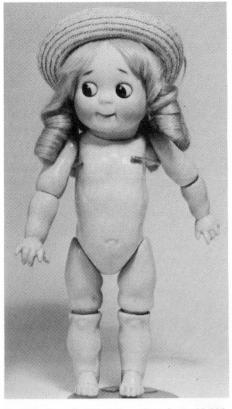

Kestner Googly 221, 16", replaced wig, $3,000.

1894 AM 7 DEP, 20", OM with four teeth, $225.

K Star R 114, 13¼", CM, blue ptd eyes, pink boy outfit, c. 1906, bald head mohair wig, $2,000-2,500.

Bald Turned-Head, 18", marked "639-9," CM, kid body, bisque lower arms. These dolls are labeled German and French, $1,200.

Simon & Halbig-K Star R 39, OM with four teeth, old French-style dress, $395.

3
German Babies and Toddlers

As a rule, the Germans were better modelers than the French. Their doll heads have more character and look like real children. The French doll with oversized cheeks and oversized eyes is a larger than life character and, for the most part, a great big beautiful doll. For this reason, I've personally felt closer to my German dolls despite their small hands and disproportionate bodies and feet. At worst, the German dolls are dwarfish; while the French dolls are masterful works of fine ingenuity and art. Their custom-made bodies, trousseaux, trunks, and accessories were indeed made to last a lifetime, not just a weekend (as many dolls and toys are now made).

When viewing an early French doll or a tiny Limoges cup and saucer, one gets the eerie feeling that they were designed not at all for the playroom but for the bibelot cabinet. The German dolls and toys, although well-made, were bona fide *playthings*. Thus, it is with little surprise that the German character dolls and babies have become so popular with collectors. They seem like real children, yearning for endearment and warmth. It is the French poupee that is untouchable. Let her stay in the bibelot cabinet!

All of the dolls listed in this chapter are in mint condition, dressed, have either original or old wigs, or remain in their preconceived bald or molded-hair state. Lesser examples cannot command these prices.

4", Maker Unknown, All-Bisque Girl. Plump body, jtd at shoulders and hips, CM, sleep eyes, indented nostrils, no lip line. Mark: "Prize Baby" **$895-995**

6¾" (head cir), Minerva Baby. Metal head, CM, incised, ptd brown hair, ptd blue eyes, red lid lines, red eye and nose dots, bisque forearms, hair-stuffed cloth body... **$95-125**

7½" (head cir), Putnam Fly-Lo. Brown glass eyes, bisque head and hands, 10½" tall, signed Putnam head, very rare **$2,500-3,000**

8" (head cir), Armand Marseille Pillow Dream Baby. Hand puppet, bisque head, CM, glass

Character Baby, incised "Made in Germany G 327 B DRGM ___ 59 A 3/0 M," 12", $300.

59

Simon & Halbig 126/6 Germany 36, 16",
$350.

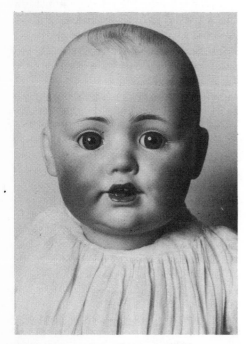

JDK, 12", made in Germany, $350.

eyes, opening in back of pillow, original tag **$600-700**

8", Schoenau & Hoffmeister Oriental Girl. Bisque socket head, OM, sleep eyes, black wig, 5-pc mache body, original Oriental costume. Mark: "4900" **$395-495**

9", Heubach Negro. Shoulder head, brown intaglio eyes with whites to the side, dark kid body and dark bisque lower arms, CM, marked **$700-800**

9", Heubach Negro. Shoulder head, brown intaglio eyes with whites to the side, dark kid body, and dark bisque lower arms, CM, marked **$700-800**

9", Heubach-Koppelsdorf Zulu Black Toddler 320. Brown sleep eyes, black wig, OM, toddler compo body, grass skirt **$400-500**

10", Heubach Baby Stuart. Sunburst mark, blue sleep eyes (some have intaglio eyes), removable bisque bonnet with round holes for ribbon ties, CM, rare **$1,500-2,000**

10", Heubach-Koppelsdorf White Baby Girl 349. Sleep eyes, CM, mld/ptd hair, celluloid hands, cloth body, c. 1925 (Heubach's answer to the Putnam Bye-Lo) **$400-500**

10", Heubach-Koppelsdorf Zulu Black Baby 399. Sleep eyes, CM, mld hair, BJ baby body, original earrings and grass skirt . . . **$400-500**

10" (head cir), K Star R Negro 126. Brown sleep eyes, OM with teeth, black hair wig, 5-pc baby body **$495-595**

10", Maker Unknown, Character Baby. All-bisque, intaglio blue eyes, bald head ptd to simulate hair. Mark: "142/0" **$495-595**

10", Schoenau & Hoffmeister Porzellanfabrik Burggrub 169. Bisque socket head character baby, OM, sleep eyes, HHW, ... **$195-295**

10½", Ellar Oriental Baby. Yellow bisque, sleep eyes, solid dome, BJ body (odd-shaped body), Oriental version of My Dream Baby. Mark: "A (star with ELLAR in the center) M Germany 8½" **$895-995**

10½", Heubach Laughing Baby. Blue intaglio

eyes, OCM with two lower teeth, mld blond hair, BJ bent limb body, c. 1910. Mark: "Heubach 7804" (in a square)..... **$795-895**

10½", Heubach Whistling Boy. Blue intaglio eyes to the side, compo forearms, mld hair, extended ears, double chin, tiny round mouth whistles when squeeze-box in tummy is pressed **$850-950**

10½" (head cir), Putnam Biskaloid Bye-Lo Baby. Blue ptd eyes, celluloid hands, cloth body, rare..................... **$700-800**

10½" (head cir), Putnam Bye-Lo Baby. Bisque head, blue sleep eyes, celluloid hands, signed cloth body **$425-525**

10½" (head cir), Putnam Negro Bye-Lo. Black celluloid hands, bisque head, glass eyes, CM, signed dark cloth body. (Watch out for reproductions!) **$900-1,000**

11", Goebel Laughing Boy. Bisque head, blue ptd eyes, OCM, blond mld hair, BJ body **$695-795**

11", Heubach Pouty Boy. Sunburst mark, CM, bisque shoulder head, bisque lower arms, intaglio blue eyes, hair molding ... **$600-700**

11", Heubach-Koppelsdorf Negro Baby Girl. Brown glass sleep eyes, OM, 5-pc BJ compo body **$400-500**

11", K Star R Negro 100...... **$975-1,200**

11", Louis Wolf & Co. Our Fairy. All-bisque, OCM with teeth, jtd arms, mohair wig. Sticker on chest reads: "Our Fairy, Germany (Louis Wolf & Co.) 1914" **$1,600-1,700**

11", O'Neill Kewpie. Bisque, rare blue glass eyes, autograph on back **$4,500-5,000**

11½", Davis & Voetsch Character Baby. Sleep eyes, CM, 5-pc compo body, ptd hair on almost-bald head, indented nostrils, no lip line. Incised: "3-Geschutz, Germany" (green ink in circle).................... **$895-995**

11½", Davis & Voetsch Lori Baby. Sleep eyes, CM, 5-pc compo body. Solid-dome head incised: "Lori D.V. 3." Mark: "GESCHUTZ Germany".................... **$950-1,100**

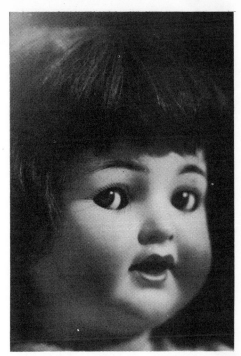

K Star R 126, 19", bisque head on 5-pc compo baby body, c. 1909, Jim and Sheila Olah Scheetz collection, $500.

A & M Oriental Baby 353, 14", olive-colored bisque, sleep eyes, CM, ptd hair, swivel neck on 5-pc compo body, c. 1900, Jim and Sheila Olah Scheetz collection, $1,500.

61

Kestner 152-5 Germany, 15", OM with mld tongue, bisque head on 5-pc compo baby body, c. 1910, Jim and Sheila Olah Scheetz collection, $450.

11½", Kestner Baby. All-bisque, swivel head, OCM, intaglio blue eyes **$1,000-1,200**

11½", Kestner Baby. All-bisque, swivel head, OCM, intaglio blue eyes,. **$1,000-1,200**

11½" (head cir), Putnam Bye-Lo Baby (in original box). Cry box, compo head, blue sleep eyes, compo hands, cloth body, label on dress, mark on head, original clothes and original pink blanket. Box inscribed: "Bye-Lo Baby, The Almost Human Doll. Modeled Corp. 1923 by Grace Storey Putnam. Geo Borgfeldt Corp" **$350-550**

11¾", Heubach-Type Boy. Blue ptd eyes, OCM, ptd/mld hair, BJ body **$525-625**

12", Amberg Newborn Babe. Sleep eyes, CM, bisque head and flange neck, compo hands, cloth body. Mark: "Germany A.R. L.A. & S." Head mark: "886-2" **$425-525**

12", Armand Marseille Baby Phyllis. Solid-dome Armand Marseille bisque head, glass eyes, CM, cloth body and limbs, made for the Baby Phyllis Doll Company, Brooklyn, New York. Mark: "BABY PHYLLIS Made in Germany 24014" **$425-525**

12", Armand Marseille Dream Baby. Sleep eyes, CM, ptd hair, BJ body, rare mld bottle in hand, made for Arranbee **$695-795**

12", C.M. Bergmann Character Baby. Armand Marseille head, OM, sleep eyes, mohair wig, BJ body **$300-400**

12", Century Doll Company Bisque Baby. Fine bisque quality, CM, PW eyes, compo hands, cloth body and limbs, possibly a Kestner for the Century Doll Company. Head incised: "Century Baby" **$795-895**

12", Heubach Pouty Baby Boy. Blue intaglio eyes, CM, flocked hair, BJ body . . **$425-525**

12", Heubach-Koppelsdorf Character Girl 262. Short mld hair with bow, OCM with mld teeth, blue ptd eyes, compo lower arms, cloth body, shoulder head type **$400-500**

12", Heubach-Koppelsdorf Gypsy 452. Sleep eyes, lt brown bisque, OM with teeth, mohair wig, compo toddler body, original brass earrings and gypsy costume **$300**

12", Heubach-Koppelsdorf Indian Toddler. Glass sleep eyes, black mohair wig, red ptd toddler body **$300-400**

12", K Star R 100. Brown glass eyes and flocked hair, very rare **$1,200-1,500**

12", Kestner Character Baby 152. Sleep eyes, OM, auburn wig, BJ body **$300-400**

12", Kestner Toddler 257. Character face, blue ptd eyes, CM, HHW, plaster pate, BJ body **$375-475**

12" (head cir), Max Handwerck Bebe Elite. Glass eyes, OM, PE, HHW, 5-pc compo BJ body **$295-395**

12" (head cir), Putnam Bye-Lo Baby. Blue ptd eyes, compo head, celluloid hands, body made of cloth **$225-425**

12", Simon & Halbig 600. Glass eyes, OM, PE, mohair wig, toddler body **$395-495**

12", Welsch Baby Doll. Sweet face, OM, fixed eyes, HHW, BJ body, in original box. Incised: "150 Welsch" **$285-385**

12½", Armand Marseille Javanese. Slanted glass eyes, CM, olive bisque, turban and wig on ptd solid dome, 5-pc compo toddler body, original print outfit. Mark: "A.M. Germany 353/2 ½K" **$895-995**

12½" (head cir), Armand Marseille Negro Dream Baby. Solid dome, CM, brown glass sleep eyes, original tissue silk dress and cape, 10½" tall **$895-995**

12½" (head cir), Putnam Betty Bye-Lo. Bisque head, blue glass sleep eyes, OCM with four ptd teeth, flange neck, standard cloth Bye-Lo body, celluloid hands (some have compo hands) **$2,000-3,000**

12½" (head cir), Putnam Betty Bye-Lo. Bisque head, blue glass sleep eyes, OCM with four ptd teeth. Flange neck, standard cloth Bye-Lo body, celluloid hands (some have compo hands) **$2,000-3,000**

Kestner Baby 260, 13½", replaced wig, Herron collection, $325.

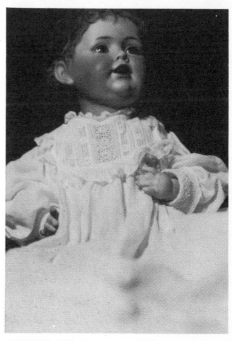

JDK 247, 17", sleep eyes, OCM, D. Kay Crow collection, $425.

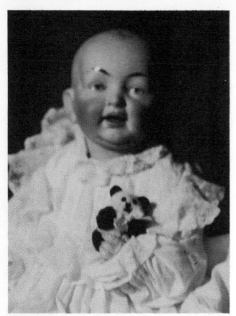

Kaiser Baby, 14", unmarked, ptd eyes, OCM, D. Kay Crow collection, $500.

Gebruder Heubach Mechanical Twins, 10", sunburst mark on back of head, squeeze tummy and doll cries and turns head from side to side, blue intaglio eyes, pouty CM, original costume, bisque head, Jim and Sheila Olah Scheetz collection, $1,500-1,700.

12½" (head cir), Putnam Bye-Lo Baby. Bisque head, rare blue ptd eyes, celluloid hands, cloth body **$1,000-1,200**

12½" (head cir), Putnam Bye-Lo Baby. Blue glass eyes, celluloid hands, body made of cloth and signed **$495-595**

12½" (head cir), Putnam Wax-Head Bye-Lo. Glass inset eyes, CM, detailed realistic face, rolls of fat around the neck, celluloid hands, cloth body, rare size **$2,000-3,000**

13", Armand Marseille Character Baby. Bisque socket head, PN, sleep eyes, OM with two teeth, BJ body, distributed by George Borgfeldt, c. 1920 .... **$395-495**

13", Armand Marseille Toddler 992. Sleep eyes, OM, mohair wig, BJ body... **$325-425**

13", Heubach Baby. Tiny eyes ptd to the right, OCM, shoulder head, mld hair, cloth body, bisque lower arms **$700-800**

13", Kestner Hilda 1070. Solid-bisque dome head, OM, blue sleep eyes. Mark: "Hilda J.D.K. Jr. 1914-N1070" **$3,200-4,200**

13" (head cir), Maker Unknown, Negro Baby. Bisque socket head, OM, sleep eyes. BJ body incised: "AMUSO" **$395-495**

13", Max Handwerck Bebe Elite. Sleep eyes, CM, HHW, 5-pc toddler body, 1900-1901 (looks very French) **$475-575**

13 1/3", Kestner Negro Girl. Bisque head, glass eyes, OM with teeth,........ **$825-925**

13½", Heubach Character Boy. Sunburst mark, bisque shoulder head type (considered rare), laughing face with squinting eyes, compo limbs, original body **$700-900**

14", Alt, Beck & Gottschalck Baby. Bisque, OM, sleep eyes, HHW, PN, jtd wrists, c. 1910. Mark: "A.B.G. 1361/32" **$225-325**

14", Armand Marseille Baby 971. Bisque head, OM with teeth, sleep eyes, HHW, BJ body **$245-345**

14", Armand Marseille Negro Baby 341. Solid dome, CM, sleep eyes, BJ body ... **$500-600**

A full view of the Early Carved Wood Creche Lady.

25", Early Carved Wood Creche Lady, cloth body, wooden spoon hands, red leather boots, carved hair, appears to be all original, D. Kay Crow collection, $2,500-3,000.

17", K Star R 117A German Bisque Pouty, D. Kay Crow collection, $2,800-3,800.

21", K Star R 65, OM, sleep eyes, PE, old wool challis dress, original wig, D. Kay Crow collection, $600-700.

18", Tete Jumeau, all original, fine pink silk dress with matching underwear, marked, D. Kay Crow collection. **$1,200-1,300**

22", S & H 1588 Lady Doll, bisque socket head, D. Kay Crow collection, **$750-850.**

13", 18th Century Creche Figures, Mary and Joseph, primitive bodies filled with straw, terracotta heads, arms, and feet, velvet robes lined with old Italian newspaper, D. Kay Crow collection, pair $1,500-1,800.

24", Solid Dome, so-called Belton, CM, blonde wig, blue PW eyes, D. Kay Crow collection, $1,500-2,000.

12", French Papier-Mache, so-called Milliners' Model, hairdo has bun in back, colored bands join limbs, tiny waist, old clothes, D. Kay Crow collection, $425-525.

10", Stone Bisque, very early, all original, D. Kay Crow collection, $295-350.

9", German Bisque Negro Girl, all original, marked "79 7/OX," D. Kay Crow collection, **$300-400**.

5", Conquistador with Metal Helmet and Sword, celluloid, ptd, all original, D. Kay Crow collection, **$45-60**.

*9", Lenci Dolls, all original, dressed doll is old, undressed doll is a later version from the same mold, D. Kay Crow collection, older, **$150-200**, newer, **$75-125**.*

*9", German Bisque Soldiers, D. Kay Crow collection, each **$125-135**.*

12", Early Queen Anne Type, ptd features, old dress, D. Kay Crow collection, $800-1,000.

20½", K Star R 255, celluloid, D. Kay Crow collection, $150-175.

14", Armand Marseille Negro Rockabye Baby. Solid dome, dark color fired in bisque (not painted on), sleep eyes, mohair wig, BJ body, OM with teeth. Incised: "A.M. 351/ Germany" **$850-950**

14", Armand Marseille 353. Yellow bisque head, glass eyes, BJ body **$650-750**

14", Bahr & Proschild Toddler. Mohair wig, OCM with two top teeth, sleep eyes, bent arms, jtd knees, BJ body **$425-525**

14", K Star R Baby 100. Solid dome, blue intaglio eyes, 10½" head cir, OCM with tongue, BJ body **$475-500**

14", Kestner Hilda 237. Sleep eyes, OM, mohair wig (sometimes bald), bent limb compo body **$3,200-4,200**

14", Kestner Hilda 245. Sleep eyes, OM, mohair wig (sometimes bald), bent limb compo body **$3,200-4,200**

14", Kestner Oriental Baby 243. Yellow bisque, OM, slanted eye sockets, dark glass eyes, black wig, silk band around head, BJ body, original costume **$1,700-2,000**

14", Revalo Character Girl. Bisque socket head, blue ptd eyes, ptd/mld short hair, OCM, compo body, c. 1920 .... **$650-750**

14½", Armand Marseille My Dream Baby Toddler. Sleep eyes, CM, mld hair, 5-pc toddler body **$475-575**

14½", Ball-Head Kestner. Blue sleep eyes, mld teeth and tongue, BJ compo body. Mark on head: "3-7" **$595-695**

14¾", Averill Bisque-Head Baby. Sleep eyes, OM, cloth body, compo limbs. Incised: "AVERILL" **$695-795**

15", Armand Marseille My Dream Baby. Blue sleep eyes, OM, bisque head. **$395-495**

15", Helen Jensen Gladdie Boy. Earthenware head, compo limbs, cloth body, old clothes, designed for Borgfeldt **$750-850**

15", K Star R Naughty Eyes 34. Bisque head, compo 5-pc body, 10½" head cir, mechanism

Large Piano Baby, 13", beautifully sculpted, blue intaglio eyes, deep hair molding, night-dress tinted in dainty pastels, heavy bisque, purchased in France during last century, Herron collection, $700-1,000.

Scheumeister & Quendt, 21", compo baby body, marked "Q" and "S," "207" on back of head, Elva Weems collection, $375.

inside head keeps eyes open when doll is flat, brown sleep eyes, OM **$895-995**

15", Kestner Character Boy 247. Bisque head, sleep eyes, OM, BJ body, HHW .. **$495-595**

15", Kley & Hahn Character Baby. Blue intaglio eyes, OCM, HHW. BJ body incised: "K & H 525" **$375-475**

15", Maker Unknown, German Character Baby. Angry face, CM, sleep eyes, 11" head cir. BJ body incised: "1428" **$695-795**

15", Maker Unknown, Screaming Baby. Large OCM revealing inner cavities, bisque socket head, squinty blue glass eyes, bald head, BJ body. Incised: "J".... **$975-1,200**

15½", Armand Marseille Negro Baby 351. Sleep eyes, OM, black wig........ **$475-575**

16", Century Doll Company Baby. Kestner head, solid dome, mld blond hair, sleep eyes, OCM, compo limbs, cloth body... **$475-575**

16", Kallus Baby Bo Kaye. Kestner bisque head, blond mld hair, glass eyes, OM with two lower teeth, celluloid limbs, cloth body. Incised: "J. L. Kallus: Copr. Germany 1394/30".................... **$1,500-1,700**

16", Kestner Baby 211. Bisque head, OM, sleep eyes, mohair wig, bent limb BJ body **$400-500**

16", Otto Reinecke Crete Baby. Sleep eyes, OM with teeth, 5-pc baby body, bent limbs, wears a mohair wig. Incised: "PM (Otto Reinecke)" **$395-495**

16½" (head cir), Armand Marseille Character Baby 518. Solid dome, OM with two upper teeth, brown glass eyes.......... **$525-625**

16½", Arthur Gerling Negro Baby. Bisque head, PN, cloth body, Gerling voice box, compo arms, brown ptd hair and eyes. Mark on back of neck: "3-Arthur A. Gerling-Made in Germany-DRG-MA".......... **$350-450**

17", Heubach Coquette. Bisque swivel head, blue ptd eyes to the side, mld short blond hair with hair band and bow at side, smiling OCM with teeth, pink twill body **$950-1,100**

17", Kestner Baby 152. Sleep eyes, HHW, OM with wobbly tongue, BJ body..... **$475-575**

17", Kestner Baby 211. Sleep eyes, OM, mohair wig, 5-pc body, well-modeled startled character face **$400-500**

17½", Averill Bonnie Babe. Similar to the 20" Bonnie Babe, except this rare doll has a wobbly tongue............... **$975-1,200**

17¾", Kestner 257. Brown fixed glass eyes, OM with two upper teeth and wobbly tongue, blond mohair wig, bent limb baby body **$500-600**

18", Armand Marseille Baby Gloria. Cloth body with squeak box, OM with two upper teeth, compo limbs. Mark: "A.M. Germany 3524"........................ **$425-525**

18", Armand Marseille Character Baby 990. Sleep eyes, OM, mohair wig, BJ body, fine bisque quality **$325-425**

18", Heubach Baby. Sunburst mark, brown sleep eyes, OM, wears a mohair wig, BJ body **$475-575**

18", Kestner Baby Jean. Solid dome, sleep eyes, OM with wobbly tongue, BJ body. Incised: "JDK 13 Germany" **$750-850**

18", Putnam Bye-Lo. Bisque socket head on BJ compo body, signed, rare .. **$1,000-1,200**

18½", K Star R 101. Blue ptd eyes, OM, HHW, BJ body............. **$2,000-2,500**

19", S & Co. Lori Baby. Sleep eyes, CM, lt mld hair. Incised: "D Lori 2." Stamped: "S and Co., Germany" **$1,400-1,500**

19½", Maker Unknown, Two-Faced Character Baby. Unusual doll, smiling face has blue glass eyes, disgruntled face has the more expressive ptd eyes, large ears, OCM, BJ body **$1,500-2,000**

20", Averill Bonnie Babe. Alt, Beck & Gottschalck bisque head, Borgfeldt cloth body, OM with two teeth, sleep eyes, mld hair, compo limbs. Mark: "Copr. by Georgene Averill, Germany"............... **$850-950**

Kley & Hahn 680, 22", antique clothing, old wig, Elva Weems collection, $600.

Heubach-Koppelsdorf, 27", marked "320/ 10," toddler body, sleep eyes, OM, Elva Weems collection, $475.

20", Hitz, Jacobs, and Kassler Kiddiejoy. Sleep eyes, OM, blond mld hair, bisque lower arms, kid body, 1918-1930s, incised on back of bisque socket head **$265-365**

20", K Star R Mechanical Baby. Arms move up and down, sleep eyes, OM, mohair wig, key........................ **$1,000-1,500**

20", Konig & Wernicke Bisque-Head Baby 98. Sleep eyes, OM, HHW **$350-450**

20½", Simon & Halbig 156. Bisque head, sleep eyes, OCM with tremble tongue, HHW, bent limb body..................... **$695-795**

21", Franz Schmidt Breather Baby. Sleep eyes, OM, HHW, PN, BJ body. Incised: "1295"........................ **$425-525**

22", Cuno & Otto Dressel Jutta Baby. Bisque socket head, OM, sleep eyes, PE, HHW, BJ body **$395-495**

22", K Star R Character 118. . . **$1,600-2,600**

22", Maker Unknown, Bisque Shoulder-Head Baby. Fixed glass eyes, OM, mohair wig, bisque lower arms, turned head, kid-gusseted body. Shoulder mark: "1127 10" . . **$695-795**

23", K Star R Character Baby 121. Bisque head, fat face, OM, sleep eyes, mohair wig, bent limb body, 1901-1920s....... **$495-595**

23½", Simon & Halbig Baby Blanche. Bisque socket head, OM with teeth, sleep eyes, PE, HHW, BJ body, c. 1900 .... **$375-475**

24", Bahr & Proschild Baby. Sleep eyes, OM, HHW. BJ body incised: "Bahr & Proschild-624-12 Germany" **$595-695**

24", Ernst Reinhardt Augusta Baby. Celluloid eyes, OM with upper teeth, HHW, BJ body, c. 1920. Incised: "Augusta" **$385-485**

24", Putnam Babykins. Bisque head, blue sleep eyes, short eyelashes on upper eye ridge only, faint brows, CM, ptd hair, compo limbs, body made of cloth, very rare. Incised: "Cop by Grace Storey Putnam. Made in Germany 7435"..................... **$2,500-3,000**

25", S & Co. Lori Baby. Solid dome with sparse ptd blond hair, sleep eyes, bent limb compo body, CM, bisque socket head incised. BJ body stamped: "Geschutz S & Co., Germany".................$1,800-2,000

26", K Star R 126. Flirty eyes, OM, mohair wig, rare toddler body $600-700

28", S & Co. Lori Baby. Solid dome, ptd blond hair, sleep eyes, OCM, BJ body. Bisque head incised: "Lori".................$895-995

31", Kley & Hahn Character Boy 166. Solid dome, OM, PW eyes, BJ body....$895-925

(L. To R.) Horseshoe mark 8900-11/0, 10", $295. Morimura Brothers, 9½", Japan, $250. Both dolls from the Herron collection.

4
Miniature Dolls
The Tinies

The most endearing dolls of all are the lovable tinies. They are the most difficult to make, yet the most adaptable. How snugly they fit into a doll's house, a bibelot cabinet, or child's tiny pocket! Their prices in recent years have become almost prohibitive, and their supply is extremely limited. The dolls listed here are in mint condition, unless otherwise stated. Nude dolls or dolls with molded-on and painted clothing are described as such. Others are dressed in old, original, or contemporary clothing. Some have molded and painted hair or bonnets; other have their original human hair or mohair wigs.

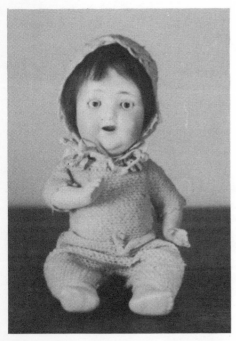

MB Japan, 10", Morimura Brothers, $200.

1¾", Maker Unknown, Bonnet Girl. All-bisque, jtd arms, ptd features, blond curls and bangs, crude, late German......... **$20-30**

1¾", Maker Unknown, Nude Bathing Beauties. Sitting, legs outstretched, ptd hair and features, one hand to the face, the other to the side, German, sold as a pair... **$150-250**

2", O'Neill Kewpie. This all-bisque Kewpie is seated and has his arms around his pet rabbit. Incised on feet: "Rose O'Neill." Paper label on back reads: "Kewpie-Reg. U.S. Pat. Off. Des-PAT. 111-4-1913" **$250-350**

2", O'Neill Kewpie on Knees. Googly eyes, wears a blond wig, jtd shoulders. Incised: "Germany"..................... **$200-300**

2¼", Maker Unknown, All-Bisque Man. Swivel neck, mld hair, mld derby hat, ptd features, jtd at shoulders and hips, fully dressed **$95-125**

2½", Maker Unknown, All-Bisque. Glass eyes, jtd at shoulders and hips, CM, mohair wig, ptd shoes and socks. Incised: "Germany 11959"......................... **$65-165**

2½", Maker Unknown, French Provincial Couple. Boy and girl, all-bisque, swivel head, blue ptd eyes, CM, brown mohair wig, jtd at shoulders and hips, original costume, sold as a pair **$350-450**

2½", Maker Unknown, Horn of Plenty Piano Baby............................ **$65-95**

2½", Maker Unknown, Parian-Type Bathing Beauty. German, mld costume **$55-95**

3", Maker Unknown, All-Bisque Baby. Movable limbs, ptd features, blond mld hair, German........................ **$50-100**

3", Maker Unknown, All-Bisque Flapper. These dolls are German unless otherwise stated as French or Japanese. Mark on leg: "Germany 17/0" **$65-95**

3", Maker Unknown, All-Bisque Man. Mustache and mld brown hair **$85-95**

3", Maker Unknown, Bottle Baby. OM for bottle, jtd at shoulders and hips..... **$55-95**

Prince and Princess Souci, 7", Nancy Ann Abbot creations, ptd bisque, mohair wigs, original costumes, $35-50 pair.

3", Maker Unknown, Boy and Girl. All-bisque, swivel head, inset glass eyes, jtd at shoulders and hips, dolls are sold as a pair **$325-425**

3", Maker Unknown, Crawling Baby. All-bisque, nude..................... **$65-95**

3", Maker Unknown, Policeman. All-bisque, jtd at shoulders and hips only, molded-on uniform, hat, German **$75-85**

3", Maker Unknown, Policeman. All-bisque, jtd at shoulders and hips.......... **$65-95**

3¼", Kestner Lettie Lane's Doll's Doll. All-bisque, brown fixed glass eyes, blond mohair wig, mld shoes and socks, all-original dress, undies, straw hat................ **$300-400**

3¼", O'Neill Negro Hottentot Kewpies. All-celluloid, white ptd wings, blue and white check blanket, Kewpie sticker on back, jtd arms, sold as a pair **$35-45**

3½", Borgfeldt Happifat Boy. All-bisque, suit, c. 1914 .... **$250-350**

Bisque Head, 7", all-cloth body, German, c. 1920, $300.

All-Bisque Girl, 5", ptd features, German,
$175.

All-Bisque Girl, 5½", German, ptd features,
$175.

3½", Maker Unknown, Little Girl. Molded-on winter cap and coat, German, all-bisque, immobile, c. 1920 .... **$20-40**

3½", Maker Unknown, Medic. All-bisque, ptd, German **$95**

3½", Maker Unknown, Nodder Boy. German, all-bisque, wears a mld cap and a mld romper, c. 1920 .... **$40-80**

3½", Maker Unknown, Santa Claus Nodder. All-bisque, German, ptd/mld costume, c. 1920. Nodders have elastic-strung heads that move. **$45-65**

3½", Maker Unknown, Tepee, Campfire & Five Indians. All-bisque, German, sold as a set **$125-145**

3¾", Maker Unknown, Little Girl. All-bisque, swivel neck, inset glass eyes, CM, jtd at shoulders and hips, German **$165-265**

4", Horsman, HEbee-SHEbee. All-bisque, blue mld shoes, rare swivel legs, label on sole **$800-900**

4", Maker Unknown, All-Bisque Boy. Sweater, trousers, mld cap with pompon, jtd at shoulders, German **$80-100**

4", Maker Unknown, All-Bisque Girl. Wired swinging legs, in seated position, mld arms folded on lap, German, c. 1920 .... **$85-125**

4", Maker Unknown, Googly. German, all-bisque, swivel head, large glass eyes glancing to the side, jtd at shoulders and hips, original clothes, Dutch-cut wig **$475-575**

4", Maker Unknown, Googly. All-bisque, movable limbs, chubby round face, HHW, glass eyes glancing to the side, CM. Incised: "217" **$450-550**

4", Maker Unknown, Piano Baby. Baby girl in nightgown with mld bonnet **$50-100**

4½", Borgfeldt Happifat Boy. All-bisque, undies, c. 1914 .... **$260-360**

4½", Borgfeldt Happifat Girl. All-bisque, pink dress, c. 1914 .... **$260-360**

4½", Butler Bros. Baby Bud. All-bisque, mld clothes on upper body, blue ptd eyes to the side, OCM, jtd at shoulders. Shirttail marked: "Germany." Incised: "Baby Bud." (This doll was later reproduced in Japan. Japanese version, **$45-65**) **$245-345**

4½", Heubach Child. All-bisque, jtd arms, ptd/mld shoes **$185-285**

4½", Heubach Dutch Boy and Girl. Sunburst mark, seated girl has mld basket on back, smiling faces, sold as a pair. Mark on boy: "3748." Mark on girl: "3964" **$425-525**

4½", Kallus Annie Rooney. Large round eyes to the side, watermelon mouth, yellow wool bangs and pigtails, mld clothes, red felt hat, arms outstretched, feet together, copyright J.L. Kallus/Jack Collins **$300-350**

4½", Louis Wolf & Co. Our Fairy. Smiling OCM with teeth, brown glass fixed eyes, all-bisque, HHW, movable arms, together legs, c. 1914. Round chest label reads: "Our Fairy-Germany" **$495-595**

All-Bisque Girl, 5½", sleep eyes, $275.

4½", Maker Unknown, Boy and Girl. All-bisque, mld rabbit costume, ptd features, wire-strung, sold as a pair. Incised: "Made in Germany" **$225-325**

4½", Maker Unknown, Breather. All-bisque, OM with two teeth, PN, blue glass eyes, old mohair wig **$175-275**

4½", Maker Unknown, Flapperette. All-bisque, mld cloche hat, mld shoes and socks, jtd arms and ptd features, wears original costume **$95-145**

4½", Maker Unknown, Little Girl. All-bisque, glass inset eyes, CM, wears a mohair wig, black booties, pegged joints. Incised: "36-10/11" **$175-275**

4½", Maker Unknown, Little Sweet Girl. All-bisque, CM, glass inset eyes, wears a mohair wig, jtd arms, mld two-strap shoes. Mark: "130" **$85-275**

4½", Maker Unknown, Piano Baby in Nightdress. Clasped hands **$85-125**

4½", O'Neill Kewpie Bride & Groom. All-

All-Bisque Child, 3½", German, D. Kay Crow collection, $275.

All-Bisque Child, 4½", D. Kay Crow collection, $150.

All-Bisque Girl, 5½", jtd limbs, sleep eyes, OM with two teeth, mld shoes and socks, hair wig with mld bows, D. Kay Crow collection, $275.

bisque, signed, jtd arms only, original clothes, sold as a pair.................. **$500-600**

4½", O'Neill Kewpie Thinker. All-bisque, jtd arms, signed................... **$250-350**

4½", O'Neill Soldier Kewpie. All-bisque, holds shotgun **$400-500**

4½", Putnam Bye-Lo Baby. All-bisque, brown glass sleep eyes, swivel neck, jtd at shoulders and hips, paper chest label, wears a mohair wig. Incised on back: "Grace Storey Putnam"...................... **$475-575**

4¾", Averill Bonnie Babe. Blue PW eyes, swivel flange neck, paper label, all-bisque, OM, pink mld shoes, jtd at shoulders and hips **$825-925**

4¾", Heubach Piano Baby. Intaglio blue eyes, satisfied smiling mouth, devilish ptd eyes, hands mld onto tummy, legs crossed in seated position........................ **$65-95**

5", Alma Dejournette My Baby Lifetime Plastic Doll. Baby has own birth certificate with paper layette, an Atlanta, Georgia, product, complete, mint, c. 1950 .... **$35-45**

5", Averill Rag. All-bisque, white with black spots, flesh colors around nose and mouth, black nose, dark red mouth (OCM with mld tongue), brown glass sleep eyes, blue mld booties, swivel head, jtd at shoulders and hips. Sticker on chest reads: "Rag TRADEMARK CORP. BY GEORGENE AVERILL 890 GERMANY"................ **$1,000-2,000**

5", Averill Tag. All-bisque, brownish-gray stripes, green fixed glass eyes, orange OM with tongue, black nose, head turns, jtd at shoulders and hips, wears mld booties, pink wool crocheted tail. Incised on back: "Tag TRADEMARK CORP. BY GEORGENE AVERILL 891 GERMANY" .. **$1,000-2,000**

5", Butler Bros. Wide-Awake Doll. All-bisque, blue ptd eyes to the side, OCM, two upper teeth, jtd at shoulders, black strap, ptd shoes, blue socks. Mark: "The Wide-Awake Doll Registered Germany" **$250-350**

5", German All-Bisque Toddler. Pink bisque, jtd at shoulders and hips, mld shoes and socks, ptd features, mohair wig **$95-125**

5", Heubach Easter Egg Piano Baby. Baby has finger to mouth. Mark: "9903" **$75-85**

5", Heubach Nude Baby. Finger to mouth, sits shyly on cobalt-blue box **$275-375**

5", Heubach Nude Baby. Finger to mouth, sits shyly on top of a cobalt-blue box . **$275-375**

5", Maker Unknown, All-Bisque Girl. Blue ptd eyes, mld bow, OCM, jtd arms, barefoot, dressed. Incised: "Germany" **$85-275**

5", Maker Unknown, Bonnet Girl. All-bisque, bonnet, long straight mld hair with uneven bangs, ptd features, very pretty face, jtd arms, mld dress, fixed legs, pink glazed ribbon mld below waist of frock, large Bertha collar trimmed with ruffles, pink flat-soled shoes. Mark: "383 German" **$125-195**

All-Bisque Boy and Girl, 7", original clothes, girl has mld hair, ptd features, jtd limbs, left leg has minor repair, $160. Boy has mld hair, ptd features, mld shoes and socks, $175. Both dolls from the D. Kay Crow collection.

5", Maker Unknown, French All-Bisque. Swivel head, CM, PW eyes, HHW, jtd at shoulders and hips, artistically designed brows and lashes, mld shoes and socks .. **$575-675**

5", Maker Unknown, Little Girl with Pink Bow. All-bisque, mld hair in curls, mld pink bow, jtd arms, white mld socks and black strap shoes **$110-210**

5", Maker Unknown, Nude Lady. Bisque, sitting position, Japanese, c. 1920 ..... **$55**

5", Maker Unknown, Sit-Down Bisque Girl. All-bisque, mld blond hair, ptd features, pink strap shoes, wire-jointed, dressed .. **$125-195**

5", O'Neill Kewpie. All-bisque, wears a pair of rare mld shoes and socks, jtd arms. Incised: "Rose O'Neill" **$200-300**

5", O'Neill Kewpie on a Vase. **$500-550**

5", Putnam Bye-Lo. All-bisque, sleep blue glass eyes, jtd arms and legs, ptd/mld shoes, legs and arms numbered. Incised: "Grace Storey Putnam" **$500-600**

Bye-Lo Baby, 8", rare size, marked "Grace Storey Putnam," original HHW, CM, sleep glass eyes, all-bisque body with shoulder joints, original label on chest, Jim and Sheila Olah Scheetz collection, $700.

5", Rohmer French Fashion. Rare size, bisque swivel head, blue ptd eyes, unpierced ears, CM, mohair wig, bisque arms to shoulders, kid body with Rohmer stamp.. **$3,000-3,500**

5½", Maker Unknown, All-Bisque Toddler.

83

German Child, 8", marked "886-2," c. 1880, bisque head on old mache body with hip and shoulder joints, sleep glass eyes, OM, original mohair wig, rare original clothes, hat, Jim and Sheila Olah Scheetz collection, $300.

All-Bisque French Doll, 5", CM, glass eyes, Jim and Sheila Olah Scheetz collection, $350.

Flirty glass eyes, mld orange romper, OM, 3-pc body, German **$375-475**

5½", Maker Unknown, Sailor Boy. All-bisque, mld hat and suit, movable limbs, mld shoes and socks, German, c. 1920 .. **$95-125**

5½", Strobel & Wilken Child. Compo body, OCM, mld hair, ptd eyes to the side, jtd at shoulders and hips **$625-725**

6", Armand Marseille Googly 324. Blue glass eyes to the side, CM, mld hair **$475-575**

6", German Bride and 6½" Groom. Dollhouse type, bisque head, hands and feet, cloth body, ptd features. bride has mohair wig, groom has ptd hair, mld and ptd shoes, both dressed in original outfits, c. early 1900s, sold as a pair **$295-395**

6", German Flapper. All-bisque, CM, blue ptd eyes, blond HHW, jtd at shoulders and hips, mld stockings and slippers, lovely original clothes, "Germany" incised on shoulder. Mark: "129-2" **$295-395**

6", Kestner Three-Faced Character. Original box contains the doll, three heads, directions, and hook for adjustment. Two heads have blue ptd eyes, the third head has brown ptd eyes, rare. Heads are marked: "178," "185," and "184" **$300-600**

6", Maker Unknown, Bisque Head. Inset glass eyes, wears a mohair wig, mache body, compo limbs, ptd shoes and socks, dressed. Incised: "19/0" **$175-275**

6", Maker Unknown, Candy-Box Doll. All-bisque, jtd arms, ptd features, mld hair, original crepe-paper dress conceals candy box, c. 1920 .... **$225-325**

6", Maker Unknown, Character Boy. All-bisque, clover mark, CM, blue glass eyes, has a swivel neck, ptd hair, jtd at shoulders and hips **$125-225**

6", Maker Unknown, Laughing Character Boy. All-bisque, nude, jtd arms are bent and raised to the chest, OCM, mld tongue and upper teeth, intaglio blue eyes glancing to the side **$150-250**

84

6", Maker Unknown, Mache Googly Boy and Girl. Original old felt clothes, mld hat, ptd features, made in Germany, sold as a pair. Boy stamped: "Made in Germany" **$200-300**

6", Maker Unknown, Scootles. All-bisque, jtd arms, ptd features, mld hair, German. Watch out for reproductions! **$500-600**

6", Putnam Bye-Lo. All-bisque, blue ptd eyes, jtd arms, legs numbered, mld hair. Incised: "Grace S. Putnam" **$325-425**

6", Schutz Marke All-Celluloid Girl. German trademark, pupil-less glass eyes, OM, mohair wig, turtles on hand and feet and back of neck **$25**

6¼", Maker Unknown, Sailor Boy. All-bisque, red eyeline marks, wears a mld sailor hat and suit, jtd at shoulders, blond mld hair, German....................... **$160-170**

German Flapper, 6", c. 1920, bisque head on mache body, black ptd stockings and shoes, CM, glass eyes, all-original outfit, rare turned head, Jim and Sheila Olah Scheetz collection, $250.

6½", Armand Marseille Character Boy 210. Similar to the Armand Marseille Googly 210, blue ptd intaglio eyes to the side, mld blond hair, CM, BJ body. (I believe these dolls are supposed to represent the Campbell Kids. Both have original old clothes, possibly Dolly Dingle and Bobby Blake) **$575-675**

6½", Armand Marseille Dream Baby. Blue glass sleep eyes, CM, reclines in cradle of wicker and wood, winding key, rocks to "Rockabye Baby," has rattle in hand, rare. Incised: "A.M. 341/Germany" **$350-450**

6½", Armand Marseille Googly 210. Intaglio blue ptd eyes, mld hair, BJ body, looks like a Campbell Kid **$575-675**

6½", German All-Bisque Child. Brown glass eyes, swivel neck, jtd at shoulders and hips, mohair wig, black mld shoes and high ribbed stockings. Incised: "620-6"....... **$295-395**

6½", Maker Unknown, Bisque Swingers. Dainty pastel coloring, character type, wears mld hat and clothes, German, dolls sold as a pair **$100-150**

6½", Maker Unknown, Bonnet Shoulder Head. White bonnet with pink and blue trim, blue bow under chin, bisque lower limbs, cloth body and upper limbs **$50-60**

Alice in Wonderland Frozen Charlotte, 5", blond hair has brush marks, black band, gold luster shoes, original outfit, $250.

*Rose O'Neill Kewpies, 10", $325-400, and 6",
$185-200, both marked, Jim and Sheila Olah
Scheetz collection.*

*French All-Bisque Couple, 3", stationary glass
eyes, long hair wig, original costumes, girl has
some foot damage, D. Kay Crow collection,
$650 pair.*

6½", Maker Unknown, Dollhouse Lady. Antique variety, bisque head and limbs, cloth body, PI, mld shoes, old clothes .. **$225-325**

6½", Maker Unknown, French Fashion. Child type, CM, bisque head, blue glass sleep eyes, swivel head on bisque shoulder plate, bisque arms to shoulders, kid body with gusseted knees, HHW **$1,200-1,300**

6½", O'Neill Kewpie with Blue Wings. All-bisque, signed, jtd arms **$150-200**

6½", Putnam Bye-Lo Baby. All-bisque, front label, intaglio blue eyes, lt brown HHW, jtd at shoulders and hips **$325-425**

6¾", Bisque-Head Baby. Blue ptd eyes, OCM with lower teeth, bent limb compo baby body. Incised: "R5G" **$95-125**

6¾", Goebel Googly 208. Glass eyes to the side, CM, wears a mohair wig, 5-pc BJ compo body, molded-on shoes, dressed in original clothes........................ **$425-525**

6¾", Goebel Laughing Girl. Bisque head, mld blond hair with flowers, compo body, jtd at shoulders and hips, mld shoes and socks, ptd features, dressed, marked **$375-475**

7", Armand Marseille Googly 323. Blue glass sleep eyes, watermelon mouth, mohair wig, 5-pc compo body **$575-675**

7", Gebruder Knoch Clown. Inset glass eyes, OM, bisque head, mache body and limbs, original clown suit and hat **$275-375**

7", German Bride. Bulbous legs with small feet and mld high-strap black shoes with tiny heels, all clothes original and detailed, 10-pc wardrobe, CM, PW eyes, HHW .. **$750-850**

7", Hermann Steiner Child. Sonneberg and Neustadt, near Coburg, Thur, 1921-1925, OM, bisque head, sleep blue eyes, HHW, 5-pc compo body, two-strap mld shoes, dressed **$125-225**

7", Heubach Googly. Blue sleep eyes, watermelon mouth, compo body, old clothes. Mark: "9573" (in a square) **$795-895**

7", Kestner Child. All-bisque, OM with four

teeth, blue sleep eyes, mohair wig, jtd at shoulders and hips, mld/ptd shoes and socks, marked, dressed **$225-325**

7", Kestner Googly. All-bisque, blue glass sleep eyes, watermelon mouth, HHW, swivel head, jtd at shoulders and hips, dressed, marked **$675-775**

7", Maker Unknown, All-Bisque Bonnet Girl. Red eyeline, ptd features, CM, jtd at shoulders and hips, wears a pair of ptd flat-heeled high-laced boots.................... **$225-245**

7", Maker Unknown, Clown. Bisque socket head, intaglio blue ptd eyes glancing to the side, mld blond hair, crude compo body, wears a blue 2-pc clown suit with two red pompons on each leg, neck ruffle, cone-shaped hat with two red pompons, ptd shoes and socks, German **$95-125**

7", Maker Unknown, Little Imp. All-bisque, ptd horns **$495-595**

7", O'Neill Kewpie. All-bisque, signed on bottom of foot, rare, mld shoes and socks, original dress, jtd arms **$300-400**

7", Simon & Halbig 1079. Blue glass eyes, OM with teeth, bisque head, mohair wig, 5-pc compo body................... **$185-285**

7½", Armand Marseille Boy 390. Bisque head, OM with teeth, glass sleep eyes, wears a mohair wig, 8-pc BJ body, wears original palace guard outfit **$125-195**

7½", Armand Marseille Child. All-bisque, CM, sleep glass eyes, mohair wig, jtd at shoulders and hips, rare, original trunk filled with original old clothes. Trunk as original stamp, leather handles and straps. Doll incised: "Germany A12/OM" .. **$1,000-1,200**

7½", Armand Marseille Girl. Blue glass sleep eyes, OM with teeth, braided HHW, BJ body, wears original peasant costume. Mark: "A12/OM".................... **$125-195**

7½", Armand Marseille Googly 323. Blue glass eyes to the side, CM, long blond sausage-curl wig, compo BJ body, original old dress and straw hat.................. **$550-650**

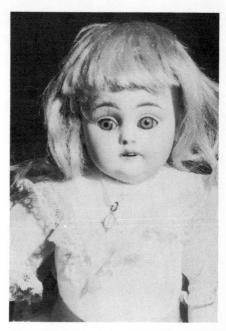

German All-Bisque, 8¾", exquisite modeling. This doll wears an elaborate 1904 French-style dress of sheer organdy and lace insertion, socks and slippers, $325.

(L. to R.) Henry, 3", $25. Molded Bisque, 4³/₄", $20. Molded Bisque, 3¹/₂", $15. Molded Bisque, 6¹/₂", $35. Molded Bisque, gold ptd hair, 5¹/₂", $30. Molded Bisque, 8¹/₄", $50. Molded Bisque, striped bathing suit, 5¹/₄", $30. Betty Boop with violin, 3¹/₄", $25. Snow White, 4¹/₄", marked "Japan" and "Walt Disney," $50. These dolls are originals, not reproductions. All are from the Herron collection.

(L. to R.) All-Bisque, 4", movable arms (this doll has original wardrobe and was the childhood doll of the author's Aunt Gussie, c. late 1880s). Opps! Nippon All-Bisque, 5¹/₂", $175. All-Bisque Bonnet, 6¹/₄", movable arms, $250. All-Bisque, 4", movable arms, $150. All-Bisque, 4¹/₄", movable arms, $175. All dolls have ptd eyes and are from the Herron collection.

(L. to R.) Hanging German Pincushion Doll, 5¼", $175. Flapper Soldier Boy, 15", flirty eyes and cigarette, bisque head, $125. Bisque Half-Doll, 5", original lace and trim, $175. Sachet Half-Doll, marked "Germany," $175. Plaster of paris Half-Doll, 4¼", original lace and trim, $50. Mache Half-Doll, 5½", original black wig, $25. Powder Puff Half-Doll, 2¾", marked "Germany," $65. Mache Santa Claus, 6", $35. Nude Bathing Beauty, marked "Japan," $100. Celluloid Sewing Doll, original oilcloth hat and outfit, $35. All dolls are from the Herron collection.

(L. to R.) All-Bisque Indian, 6", Japanese, $35. Skippy, 6½", Japanese, $50. Baby with movable arms, 6½", damaged foot, Japanese mark, $35. All dolls are from the Herron collection.

Japanese Happifat, 4", orange bow in mld hair, lavender striped dress and orange shoes, D. Kay Crow collection, $125-135.

7½", P.J. Gallais & Co. French Hansi Character Boy. Earthenware, ptd features, ptd hair, CM, 5-pc BJ earthenware body, ptd shoes and socks, original costume, c. 1921-1925. (Gretel is his mate)........ **$240-340**

7½", Heubach on a Sled. Bisque head, attached to old candy-box lid, box intact and marked **$395-495**

7½", Heubach-Koppelsdorf 399. Brown glass eyes, CM, PE with large original earrings, BJ compo black body, original grass skirt. This is the familiar African toddler **$325-425**

7½", Maker Unknown, Buster Brown-Type Googly. All-bisque, intaglio blue ptd eyes, mld clothes, mld shoes and socks, 2-pc white Buster Brown suit, mld blue belt and blue necktie, Buster Brown hairstyle, OCM with teeth **$500-600**

7½", Maker Unknown, French All-Bisque. Brown fixed glass eyes, CM, mohair wig, mld socks with red band, high mld boots with black tassels, unmarked.......... **$750-850**

7½", Maker Unknown, Upstairs-Downstairs Dollhouse Lady. Arms bent at elbows, wears mld shoes with ptd bows, all-bisque, original old clothes **$175-200**

7½", O'Neill Kewpie. All-bisque, labeled front and back, labeled original box, jtd arms. Incised on foot: "O'Neill" **$600-700**

7½", Pre-Greiner Shoulder Head. Papier-mache, ptd hair and features, leather arms, cloth body, dressed, rare size **$350-495**

7½", Recknagel of Alexandrinenthal Bisque Head. Blue sleep eyes, OM with mld teeth, wears a mohair wig, compo body. Incised: "R.A.".................... **$125-225**

7½", Recknagel of Alexandrinenthal Googly. Bisque head, mld white cap with pompon, jtd compo body, CM, blue ptd eyes to the side, jtd at shoulders and hips, original clothes (called "Character Baby" by collectors). Incised: "R.A.".................... **$525-625**

7½", S.F.B.J. 247. Blue glass eyes, mld hair, BJ body **$1,000-1,200**

7¾", Heubach Girl. All-celluloid, sunburst mark, jtd at shoulders, mld hair, ptd features **$35-45**

7¾", Unis France Little Girl 301. Mohair wig, 10-pc BJ body, CM, PW eyes **$600-700**

8", Armand Marseille Character 500. Blue intaglio eyes, CM, mld hair **$250-350**

8", Armand Marseille Oriental Girl. Fixed slanted brown glass eyes, bisque socket head, BJ body, shoulder and hip joints, tiny bound feet (Manchu Dynasty), original HHW, OM with teeth, original costume **$650-750**

8", Heubach Boy. Blue ptd intaglio eyes, OCM, all-bisque. Mark: "14D Germany" (inside a square) **$600-700**

8", K Star R Girl. Bisque head, glass eyes, compo body, baby type, CM **$325-425**

8", Kestner Toddler 260. Bisque socket head, OM, sleep eyes, mohair wig, 5-pc toddler body, red Kestner stamp on back, original clothes and labeled box **$450-550**

8", Maker Unknown, Bonnet Baby. Bonnet has three mld ribbons, mld blond hair, blue ptd eyes, OCM with two top teeth, compo body, German, looks Heubach **$500-600**

8", Maker Unknown, Bonnet Bisque Shoulder Head. Bonnet has mld pink roses, green leaves and blue ribbon, bisque limbs, cloth body **$175-275**

8", Maker Unknown, Celluloid Boy. Turtle mark, mld/ptd clothes and hat, compo arms, wooden feet, all original **$22.50**

8", Maker Unknown, French Socket Head. Brown pupil-less glass eyes, OM with teeth, old mache body, jtd at shoulders and hips, familiar heavy dark brows feathered together. Incised: "185-18/0" **$395-495**

8", Maker Unknown, German Character Baby. Sleep eyes, OCM, cloth body, bisque head, compo arms, all original **$95-125**

8", Maker Unknown, Mache Lady Doll. Pink kid body with tiny waist and large hips, leather arms, early black mld/ptd hair, ptd features, German or French **$400-500**

Rare Marked Meissen Pincushion Half-Doll, 2½", gray hair with brush marks, gold straps on pink bodice, mld bosom, fine facial detail, crossed swords mark, D. Kay Crow collection, $400-500.

91

Indian Bisque Girl, 7", original costume, D. Kay Crow collection, $225-250.

8", Motschmann-Type Enigma Baby. Compo head and lower limbs, fabric insets hold limbs to body, dark brown pupil-less glass eyes, rare size **$395-495**

8", O'Neill Kewpie Bride. All-bisque, jtd arms **$400-500**

8", Simon & Halbig 1079. Bisque head, CM, glass inset eyes, wig, BJ body **$495-595**

8", Unis France. Black sleep eyes, CM, blond mohair wig, 5-pc compo body, original old French Provincial costume, some made by S.F.B.J. **$225-325**

8", Walt Disney Snow White & the Seven Dwarfs. All-bisque, ptd, no joints, boxed, c. 1930. Incised: "Walt Disney" and the name of each character **$300-400**

8¼", Unmarked Heubach Child. Head slightly tilted to the side, intaglio brown eyes looking upward, glazed blue ribbon encircles lt brown mld hair, smiling OCM with realistic-looking teeth **$600-700**

8½", Armand Marseille Googly 200. All-original, including clothes **$650-750**

8½", Armand Marseille 322. Smiling CM, mld hair, blue intaglio eyes to the side, bent limb compo baby body **$375-475**

8½", Heubach-Koppelsdorf Child. Blue sleep eyes, ptd bisque swivel head, OM with four teeth, mohair wig, BJ body, ptd shoes and socks. Incised on back of head: "Heubach-Koppelsdorf, 2511-7-Germany" **$95-145**

8½", Heubach-Koppelsdorf Googly 322. Blue sleep eyes, watermelon mouth, BJ toddler body **$550-650**

8½", Jumeau Child. Large blue PW eyes, CM, mohair wig, BJ body, straight wrists, old clothes.................... **$1,300-1,500**

8½", K Star R Child. Bisque head, 5-pc BJ compo body, glass eyes, wears a mohair wig, CM **$225-325**

8½", K Star R 126. Toddler with rare Kewpie hands, all-bisque, dressed **$495-595**

8½", Maker Unknown, Art Deco Lady. All-bisque, arms outstretched, legs mld together, CM, intaglio blue eyes, beaded toga. Incised: "972" **$325-425**

8½", Maker Unknown, Baby. Solid dome, OM, blue glass eyes, all-bisque, jtd at shoulders and hips. Mark on body "1924 15/0" **$185-285**

8½", Maker Unknown, French Wrestler. Plump little girl, all-bisque, CM, PW eyes, mld yellow 5-strap booties with black gussets and yellow soles, ribbed stockings with blue trim, joints and wooden pegs at shoulders and hips, rare swivel neck, wig........ **$800-900**

8½", Maker Unknown, Painted All-Bisque. Blue glass sleep eyes, blond mohair wig, c. 1920. Stamped: "Germany"........ **$95-250**

8½", S.F.B.J. Character Baby 251.. **$600-700**

8½", Simon & Halbig 1160. Lady doll, CM, PW eyes, mohair wig, cloth body, dressed, bisque shoulder head, bisque arms and legs, mld boots, c. 1900. Often called "Little Women" by collectors **$265-365**

8½", Steiner Child. Series A, size 1, very rare, CM, glass eyes, HHW, compo body, straight wrists...................... **$1,000-1,400**

8¾", Armand Marseille Child. Bisque socket head, inset glass eyes, mohair wig, OM with teeth, BJ body, ptd shoes and socks. Mark: "10/0 DEP Ger. 1894".......... **$125-225**

9", Armand Marseille Googly 323. Blue glass eyes to the side, CM, mohair wig. 5-pc toddler body **$650-750**

9", Armand Marseille Just Me. Bisque socket head, fixed blue glass eyes, HHW, CM, BJ body, ptd bisque, c. 1925........ **$325-425**

9" Armand Marseille Googly 323. Blue glass eyes to the side, CM, mohair wig, 5-pc toddler body **$650-750**

9", Armand Marseille Oriental Toddler. Bisque head, CM, sleep glass eyes, mohair wig, compo hands, cloth body and limbs, original costume **$450-550**

9", Armand Marseille 370. Sleep glass eyes,

All-Bisque German Girl, 3", ptd features, ptd shoes and socks, old long hair wig, original dress, D. Kay Crow collection, $125-150.

Carved-Wood Negro Girl, 6", glass inset eyes, earrings, fine carving detail, original costume, D. Kay Crow collection, $225-250.

OM with teeth, mohair wig, BJ body, straight wrists, original Volendam costume, wooden shoes **$145-195**

9", Armand Marseille 390. Blue fixed glass eyes, OM with teeth, mohair wig, BJ body, mld shoes and stockings, original Scottish outfit (plaid kilt and scarf, velvet jacket, tam, lace blouse), c. 1930 . . . . **$145-195**

9", Heubach Indian Boy. Dark bisque, CM, brown glass eyes, black mohair wig, original red headband, original costume . . . **$500-600**

9", Maker Unknown, Belton Boy. French, CM, bisque head, ptd blue eyes, compo limbs, wooden body, mohair wig **$600-700**

9", Maker Unknown, Black Bisque Head. Old black mohair wig, dressed, 8-pc BJ compo body. Incised: "1000" **$325-425**

9", Maker Unknown, Stone-Bisque Bonnet Shoulder Head. Blue and white bonnet with pink ribbon, stone bisque limbs, old cloth body **$95-145**

9", Simon & Halbig 1078. Bisque socket head, OM, HHW, blue glass sleep eyes, BJ body with mld shoes and socks **$195-295**

9½", Armand Marseille Googly Baby Boy. Watermelon mouth, gray intaglio eyes to the side, mld hair, BJ compo baby body. Mark: "GB (written in script) 252 Germany A5/OM DRMR" **$375-475**

9½", Armand Marseille Googly Baby Girl. Large blue glass eyes to the side, watermelon mouth, mate to the Googly Baby Boy. Mark: "GB (written in script) 253 Germany A6/OM DRMR" **$375-475**

9½", Armand Marseille Oriental Baby. Olive bisque, CM, brown glass sleep eyes, original costume, hat, shoes, pre-Ellar **$600-700**

9½", Maker Unknown, Paris. All-bisque, CM, PW eyes, mohair wig, high white mld/ptd stockings, black ptd/mld boots, arms bent at elbows. Incised: "Paris" . . . **$800-900**

9½", Maker Unknown, Piano Baby. Lies on stomach and holds kitten in arms beneath head, blue nightshirt **$175-275**

9½", Putnam Bye-Lo. Bisque head, brown glass sleep eyes, celluloid hands, cloth body, stamped **$500-600**

10", AHW/SH Baby 156. Bisque head, glass sleep eyes, compo body, CM **$325-425**

10", Armand Marseille Googly 200. Blue intaglio eyes, watermelon mouth, mohair wig, BJ compo body **$750-850**

10", German Baby. Looks like a Kaiser baby with grooved flange neck and mld stringing loop, two-part mld head, ptd eyes and hair, OCM, double chin, large ears, BJ compo body, dressed. Base of flange incised: "2.2.9-23" **$695-795**

10", Kestner Baby 142. Solid-dome head, CM, blue ptd eyes, kid and compo baby body, swivel bisque head **$325-425**

10", Kestner Gibson Girl. Shoulder head, CM, brown fixed glass eyes, HHW, bisque limbs, cloth body. Mark: "2/0-172" . . . **$900-1,200**

10", Maker Unknown, Bonnet Bisque Shoulder Head. Orange ptd bonnet, bisque limbs, cloth body **$210-235**

10", Maker Unknown, Doughboy. Bisque head, mld handlebar mustache, helmet, blue ptd eyes, brown ptd/mld hair, compo body and limbs, dressed **$95-125**

10", Maker Unknown, WWI Soldier Boy. Bisque head, CM, gray glass eyes, gray ptd/mld hair parted down the center, open crown, mld gray mustache, 5-pc compo body, original clothes **$495-595**

10", Revalo Toddler. Brown mld short hair with mld red ribbon across front, bows on each side, blue intaglio eyes, OCM, 5-pc toddler body, bisque head **$495-595**

10½", Armand Marseille Googly 323. Blue sleep eyes, HHW, CM, 5-pc Marseille toddler body **$750-850**

10½", Cuno & Otto Dressel Poppy Doll. Bisque shoulder head boy, blue glass fixed eyes, CM, mld and flocked blond hair, blue cotton body, compo arms, cloth legs, dressed. Body mark: "Poppy Doll" **$225-325**

Bisque Shoulder-Head Boy, 4½", mld hair, bisque lower limbs, cloth body, dressed in blue velvet, D. Kay Crow collection, $125-135.

China Half-Doll, 4½", gray ptd hair, marked "GERMANY," D. Kay Crow collection, $110-125.

12", Armand Marseille Indian. Dark bisque, brown glass eyes, black mohair braided wig, BJ body, shoulder and hip joints, dressed in Iroquois costume, c. 1930 . . . . **$200-300**

12", Armand Marseille 390. Bisque socket head, OM with teeth, blue fixed glass eyes, mohair wig, 1865-1930s **$145-195**

12", Heubach Coquette. Bisque head, mld blond hair, mld blue ribbon, BJ body, original clothes, shoes, rare **$750-850**

7½", Maker Unknown, Googly GB 253. Sleep eyes, toddler body **$495-595**

American and English Tinies

3", Amberg Pink-Bisque Girl. Blue ptd eyes, mld blond hair, movable arms, stationary legs, mld ankle-strap green shoes, rose-colored socks, dressed in red and white handmade polka dot frock. Incised: "Louis Amberg & Son" **$65-95**

3", German Snow Baby. Plays musical instrument, all-bisque, c. 1900s **$50-100**

4", Maker Unknown, Snow Baby on Sled. All-bisque, c. 1920 . . . . **$65-125**

5", J.I. Orsini Child. All-bisque, OM, sleep eyes, HHW, jtd at shoulders and hips, arms bent at elbows, chest label **$1,100-1,500**

5", J.I. Orsini Vivi. All-bisque, HHW, character face, mld shoes, rare. Incised on shoulder: "J.I.O." Round chest label reads: "Vivi Reg. U.S. Pat Office Corp. 1920 Orsini Pat. app. for" **$1,200-1,600**

5½", Maker Unknown, Snow Baby. All-bisque, jtd at shoulders and hips. (Snow babies were manufactured in the early 1900s, although similar types were found and used on Christmas trees in the 1890s. They are still manufactured to this day. Many were made in the 1920s and 1930s) **$225-325**

6½", Maiden Little Bo Peep. All-celluloid, movable arms, blond mld Dutch bob, ptd features. Incised: "America 207" **$15**

8", Maiden America. All-compo, mld blond hair with topknot, smiling CM, dot eyebrows, large blue ptd eyes to the side, patriotic ribbon tied in bow around lower part of body, c. 1916, made by Maiden Toy Co., N.Y. (This doll was a war bond prize. War savings stamp is pasted to chest) **$95-125**

8½", Maker Unknown, Queen Anne. English, ptd eyes, HHW, wood, good condition, very old clothes, c. 1900 . . . . **$700-800**

Oriental Tinies

4", Heubach Chin-Chin Baby. All-bisque, jtd arms, sticker on chest **$160-200**

4½", Maker Unknown, Little Girl. Japanese, jtd bent arms, mld blond hair with red headband and bows, mld/ptd clothes, paint clear and not faded **$25-35**

4½", Morimura Bros. Queue San Baby. All-bisque, CM, jtd at shoulders only, legs mld together, mld cap, queue, shoes, green cap trimmed with lavender. Chest sticker reads: "QUEUE SAN BABY" **$95-125**

4½", Nippon Baby. All-bisque, character face, OCM with two teeth, jtd curved arms, blue ptd eyes to the side, sucks index finger . . **$45-65**

4½", Nippon Bonnet Girl. Jtd arms, ptd features, mld/ptd clothes, c. 1920 . . . **$45-65**

4¾", Morimura Bros. Baby Darling. All-bisque, jtd at shoulders, bent arms, legs mld together, blond mld hair and hair band, label with "MB Baby Darling" **$95-125**

6", Maker Unknown, HEbee-SHEbee. All-bisque, Japanese **$125-145**

6", Nippon HEbee-SHEbee. **$165-185**

8", Maker Unknown, Old Chinese Bisque-Head Baby. Sleep brown eyes, compo body, CM, ptd shoes, wears old clothes, Chinese mark **$225-325**

13½", Maker Unknown, Japanese Boy and Girl. Baby type, OCM, inset brown glass eyes, black hair wig, cry box in center of tummy, kimonos, red cloth slippers, stucco-chiffon type, ptd mache. 1920-1960, older types of better quality, later types often chipped and cracked **$25-65**

Bisque Half-Doll, 4", bald head and original wig, marked "2470 Germany," D. Kay Crow collection, $125-150.

13½", Maker Unknown, Old Chinese Boy. All-compo, inset glass eyes, CM, HHW, original costume, c. 1920 . . . . **$125-145**

15", Maker Unknown, Chinese Boy and Girl. Mache heads, hands and feet, cloth body and limbs, ptd features, HHW, CM, old Chinese clothes, c. 1900, sold separately **$65-85**

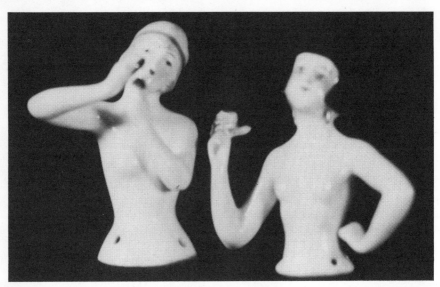

(L. to R.) Blond China Flapper Half-Doll, 2½", blue bandeau, marked "GERMANY," $135-155. Black-Haired Flapper, 2½", gold earrings, rose in hand, marked "GER-MANY," $200-225. Both dolls are from the D. Kay Crow collection.

Choice selection of half-dolls from the D. Kay Crow collection.

(L. to R.) German All-Bisque, 4³/₄", mache arms, ptd eyes, $125. Rare Kestner Tiny, 4¹/₄", crown stamp on tummy, sleep eyes, original wig and clothes, $500. German All-Bisque, 4¹/₂", movable limbs, glass eyes, old clothes and wig, $275. All dolls are from the Herron collection.

(L. to R.) All-Bisque, movable limbs, glass eyes, original wig and clothes, $600. Late French Dolls, rough bisque heads, ptd features, mache bodies, crude original costumes, movable limbs, $150 each. All dolls are from the Herron collection.

5

China Head Dolls

The old-fashioned china head doll is the true aristocrat of the doll collecting hobby. If age and antiquity denoted worth and value, this doll alone would glean all the honors, for here we find not only an ageless doll of the highest quality but a doll conceived in more varieties than any other. From rare hairdo arrangements to signed specimens and chinas of various tones—pink, black, white, creamy ivory—the vagaries abound, and we discover a doll standing head and shoulders above all others. The chinas listed here are all original and well-dressed.

Blond Dolly Madison China, 20", blue bow, Jim and Sheila Olah Scheetz collection, $450-550.

Name Chinas

6½", Kling China. Black hair, flesh-tinted, unusual facial modeling, china limbs, cloth body. Mark: "KLING BELL" **$125-145**

7", Ruth Gibbs Pink China. These are not reproductions. They are original china head dolls, distinguished by their heart-shaped mouths, eyelashes, hair color, pink cloth bodies, c. 1945. Incised: "R," "G" .. **$95-145**

7½", Maker Unknown, Peg-Jointed China. China head secured by dowel, china lower limbs, hair ptd black, German, dressed in Empire-style costume (which might be original), c. early 1800s **$795-895**

8", Maker Unknown, Age & Youth China. Rare two-faced china has the face of a black-haired child on one side and the face of a wrinkled gray-haired hag on the other side, ptd hair and features, old china limbs, original cloth body, original costume... **$1,000-1,200**

8", Maker Unknown, Jeweled China. Black ptd hair in low-brow hairdo, shoulder plate has rare mld/ptd gold necklace, bisque lower arms and legs, original cloth body, no red lid lines, c. 1900s.................. **$195-295**

10", Maker Unknown, Jenny Lind Autoperipatetikos. Key-wound walking doll, brass clockwork-type feet. Patent on base: "1862. E.C. Spirin, London"... **$1,000-1,200**

10", Maker Unknown, Nursery Rhyme China. Low-brow blond hairdo, old china limbs, old cloth body imprinted with nursery rhyme figures, c. 1900. (These bodies are often found on name china shoulder heads and are not considered rare.) "Bertha" in gold letters on front shoulder plate. "Patent App'd For 11 Germany" incised on back **$185-285**

10", Maker Unknown, Patriotic China. Common low-brow type, shoulder head glued to body, china lower limbs, muslin body printed with names of states in red and blue, U.S. emblem printed in the center of the torso, c. WWI...................... **$200-300**

11", Maker Unknown, Biedermeier China. Solid-dome head, no tonsure spot, skin wig, PI, leather arms, old cloth body .. **$395-495**

11", Maker Unknown, Bonnet China. White ribbon around center brim, blond hair with mld bangs, old china limbs, old cloth body, c. 1880 .... **$350-450**

11", Maker Unknown, Kindergarten China. Blond low-brow hairdo, cloth body imprinted with multiplication tables, a drum, horse, and cart, c. 1900. The various colors on the cloth body together with the tables and objects made this doll invaluable to the young preschool child **$225-325**

11½", Maker Unknown, Peg-Wooden China. This 1840s head is the type seen on most of the Milliners' papier-mache dolls (flat-parted top with long black sausage curls on back shoulders), red lid lines, peg joints hold the china head intact, wooden body... **$595-695**

12", Emma Clear Pink Luster China. Pink luster limbs, cloth body **$300-350**

12", Maker Unknown, Bald-Head Enigma Baby. Motschmann-type body, HHW, china shoulder head, rare.......... **$1,800-2,500**

12", Maker Unknown, Black Beret China Boy. Beret trimmed with pink and white plaid band, short blond mld hair in Scottish style, blue ptd eyes, red lid lines, old china limbs,

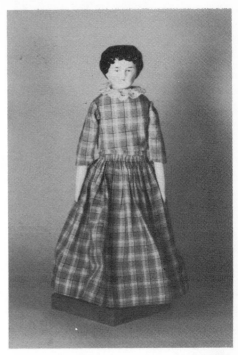

China Shoulder Head, 13", marked "2," $250.

Ruth Gibbs Godey-Style China, 12", china limbs, cloth body, $175.

black ptd boots with heels, old cloth body, original Scottish outfit **$850-950**

12", Maker Unknown, Empress Eugenie Autoperipatetikos. Blond hair, brown leather arms, gilt tin feet, dressed like others in this choice group **$1,200-1,500**

12", Maker Unknown, Enigma Baby. Motschmann-type body, china head pivots on china shoulder plate, china limbs, black ptd shoes, cloth and china body . . . **$1,700-2,000**

12", Maker Unknown, Green Bonnet China. Green bonnet trimmed in red and pink, black hair, blue ptd eyes, very sweet little mouth, leather arms, old cloth body. Blue mark inside shoulder plate: "Guta" **$895-995**

12", Maker Unknown, Nancy Hanks Lincoln. Black hair, very pale china with red lid lines, red nose and eye dots, fully exposed ears, old china limbs, old cloth body. **$395-525**

12½", Maker Unknown, Dotter China. Black common low-brow hairdo, corset body, china limbs, dressed **$195-295**

13", Maker Unknown, Whistling China. Black ptd hair, blue ptd eyes, red lid lines, china limbs, cloth body. The whistle is in the head **$495-595**

13½", Unmarked Rohmer China. Brown glass eyes, leather arms, kid body . . . **$2,000-3,500**

14", Maker Unknown, Enigma Baby. Black hair, fine brush marks, baby face, swivel neck on bisque shoulder plate, cloth upper body, china body from waist to upper thigh, cloth thighs, lower limbs made of china, sculpted feet **$2,000-2,500**

14", Maker Unknown, Liberty Boy China. White mld cap on head with the word "Liberty" across the front, blue ribbon with white stars on mld neckerchief (tied with bow at the back), OM with mld teeth, blue ptd eyes with eyelashes, OM with mld teeth. Incised across the front shoulder plate: "Made in U.S.A." **$395-495**

14", Maker Unknown, Pink Snood China. Trimmed with twisted band and gold bow, blue beads, large blue shadowed eyes, PE, gusseted kid body, leather arms . . . **$795-895**

14", Maker Unknown, Red Bonnet China. Bonnet mld flat to head, black hair, tie-string under double chin, bonnet trimmed in green, one-stroke black brows, blue ptd eyes with red lid lines, deeply mld shoulder plate with two sew holes front and back, leather arms, leather body and legs, dressed as a pioneer woman, c. 1850 . . . . **$695-795**

14", Rohmer Signed China. Fashion child type, cup and saucer neck, CM, blue ptd eyes, mohair wig, pink luster head and lower arms, wood above china arms, circular wooden knee joints, kid body. Label reads: "Mme Rohmer-Brevete SGDG-A-Paris" **$5,000-10,000**

14½", Maker Unknown, Little Girl. Curl in the middle of her forehead, back of hairdo has elaborate mass of black curls held by a band, china limbs, cloth body **$395-495**

14¾", Maker Unknown, Necklace China. Black ptd Civil War flattop hairstyle, mld necklace with blue and white beads, red lid lines, rosy cheeks, kid arms, cloth body and legs, sewed-on leather shoes **$425-525**

15", Maker Unknown, Bonnet China. Fine china quality, chubby child face, blond undercurled bangs, blue ptd eyes, bonnet has bow beneath chin, bow and bonnet trim of luster quality, china limbs, purple luster high-heeled boots, old cloth body **$695-795**

15", Maker Unknown, Turkey Ridge China. Black ptd hairstyle mld high on top of head in ridged waves (this was the era when hairstyles were higher on the head, c. 1886), blue ptd eyes, red lid lines, rosy cheeks, original china limbs, cloth body, bulbous lower legs, black ptd shoes. A pink ribbon is painted at the knees **$300-400**

15½", Maker Unknown, Clown China. Blond mld hair, mld white cap trimmed with blue and red, brown mustache and goatee, blue ptd eyes, china limbs, cloth body **$795-895**

15½", Maker Unknown, Dolly Madison. Blond hair, blue bow and band, blue ptd eyes, PI, exposed ears, leather arms, body made of cloth **$425-525**

16", Maker Unknown, Alice China. Swivel neck, black hair with fine brush marks, mld band, exposed ears, ptd features, red lid lines,

China with 1868 hairstyle, 21", D. Kay Crow collection, $350-450.

103

China with 1880 hairstyle, 21", D. Kay Crow collection, $250-350.

china limbs, cloth body **$1,250-1,350**

16", Maker Unknown, Biedermeier China. Solid-dome head with tonsure spot, old HHW, PI, old china limbs, old cloth body, flat-soled ptd shoes, c. 1840 ...... **$550-650**

16", Maker Unknown, Empress Josephine. Black hair with mld crown, old china limbs, old cloth body **$895-1,100**

16", Maker Unknown, Gold Snood China. Black ptd hair, mld netting, blue ptd eyes with red lid lines, sloping shoulders, leather arms, cloth body **$495-595**

16", Maker Unknown, Jenny Lind. Black center-parted hair mld into rear bun, long oval portrait face, sloping shoulders, old china limbs, old cloth body **$350-450**

16", Maker Unknown, Kate Greenaway Bonnet China. Blond hair, red lid lines, orange bonnet with blue ribbon and bows, white ruffle around the face, bisque lower arms, cloth body **$495-595**

16", Maker Unknown, Pink Ribbon China. This china has a pink ribbon with a pink bow over each ear, black net with black band down the middle, blond ptd hair, round face, smiling mouth, leather arms, cloth body .. **$795-895**

16", Maker Unknown, Snood China. Portrait face, deep shoulder slope, snood attached to raised headband with a bow at each ear, black ptd hair, long neck, old china limbs, old cloth body **$975-1,200**

16", Maker Unknown, Snood China. Hairdo has plumes and mld ribbon, blond hair, old china limbs, cloth body **$625-725**

16", Maker Unknown, Tiara China. Black ptd hair with mld tiara and rose, no red lid lines, wooden limbs, kid body **$795-895**

16", Rohmer Signed China. French, original BJ kid body, green oval stamp on chest, eyelet holes below, Rohmer knee joints, swivel neck, pink china arms, kid joining arms to shoulders, swivel is cut straight, blue ptd eyes, unpierced ears, mohair wig ... **$5,000-10,000**

16½", Carrie Ordway. Black hair, brush

marks, mld band through two top clusters of curls, two other large curls roll down through the center of the back hairdo, leather arms, old cloth body **$750-850**

16½", Jacob Petit Signed China. French, creamy pink china, 3½" head cir, black ptd/mld hair in 1840s style, exposed ears, long slender neck, sloping shoulders, eight sew holes, leather arms, kid fashion body, gorgeous clothes. Mark inside head: "JP" in blue under the glaze, one dot over the J and one dot below the P. (Petit started a porcelain factory at Belleville in 1790) . . . **$2,500-5,000**

17", Huret Signed China. Blue ptd eyes, BJ hard leather body. Stamp on body: "Poupee Paris" **$3,795-5,795**

17", Huret Signed China. Gutta-percha body, blue ptd eyes with black liner on upper lid, lt brown feathered brows, pegs at hips and shoulders, bisque Bru-type hands and wrists, fingernails outlined in bright pink, separated fingers, c. 1885. Strip across chest reads: "54 Boulevard Haussmann" **$4,000-7,000**

17", Maker Unknown, Agnes China. Goldsmith red corset body, leather arms, cloth body **$250-350**

17", Maker Unknown, Dresden Portrait China. Brown ptd hair, blue ptd eyes, feathered eyebrows and lower eyelashes, slightly parted lips, long slender neck with hollow throat, deep bangs. The finely detailed hairdo is swept high off her graceful neck and gathered into looped curls (the overall effect is "windblown"—a lovely lady caught at the seashore perhaps), old china limbs, old cloth body **$1,750-1,850**

17", Maker Unknown, Helen China. Common black ptd hairdo, mld yoke, name in gold, china limbs, cloth body. (Other names in this series are: Ethel, Agnes, Bertha, Dorothy, Daisy, Edith, Esther, Florence, Mabel, Marion, and Pauline. Heads were often marked "Germany." There are blonds as well as brunettes. Some heads are found on unusual bodies, c. early 1900s) **$200-250**

17", Maker Unknown, Queen Victoria. This authentic Victoria china has the familiar hairstyle popular in 1837, pink luster china limbs, blue ptd eyes, red lid lines, red half-

Unusual China, 24", little girl face and hairdo, unusual old arms, marked "1046-9," ribbon winner, D. Kay Crow collection, $400-500.

Civil War Flattop China, 27½", deep breastplate, three sew holes, very heavy head, D. Kay Crow collection, $400-500.

circles at nostrils, old clothes. The face resembles the young queen **$895-995**

17", Maker Unknown, Spill-Curl China. Lovely black hair, pink luster limbs, old cloth body **$795-895**

17½", Maker Unknown, Beau Brummel or F.P. China. Fine china with brush marks, mld shirt and tie, leather arms, cloth body, dressed as a fine gentleman **$795-895**

18", Currier & Ives Child. Black hairdo modeled onto shoulders in pointed sausage curls, scalloped bangs, exposed ears, old china limbs, old cloth body **$300-450**

18", Maker Unknown, Fashion China. Black ptd hair brushed into rear bun, large flat PE, blue ptd eyes, red lid lines, leather arms, stitched fingers, fashion kid body similar to the bisque type **$975-1,200**

18", Maker Unknown, Fortune-Telling China. This typical Civil War flattop version of the German china shoulder head was designed by a French artist for the French market. Exquisite detail and flair, mache limbs, flat-soled ptd slippers, velvet jacket with cloth upper torso, red cotton outer skirt trimmed with lace, folded sheets of pastel-colored paper from an inner petticoat, messages in French, c. 1860 . . . **$1,500-2,000**

18", Maker Unknown, Martha Washington. Strawberry blond ptd hair, blue ptd eyes, red lid lines, nose and eye dots, tiny pink mouth, capo di monte-type, old china limbs, old kid body **$1,250-1,400**

18", Nymphenburg China Shoulder Head Lady. Court type, mld/ptd white hair in 1770s style, prim features, long neck, long forearms with lovely sculpted hands, kid body, original costume. (Similar chinas can be found with different hair colors. They actually date from 1908 and not the 1700s) **$1,600-2,000**

19", Jacob Petit Jenny Lind China. Rare portrait china of the famous singer (not to be confused with usual china of this name), faintly smiling mouth, delicate modeling, said to be the work of Parisian potter, Jacob Petit, who sculpted doll heads for the porcelain market in 1843. He also made a china head of

Queen Victoria. This head has the singer's familiar hairstyle (there is a slight portrait resemblance), old china limbs, old cloth body, dressed in Lind style......... **$3,000-5,000**

19", Maker Unknown, Countess Dagmar. Black hair, PE, fully exposed ears, no red lid lines, no eye dots, brush marks, old china limbs, old cloth body............ **$395-495**

19", Maker Unknown, Lola Montes. This rarely seen china has black ptd hair and a sweet portrait face, delicate long fingers and flat-soled slippers with ptd bands around her ankles, leather body, c. 1860... **$1,500-2,000**

19", Maker Unknown, Pillbox China. Rare red ptd hair with mld pillbox hat and turned head, ears exposed, hair mld into curls brushed behind the ears and sculpted onto shoulders, blue ptd eyes, leather arms, old cloth body and legs **$795-895**

19", Maker Unknown, Prince Albert. Excellent likeness of Albert with mld and ptd gray hair and mustache, mld gray beard, pink luster head and limbs, old cloth body, old costume **$1,000-1,200**

1860 China, 32", deep breastplate, three sew holes, exquisite costume, D. Kay Crow collection, $400-500.

19", Maker Unknown, Spill-Curl China. Cafe au lait ptd hair, tiny corkscrew curls around forehead and cascading onto rear shoulders behind fully exposed ears, mld ribbon across top of head, blue ptd eyes, faintly smiling mouth, short neck, sloping shoulders, china limbs, old cloth body............ **$650-750**

19", A. Metayer Waterfall China. Black hair mld into high waterfall hairdo, oval-shaped face, short one-stroke brows, sloping shoulders and deep shoulder plate, no sew holes, shoulder plate glued inside well-shaped lady-style kid body, well-shaped buttocks, tiny waist, straight 1-pc legs, movable leather arms. Label inside head reads: "BAZAR DES HALLES—A. METAYER—22 Rue S. MARTIN" **$1,750-1,850**

19½", Maker Unknown, Adelina Patti. Black ptd hair, ears partly exposed, round face with faintly smiling lips, old china limbs, old cloth body **$425-595**

19½", Sophie Smith Pink Rose China. Finest quality, black center-parted hair with thirteen

107

Milliners' Model China, 18", hairdo has bun at rear, all-original body, Jim and Sheila Olah Scheetz collection, $400-500.

vertical curls ending sharply in the middle of the neck, marked with small script under shoulders. This rare lady type has china limbs and flat-soled slippers mld onto feet, cloth body **$850-950**

20", Emma Clear Jenny Lind. Reproduction, signed and dated, original limbs and originial body **$200-300**

20", Maker Unknown, Curly-Top China. Blond version of familiar brunette type, deeply sculpted curls mld around forehead and shaped into points, leather arms, old cloth body **$395-495**

20", Maker Unknown, Flower China. Black ptd hair with flowers on each side of puffed hairdo, rare swivel neck, old china limbs, old cloth body **$1,200-1,300**

20", Maker Unknown, Pink Scarf. This choice doll has a pink scarf mld across the top of her head, a blue feather is mld/ptd down the side, red lid lines, cafe au lait ptd hair, smiling mouth, china limbs, cloth body ... **$895-995**

20", Maker Unknown, Snood Child. Yellow ptd hair styled short and held by snood trimmed with blue bows on each side, ribbon down back of snood, round chubby face, blue ptd eyes, red lid lines, tiny smiling mouth, old china limbs, cloth body **$725-825**

20", Maker Unknown, Soft-Paste China. Although soft-paste china was used before hard china, this head is dated 1850s. Center-parted hair, side puffs conceal ears, braided wreath high off neck exposes long neck and graceful sweep of the shoulders, double chin, coy facial expression, red lid lines, leather arms, old cloth body **$975-1,100**

20", Pre-Greiner China. Resembles papier-mache type, black ptd center-parted hair smoothly modeled over fully exposed ears, large blue glass eyes with upper and lower ptd eyelashes, eyelid modeling, red lid lines, tiny expressive mouth, leather arms, cloth body. (The discovery of this china leads one to speculate whether the pre-Greiner papier-mache dolls came from these china head molds).................... **$1,750-1,950**

21", Emma Clear Dolly Madison. Pink luster,

black hair, blue and gold luster ribbon, PE, blue ptd eyes, pink china limbs, blue ptd boots, cloth body **$350-595**

21" Maker Unknown, Berlin China. Black hair, neck modeled forward, old china limbs, kid body, hands not as delicately modeled as others of this period, original Bavarian national costume, dirndl skirt, hand-embroidered blouse, hair ptd brown beneath glaze, c. 1830. (Many of these early chinas have brown or auburn hair. Many also have gray eyes) **$1,500-1,600**

21", Maker Unknown, Dolly Madison. Black hair with mld ribbon and band, china limbs, cloth body **$395-495**

21", Maker Unknown, Empress Eugenie. Blond ptd hair, pink and white scarf on right side of head, white feather on left side, black hairnet covers back of hairdo, red lid lines, red nose and eye dots, old china limbs, old cloth body **$1,000-2,000**

21", McPerk 1953 China. Unusual plump face, fine quality, all original **$200-350**

21½", Maker Unknown, Grape Lady. This rare china has a white gold-edged ruffle around her head, a net covering the back of her black hairdo, PE, rare "spoke eyes" and eyelashes, a long oval portrait face, old china limbs, old cloth body **$1,000-1,200**

22", Maker Unknown, Empress Josephine. Black hair with mld crown, exposed ears, original body and limbs **$1,300-1,500**

22", Maker Unknown, Queen Victoria. Black center-parted hair draped in front of the ears with the ends braided and coiled into rear bun, detailed ears fully exposed, blue ptd eyes, red lid lines, red nose and eye dots, old china limbs, old cloth body stuffed with horse hair, old clothes, c. 1840 .... **$1,500-1,700**

23", Maker Unknown, Apple Cheek China. Black hair, character face, blue ptd eyes, red lid lines, vivid red splotches on each cheek, china arms, original cloth limbs and original body **$265-365**

24", Maker Unknown, Mona Lisa. This lady has a definite smile, black ptd hair, red lid

Civil War China, 22", fat child's face, all-original condition, old clothes, Jim and Sheila Olah Scheetz collection, $350-400.

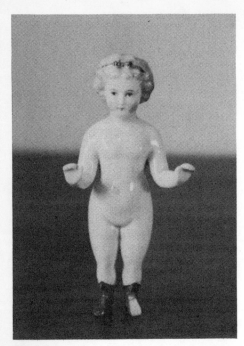

Frozen Charlotte, 5", $150.

lines, Civil War hairdo, cloth body and limbs, sewed-on leather shoes and stockings, well-made homemade body **$450-550**

25", Maker Unknown, Biedermeier China. Pink luster shoulder head and lower limbs, HHW, old cloth body **$1,000-1,200**

25", Maker Unknown, Duchess with a Goiter. This Civil War flattop china has a large swelling of the neck, more than a fat double chin, sweet faintly smiling mouth, creamy tone, leather arms, cloth body **$495-595**

25", Maker Unknown, Mary Todd Lincoln. Pink luster, black center-parted hair, red eyelines, pink luster limbs, old cloth body, floral lace corset and old clothes .. **$695-795**

25", Sophie Smith China. Brown eyes, all original **$495-595**

36", Emma Clear Lady China. Blue ptd eyes glancing downward, short curly blond hair, spill curl on forehead, gold buckle and snood, gold bow on top of head, exquisite china hands and feet, black shoes, mld bosom, china limbs, cloth body **$1,000-1,200**

Common and Rare Featured Chinas

1", Maker Unknown, Frozen Charlotte. A Cracker Jacks prize, metal **$10-25**

2", Maker Unknown, Frozen Charlie. Black hair, in tub **$100-125**

2", Maker Unknown, Frozen Charlotte. Black hair, in tub **$100-125**

2", Maker Unknown, Negro Frozen Charlotte. Rare, mld white chemise and pleated skirt **$265-300**

2½", Maker Unknown, Frozen Charlotte. Black hair, molded-on bonnet with red ribbon ties, bouquet, nude **$140-200**

3", Maker Unknown, Baby Girl Frozen Charlotte. Black hair, in seated position, fits into high chair, nude **$150-250**

3", Maker Unknown, Frozen Charlotte. Soap, c. 1895 .... **$15-25**

Rare Black Chinas, 7" and 7½", all-original, Herron Collection, $1,000 pair.

(L. to R.) Frozen Charlotte, 2", $95. Frozen Charlotte, 5", $175. Frozen Charlotte, 3½", $225. All dolls from the D. Kay Crow collection.

China with 1860 hairstyle, 26", all-original, pink-tinted, D. Kay Crow collection, $500-600.

3½", Maker Unknown, Frozen Charlie. Rare all-bisque version, black ptd hair . . . **$95-125**

3½", Maker Unknown, Frozen Charlie Harlequin. Green ptd cap with gold tassel, mustache and goatee, ptd garters and shoes, nude **$150-250**

3½", Maker Unknown, Frozen Charlotte. Rare mld dress, stockings, shoes, rare mld long yellow braids, pink bows **$795-895**

3¾", Maker Unknown, Negro Pincushion Doll. This well-dressed lady has mld earrings, hat, fancy mld blouse (1920s style), arms away from body, cushion bottom decorated to harmonize with upper part of dress, all original, rare **$200-300**

4", Maker Unknown, Frozen Charlotte. This old doll has one arm straight at side with palm facing forward, mld shoes and socks, nude, German, brown rubber **$60-70**

4", Maker Unknown, Negro Frozen Charlotte. Brown ptd eyes with whites, nude **$395-450**

4½", Maker Unknown, Brown-Eyed China Shoulder Head. Black flattop, bisque limbs, original cloth body, dressed, dollhouse type doll **$50-85**

4½", Maker Unknown, Frozen Charlotte. Rare red ptd hair, gold hair bow, gold shoes with green tassels **$395-450**

4½", Maker Unknown, Pink Luster Frozen Charlie. Black hair, fine brush marks, nude **$200-300**

4⅝", Maker Unknown, Negro Women Chinas. Mammy type, short black mld/ptd hair, black china shoulder head and limbs, black cloth body, old clothes, sold as a pair, c. 1860 . . . . **$695-795**

5", Maker Unknown, Frozen Charlotte. Black hair, one arm straight at side, the other arm mld to chest, both arms mld in one with the body **$200-300**

6", Maker Unknown, Frozen Charlie. Black ptd hair, one arm mld to chest, genital detail, nude, rare. Mark on body:"GERMANY 4433" **$1,300-1,500**

112

6", Maker Unknown, Frozen Charlotte. Rare shoulder and hip joints, black hair, red lid lines, rosy cheeks, Civil War flattop hairdo, arms almost straight at sides... **$1,000-1,200**

6¼", Maker Unknown, Swivel-Neck Black Hair China. Common hairdo, blue ptd eyes, china limbs, cloth body **$350-450**

7", Maker Unknown, Pincushion Doll. Typical china half-doll sewn to pincushion bottom, china lower arms, sawdust bottom covered with same material as outer skirt, upper arms cloth-stuffed, bonnet, flannel apron serves as pin holder........ **$350-650**

8", Maker Unknown, Frozen Charlotte. Yellow old-fashioned bathing suit with pink belt, black ptd shoulder-length hair and green headband, red lid lines, blue ptd eyes, hands mld in diving position **$395-450**

8½", Maker Unknown, Frozen Charlotte. Rare bald head, HHW, flat-heeled boots and ribbed mld stockings, nude **$1,500-1,700**

10", Maker Unknown, Blond Low-Brow China. Red lid lines, original china limbs, original cloth body **$95-125**

10½", Black Hair Fancy Hairdo China. Exposed PE, blue ptd eyes, china limbs, cloth body, made in Japan, c. WWI **$225-250**

10½, Maker Unknown, Black Hair China Lady. Pink kid body with stiff legs, mld bosom, brown leather arms, 1840s hairdo, fine china, rosy cheeks.............. **$595-795**

12", Maker Unknown, Frozen Charlotte. Chubby little girl with protruding tummy and buttocks, fat legs and arms, arms extended, mld bonnet with white fluting around the edges **$595-695**

12", Maker Unknown, Man China. Brown ptd hair, mld black top hat, exposed ears, ptd features, china limbs, cloth body, original coachman outfit **$795-895**

12¼", Maker Unknown, Pink China. French type, artistically ptd face, fine eyebrow lines, finely stroked upper and lower lashes, very expressive blue ptd eyes, fine hairline brush marks accentuating black mld curls, French

1860 China, 27", rare intaglio eyes, looks like a child, D. Kay Crow collection, $1,000-1,200.

Boy China, 32", exposed ears, c. 1870, D. Kay Crow collection, $500-600.

cloth body, pink kid arms, very beautiful costume **$1,250-2,250**

12½", Blond Fancy Hairdo China. Japanese look to features, PE, china limbs, cloth body, exposed ears. Paper sticker on back reads: "MADE IN JAPAN"........... **$200-250**

13", Maker Unknown, Frozen Charlie. Black ptd hair, brush marks, pink luster face, white china body and limbs, arms forward and bent at elbows **$425-525**

13", Maker Unknown, Frozen Charlie. Black ptd hair, brush marks, white china face, body, and limbs **$395-450**

13", Maker Unknown, Turned-Head China. Black ptd hair, low-brow style, original china limbs, cloth body **$115-195**

13¼", Maker Unknown, Black Hair China. Center-parted hair with high waves, ringlets, curls mld high over back of head, PE, china limbs, gold ptd low-heeled slippers, blue clocks on each side **$495-595**

14", Maker Unknown, China Shoulder Head. Black center-parted hair modeled with long narrow sausage curls similar to early Milliners' Models, long slender oval face, delicate features, pale china, wooden limbs, kid body **$1,000-1,100**

14", Maker Unknown, Pink Luster China. Low-brow hairdo, mld front bow ptd black, leather arms, cloth body **$395-495**

14½", Maker Unknown, Black Hair China. Center part, full on sides, leather arms, cloth body, c. 1870 .... **$265-365**

14½", Maker Unknown, Glass-Eyed China. French type, black ptd hair, PW eyes, kid fashion body, PE **$1,000-2,000**

15", Maker Unknown, Common Low-Brow China. Black hair, new body, old leather arms, c. 1880 .... **$145-195**

15", Maker Unknown, Frozen Charlie. Brown ptd eyes, brush marks, well-defined ears, usual arm and leg positions, nude body, black hair **$595-695**

15", Maker Unknown, Frozen Charlotte. Black hair, white china, arms forward, elbows bent, common variety **$350-400**

15", Maker Unknown, Late Blond China. Low-brow hairdo, exposed ears, original china limbs, cloth body, c. 1920... **$110-195**

15½", Maker Unknown, Black Hair China. Center part and flattop, not the usual Civil War style, PE, arms made of leather, body made of cloth **$350-450**

16", Maker Unknown, Brown-Eyed China. Rare bulging mld/ptd eyeballs, covered wagon hairstyle, exposed ears, red lid lines, red eye dots, red nose dots or circles, leather arms, old cloth body **$595-695**

16", Maker Unknown, Frozen Charlie. Blond ptd hair, arms mld forward in common position, lid lines, blue ptd eyes ... **$695-795**

16", Maker Unknown, Frozen Charlie. Black hair, pink china................ **$850-950**

16", Maker Unknown, Pink China Shoulder Head. Two rows of teeth, shadowed eyes ptd blue and deeply mld for realism, short upper and lower lashes, wide nose with large red nose dots, no red lid lines. This ugly doll resembles the J.N. Steiner with two rows of teeth, bald head, auburn HHW, pink china arms, pink kid body, French **$3,500-4,500**

16", Maker Unknown, Portrait China. Black hair sculpted off forehead in soft waves and swirled into large bun, one long black curl sculpted to right side of shoulder, fully exposed and well-sculpted ears, deep sloping shoulders, leather arms, body made of cloth, c. 1870 .... **$895-1,100**

16", Unmarked Rohmer Pink China. Blue fixed glass eyes, pink china arms, cork pate, HHW, rare. This well-dressed lady has her own personal wardrobe trunk with extra clothes, hats, shoes, fan, and mirror. Mark: "BREVETTE SGDG" **$3,500-6,975**

16½", Maker Unknown, Civil War Flattop China. Applied flowers, old china limbs, old cloth body **$350-450**

16½", Maker Unknown, Pink Civil War Flattop China. Pink china limbs, long oval

Biedermeir China, 18", c. 1840, original old body and limbs, original hair wig, black spot on head, Jim and Sheila Olah Scheetz collection, $800-900.

Jenny Lind China, 22", D. Kay Crow collection, $400-500.

face, looks like a young girl, leather arms, cloth body **$695-795**

17", Maker Unknown, Bald Pink China. Deep slit on top of head for hair insertion, HHW, top of head unglazed for glue, blue ptd eyes, red lid lines, short black ptd brows, tiny prim mouth, deeply sloping shoulders, six large sew holes, cloth body has wasp waist, china limbs, appears to be a late 1800s type.... **$850-950**

17", Maker Unknown, Blond Child China. Exposed ears, short curls fringing forehead and back area, black ribbon encircling uppermost section of hair, thin black brows, blue ptd eyes, red lid lines, PE, old china limbs, body made of cloth. Head incised: "137 10"........................... **$475-575**

17", Maker Unknown, Blond China. Blue ptd eyes, Civil War flattop hairdo, old china limbs, old cloth body **$350-450**

17", Maker Unknown, Early Pressed Boy China. Black hair conceals ears, brush marks, fine eyebrow lines, slightly mld eyelids, blue ptd eyes, tiny mouth, blue leather arms, old cloth body..................... **$495-595**

17", Maker Unknown, Low-Brow Laughing China. Rare mld teeth, black hair, original china limbs, original cloth body imprinted with flags of all nations, c. 1908... **$600-700**

17", Pink Swivel-Neck China. Shoulder plate, lt eyebrows, deep blue eyes, delicate eye shadowing, lashes, cork pate, skin wig, leather arms, kid-gusseted body is of the Rohmer type **$2,500-5,500**

17½", Maker Unknown, Black Hair China. Rare hairdo (vertical curls bordering forehead), exposed ears, long sausage curls mld onto back shoulders, leather arms, muslin body......................... **$695-795**

18", Jeannie June China Shoulder Head. China lower arms and legs, cloth body. (These modern china head dolls were sculpted by Aida Hubbard for the Mark Farmer Company California Centennial in 1949, sizes ranged from 4" to 28")............ **$60-95**

18", Koenigliche Porzellan Brown Hair China. Flesh-colored, thin curved brows, large blue ptd eyes, well-sculpted smiling mouth, china limbs, cloth body, c. mid-1800s. Mark: "K.P.M." **$3,000-5,000**

18", Maker Unknown, Baby China Shoulder Head. Black ptd hair with many fine hairline brush marks, exposed ears, fine brows, large blue ptd eyes, OCM with white line between lips, chubby baby china limbs, bare feet with toe detail, cloth body, rare **$2,000-3,000**

18", Maker Unknown, Blond China Shoulder Head. Old china limbs, old cloth body, OM with mld teeth, c. 1880 . . . . **$675-775**

18", Maker Unknown, Boy China. Flesh tones to china shoulder head, exposed ears, black ptd hair, loose locks of hair feathered around face, straight-line black eyebrows, some eyelid modeling, red lid lines, Cupid-bow mouth, round shoulders, old china limbs, old kid body **$495-595**

18", Maker Unknown, Child Fashion China. Cup and saucer neck, fixed glass eyes, large flat PI, HHW, leather arms, cloth body, clean-cut professional appearance. . . . **$1,500-1,700**

18", Maker Unknown, China Shoulder Head. Black scalloped curls around face, lower ears exposed, grayish eyebrows, large brown ptd eyes with red lid lines, delicate nose modeling, lovely lips, eyes have rare lower ptd lashes, old china limbs, cloth body, c. 1850 . . . **$795-895**

18", Maker Unknown, Common Low-Brow China. Black hair, red lid lines, original china limbs, cloth body, c. 1890 . . . . **$125-225**

18", Maker Unknown, Countess Dagmar. Similar to the 13" Dagmar **$525-625**

18", Maker Unknown, Little Boy China. Black ptd hair accentuated by many fine brush marks, red lid lines, blue ptd eyes, exposed ears, somber facial expression, original china limbs and cloth body **$695-795**

18", Nymphenburg China Lady Doll. Portrait face, cafe au lait hair, unevenly ptd eyebrows, thin lips, broad nose, an individual look, white china shoulder head and limbs, pale tint to features, exquisite hands with long unbroken expressive fingers, leather body, undressed, c. 1840 . . . . **$2,000-5,000**

Brunette Dolly Madison China, 16", mld hair bow, leather body, individually stitched fingers, Jim and Sheila Olah Scheetz collection, $300-400.

19", Maker Unknown, Black Hair China. Two-toned eyebrows (black on brown), center-parted hair smooth to tops of ear and coiled into braids, rare circular or flared nostrils, Cupid-bow mouth, blue ptd eyes, round face with rosy cheeks, leather arms, cloth body..................... **$895-995**

19", Maker Unknown, Black Hair Portrait China. Slightly mld bosom, center-parted hair draped over upper part of ears only and sculpted into bun pierced by hair ornament, large blue ptd eyes, red lid lines, tiny Cupid-bow mouth, sloping shoulders, high-quality china, original china limbs, cloth body stuffed with horsehair **$925-1,100**

19", Maker Unknown, Blond China. Common low-brow hairdo, no red lid lines, original china limbs, original cloth body, c. 1900........................... **$250-300**

19", Maker Unknown, Blond Portrait China. Hair mld into double rows of curls around face, green band across top of head, black hairnet, china limbs, kid body, mld eye-lids, boudoir or sleepy look to blue ptd eyes **$925-1,100**

19", Maker Unknown, Brown Glass Sleep-Eyed China. This very rare lady has an open crown with plaster pate, old mohair wig, chubby round face with double chin and well-sculpted ears, arms made of leather, body made of cloth............... **$3,500-4,500**

19", Maker Unknown, China Boy Shoulder Head. Bald dome head, HHW, faintly modeled ears, very large French eyes, red lid lines, kid limbs, c. 1858. Original kid body marked: "D'Autrement"....... **$1,800-2,800**

19", Maker Unknown, Civil War China. Black hair, old cloth body, original china limbs, rare bare feet with toe modeling..... **$950-1,250**

19", Maker Unknown, Cream-Tinted Portrait Lady. Long graceful neck set forward on well-modeled shoulder plate, bosom, four large sew holes, fine portrait features, early pressed head, black hair brushed back and decorated on each side with flowers and leaves, swirled bun at rear, fine brush marks around front hairline, thin nose modeling, fine upper lip detail, well-sculpted chin, china limbs, old cloth body................... **$925-1,200**

19", Maker Unknown, Early Lady Portrait China. Delicate high-quality pink china, French type, large blue ptd eyes, single-stroke brows, sensitive mouth, cheek fullness, long neck, shoulder modeling and some back detail, brown hair has tinge of luster, brush marks at nape, draped black ptd hairstyle covers ears, ungusseted kid body and kid arms **$1,800-1,900**

19", Maker Unknown, Flirty-Eyed China. Blue ptd eyes to the side, red lid lines, white line between lips, leather arms, body made of cloth......................... **$950-1,100**

19", Maker Unknown, Pink China. Dark brown hair, blue ptd eyes, red lid lines, brush marks, gold band around hair, wooden limbs, kid body.................... **$1,000-1,200**

19", Maker Unknown, Wire-Eyed China. Glass sleep eyes, open crown, old HHW, leather arms, kid body, wire lever to open eyes **$2,250-5,250**

19½", Maker Unknown, Civil War Flattop China. Blue ptd eyes, red lid lines, new china limbs, new body................. **$245-345**

20", Maker Unknown, Black Hair China. Low-brow hairdo higher on top of head than most, known as Gibson Girl china, original china limbs, cloth body, c. 1900... **$195-295**

20", Maker Unknown, Blond China. Deeply mld elaborate hairstyle, exposed ears, blue ptd eyes, red lid lines, red nose dots, deeply mld sloping shoulders, old china limbs, body made of cloth....................... **$595-695**

20", Maker Unknown, Boy China. Exposed ears, black ptd hair mld very short with center part, definite boy face, old china limbs, old cloth body.................... **$550-650**

20", Maker Unknown, Brown-Eyed China. Black 1880s hairstyle, kid arms, original old cloth body **$450-550**

20", Maker Unknown, Covered Wagon China. Severe hairdo, white part down center of black ptd hair, sloping shoulders, two-tone eyebrows (black and brown), red lid lines, circular nostrils, old china limbs, original old cloth body **$495-595**

20", Maker Unknown, Early Lady Portrait China. Slender face with delicate classical features, blue ptd eyes, red lid lines, black center-parted hair draped smoothly over covered ears and coiled into a braided bun at back of head, china limbs, feet have modeled and ptd low-heeled shoes, ptd pink garters, old sawdust-filled body, c. 1840. . . . **$1,000-1,200**

20", Maker Unknown, Man China. Definite male face, deep shoulder plate, blue ptd eyes, sparsely ptd black hair with brush marks, red lid lines, exposed ears, leather arms, old cloth body, dressed as a man **$695-795**

20", Maker Unknown, Negro China Shoulder Head. Teeth, black china limbs, black cloth body, black ptd hair, brown ptd eyes with whites, old clothes, very rare . . **$2,000-2,500**

20", Maker Unknown, Portrait China. Black mld/ptd hair with rear bun, brush marks, delicate facial modeling, long slender neck, red lid lines, blue ptd eyes, red eye and nose dots, old china limbs, cloth body. . **$895-995**

21", French China. Blue glass eyes, HHW, kid body and arms, stitched fingers, clear china quality with no imperfections, c. 1960. Incised: "FG" **$225-325**

21", Maker Unknown, Bald or Ball-Head China. Original elaborate HHW in 1930s style, bald pate, ptd features, four large sew holes, deeply rounded sloping shoulders, semi-long neck, rosy cheeks, tiny smiling mouth, large blue ptd French eyes, red lid lines, slightly mld eyelids give eyes the desirable sleepy or boudoir look, red lid lines ptd higher than usual, leather arms, kid body. These heads were often used in salons in Paris as hairstyle display heads. **$1,275-1,375**

21", Maker Unknown, Black Hair China Shoulder Head. Hair mld into a mass of curls, exposed ears, Mary Steuber legs (the Mary Steuber leg was patented in 1878 and sold commercially for homemade doll bodies) **$395-495**

21", Maker Unknown, Late French Bald-Head China. Blue ptd eyes, no red lid lines, blond mohair wig, rosy cheeks, red mouth, shoulder plate sculpted with portion of upper arms, china lower arms. Kid body stamped: "BREVETE" (in an ellipse). . . . **$1,250-1,500**

21", Maker Unknown, Pink China. Black ptd hair, blue ptd eyes, red lid lines, china limbs, black boots and green garters, cloth body **$595-695**

21", Maker Unknown, Pink China Fashion Lady. Brown glass eyes, swivel neck, finely stroked eyebrows, ptd upper and lower eyelashes, PE, rare cutout crown, HHW, CM, kid arms with stitched fingers, kid fashion body **$2,795-3,795**

21", Unmarked Thuringian China. Hear swept high off forehead, braids around crown, hair decorated with black comb, fine china with high glaze, black lines for eyebrows, red lid lines, deep slope to shoulders, old china limbs, cloth body, c. 1700s **$3,000-5,000**

21½", Maker Unknown, Pre-Civil War China. Deep shoulder modeling, comb marks, vertical sausage curls, leather arms, body made of cloth **$495-595**

22", Maker Unknown, Ball or Bald-Head China. Brown ptd eyes, deep shoulder modeling, leather arms, cloth body with small waist, skin wig **$1,000-1,200**

22", Maker Unknown, China with Turned Head. Brown eyes, blond hair, old china limbs, old cloth body, c. 1880 . . . . . **$395-495**

23", Maker Unknown, Blond Child China. Slightly bulging blue ptd eyes, mld eyelids, PE, deeply mld waves brushed away from center part, short hairdo, fully exposed ears, leather arms, cloth body and legs, resembles Bette Davis **$595-695**

23", Meissen China Shoulder Head. Flesh-tinted, long neck leaning forward, neck lines, throat hollow, sloping shoulders and sloping chest plate with mld bosom, back shoulder plate flatter than front, six sew holes, brown streaked center-parted hair draped over ears and modeled into rear braided bun, original china limbs, kid fashion body, shoulder plate nailed to body, 1840s hairdo. Mark: "756 2 pap" **$3,000-6,000**

24", Maker Unknown, Girl China. Slightly turned head, similar to 26" Boy china, could be dressed as twins, old china limbs, old cloth body, feet have unusual mld boots with tiny rosettes and mld buttons **$350-450**

24½", Maker Unknown, Pink Luster China. Brown eyes, black hair, PE, unusual face, old china limbs, cloth body **$895-995**

25", Maker Unknown, Glass-Eyed China. Short center-parted black ptd hair, blue PW eyes, china limbs, cloth body ... **$925-1,200**

26", Maker Unknown, Boy China. Black ptd center-parted wavy hair, exposed ears, old china limbs, old cloth body, dressed in boy's clothes........................ **$350-450**

26", Maker Unknown, Pink China Portrait Lady. Long neck attached to narrow sloping shoulders, some bosom modeling, short curly dark brown hair, blue ptd eyes, red lid lines ptd higher than usual, dark red lip lines, china lower arms with exquisite hands, kid body, c. late 1700s **$2,795-3,795**

27", Maker Unknown, Black Hair China. Blue enameled eyes, red lid lines, one-stroke brows, lovely smiling mouth, leather arms, body made of cloth **$975-1,200**

29", Maker Unknown, Black Hair China. Hair scalloped around face, large blue ptd eyes, eyes ptd looking up, deep shoulder plate, leather arms, old muslin body with stains, lovely doll, unusual face **$500-600**

30", Maker Unknown, China Shoulder Head. Gray eyes, blond hair, curly hairstyle with bangs, new china limbs, new cloth body, c. 1880......................... **$495-595**

31", Maker Unknown, Flattop Civil War China. Black hair, new body, lovely new china limbs **$350-450**

34", Maker Unknown, Black Hair China. Blue ptd beads mld around neck, blue ptd eyes, red lid lines, leather arms, cloth body.. **$795-895**

(L. to R.) Rare Civil War China, 15", blue mld necklace, $350-400. Turkey Ridge China, 15", old clothes all-original body, $300-400. Blond China, 12", original body and undies, $200-225. All dolls are from the Herron collection.

6
Parians

Call them Parians (which they are not) or Fancies (which most of them are) or simply untinted or molded bisques, they are still among the most underrated, beautiful, and fascinating of the old dolls. On the pricing yardstick, they are underpriced when compared with the overpriced poor quality of late French dolls. And fortunately for those who cherish them, the Fancies of yore can still be found. The dolls listed in this chapter are "old" in every way, including head, limbs, body, and clothing. Cracked or refired heads and limbs cannot command these top prices. A new body does not detract much from a doll's value, but it is always best to leave an old body intact and merely reupholster. To do so retains a doll's value fully and makes her even more coveted in the most competitive field in the world.

Note: Many of the unmarked Parians were made by J.D. Kestner. Some are found with Kestner size numbers.

2½", Maker Unknown, Bathing Beauty. Mld swimsuit, ptd hair and features. Body Mark: "Germany" **$150-175**

4", Maker Unknown, Snood Parian. Dollhouse type, mld/ptd hair with feather, ptd features, blond hair, bisque lower limbs, cloth body **$125-225**

6", Maker Unknown, Baby Jesus Parian. In swaddling clothes **$300-350**

6", Maker Unknown, Corset Parian. Blond hair, ptd features, Parian limbs, mld corset, drawers trimmed with gold, cloth inserts for shoulder and thigh movement, ptd/mld boots. Mark: "8" **$300-400**

7", Maker Unknown, Parian with Elaborate Molded Bonnet. Bonnet decorated with huge bows, huge bow under fat chin, blue and pink decoration, ptd features, Parian limbs, brown glazed boots, body made of cloth. Mark: "Germany" **$195-225**

Rare Glass-Eyed Parian, 16", bisque forearms, kid body, French quality, $895.

Alice in Wonderland, 23", all-original, Jim and Sheila Olah Scheetz collection, $750.

Emma Clear Reproduction Parian, 18", marked "Clear 65," D. Kay Crow collection, $195-250.

7½", Maker Unknown, Parian. Gold bead trim, mld guimpe, blond mld hair, ptd features, Parian limbs, cloth body ... **$165-195**

8", Maker Unknown, Portrait Lady Parian. Long oval face, fine ptd features, PE, blue band across front of fancy hairdo, leather arms, cloth body **$165-195**

8½", Maker Unknown, Corset Parian. Blond mld hair, blue ptd eyes, orange lid lines, cloth upper arms, cloth upper legs and lower body, Parian limbs, rare molded-on white corset with gold trim, blue ptd slippers .. **$350-450**

10", Maker Unknown, Green Hat Parian. Blond hair, mld green hat with pink plume and luster trim, Parian limbs, body made of cloth **$395-495**

10½", Maker Unknown, Pillbox Parian. Blond hair, Parian limbs, cloth body, mld green pillbox hat with glazed lavender plumes on top, black edging and black bow in the back ....:....... **$495-595**

10½", Maker Unknown, Rare Hairdo Blond Parian. Ten fat sausage curls and band in hair, long portrait face, Parian limbs, early flat-heeled slippers, cloth body....... **$725-825**

11", Maker Unknown, Little Girl Parian. Inset blue glass eyes, short curly blond mld hair, earlobes exposed and pierced, bisque lower limbs, glazed socks and purple luster boots........................ **$695-795**

11¾", Maker Unknown, Elegant Blond Lady Parian. Parian limbs, mld blond hair brushed into waves over ears and fashioned into low neck bun with thick braid across middle, ptd features, heel-less black ptd boots. Incised on shoulder: "12.B"................. **$385-485**

12", Maker Unknown, Glass-Eyed Parian Child. Little girl, short blond mld ringlets, earlobes exposed, ptd features, Parian limbs, kid body...................... **$595-695**

12", Maker Unknown, Regional Parian. Black hair, mld "regional" white cap, mld yoke, mld cross and chain, original Provincial costume, Parian limbs, cloth body (head resembles the glazed china head of the 1870s) **$395-495**

12½", Maker Unknown, Parian. Double bands, blond ringlets at back of hairdo, chubby face, bisque limbs, black ptd/mld boots with tiny heels **$395-495**

13", Maker Unknown, Countess Dagmar. Similar to the 22" Countess Dagmar with leather arms and cloth body **$395-495**

13", Maker Unknown, Parian Man. All-wood body, mld mustache, ptd eyes, open crown, hair mld on sides of head, Parian limbs, mld shoes, mohair wig, rare type ... **$1,000-1,200**

15", Emma Clear Parian. Pale blue mld hair ribbon, gold luster trim, pale blue drop earrings, elaborate blond hairstyle, mld blouse with pale blue trim, Parian limbs, body made of cloth **$300-400**

15", Maker Unknown, Alice in Wonderland Parian. Black band across front of hairdo, exposed ears, Parian limbs, body made of cloth **$425-525**

15", Maker Unknown, Glass Jewel Parian. Rare mld necklace with a real glass jewel, ptd features, blond mld hair, exposed ears, Parian limbs, cloth body **$750-850**

15", Maker Unknown, Tam o'Shanter Parian. Blond hair, mld yoke and necklace, mld tam, Parian limbs, cloth body **$425-525**

15", Unmarked Huret Shoulder Head Parian. Ball head with skin wig, ptd features, original articulated wooden body, rare. . **$3,000-5,000**

16", Kling Turned-Head Parian. Blond mld hair, ptd features, Parian limbs, cloth body. Mark on back: "Kling" **$425-525**

16", Maker Unknown, Parian Boy on Bicycle. Blond short mld hair, mld Scottish cap ptd with blue stripes and red and blue lines, mld black buttons, mld blue ribbons on cap (ribbon end mld onto shoulder), blue ptd eyes, wooden body, tin legs, feet, arms and hands, hands flesh-tinted, original costume, bike has red metal ptd frame with tin wheels, seat and handles also metal, unmarked **$685-785**

16", Maker Unknown, Parian with Molded Black Beads in Blond Hair. Parian limbs, PE, ptd features, cloth body.......... **$425-525**

Emma Clear Blue-Scarf Parian, 16", marked "Clear 49," D. Kay Crow collection, $225.

Rare Black-Hair Parian, 20", marked "8552" and "Clover," mld breastplate and hair bow, mld gold brooch on the ruffled high-fitting neckline, rare intaglio eyes, OM with teeth, corset, D. Kay Crow collection, $3,000-5,000.

16", Maker Unknown, Sarah Bernhardt Parian. So-called because Miss Bernhardt once owned a similar doll. Bernhardt dolls can still be found, however, with gold mld beads entwined throughout elaborate hairdo, narrow portrait face, Parian limbs with flat-soled shoes mld onto feet **$695-795**

16", Maker Unknown, Swivel-Neck Parian. Cobalt-blue glass eyes, Parian limbs, mld hair, ptd features, cloth body...... **$1,200-1,500**

16", Maker Unknown, Turban Parian. Black hair, fine brush marks, Turban draped around crown and back bun and tied on right side, mld fringe sculpted onto right shoulder, Parian limbs, heel-less ptd boots, body made of cloth **$895-995**

16", Maker Unknown, Turned-Head Parian. Glass eyes, short blond mld hairdo with tiny ringlets, ptd features, Parian limbs, body made of cloth **$925-1,100**

17", Dresden Parian. Elaborate hairstyle, mld flowers around crown, long curls at rear cascading onto neck, Parian limbs, cloth body, mld necklace............. **$750-850**

17", LaMotte 65 Marked Parian. Modern, good quality, well-modeled hairstyle with gold luster comb, blue ptd eyes, PE, gold luster mld necklace, cloth body............ **$195-295**

17", Maker Unknown, Alice Parian. Black hair, mld band with "Alice" across front, exposed ears, blue ptd eyes, sloping shoulders, Parian limbs and heel-less mld slippers, cloth body **$650-700**

17", Maker Unknown, Lady Parian. Blue glass eyes, PE, elaborate blond hairdo with clusters of curls on back, swivel neck on deep shoulder plate, articulated twill-covered wooden body, dressed in original bride costume with veil **$2,250-4,250**

17", Maker Unknown, Lady Parian. Brown glass fixed eyes, OM with teeth, PE, blond mld hair with comb marks, sculpted high waves on top of head, clusters of curls in rear, applied pink roses on top of head, stationary head on deep shoulder plate, Parian limbs, pink kid body, dressed as bridesmaid ... **$3,000-5,000**

17", Maker Unknown, Man Parian. Swivel neck, blue fixed glass eyes, mld black hair, CM, articulated twill-covered wooden body, dressed as bridegroom **$2,795-4,795**

17", Maker Unknown, Parian Portrait Lady. Black and gold hair bands, mld glazed earrings, ptd features, Parian limbs, cloth body **$465-565**

17", Maker Unknown, Pauline. Sister to Napoleon, portrait type, gray ptd hair, fully exposed ears, mld hair brushed off neck, braids crossed to form a small coronet on top of head, narrow green band trimmed with gold luster encircles hair, expressive face, lightly parted lips turned up at corners, upper and lower lashes, detailed eye and ear sculpture, Parian limbs, kid body **$1,200-1,300**

17", Unmarked Huret Parian. Bald head, blue ptd eyes, mohair wig, Parian arms, original kid body **$1,700-3,700**

18", Dernheim, Kock, and Fischer Parian Child Shoulder Head. Elaborate hairstyle with bangs and side waves, black hair mld onto shoulders, large ears, large blue glass eyes, short upper and lower eyelashes, bisque lower arms and lower legs, glazed boots, cloth body. Incised: "674 x 6". **$895-995**

18", Empress Augusta Victoria of Germany Parian. Dark hair waved high on head, exposed PE, enameled jewels in hair, iron cross on neck, brown leather arms, cloth body, c. 1880. .... **$1,000-1,200**

18", Empress Augusta Victoria of Germany Parian. Blond hair, enameled jewels in hair, iron cross, leather arms, body made of cloth **$1,250-1,500**

18", Leipold Round-Face Common Parian. Side-parted 1860s style windblown hairdo, blue ptd eyes, shoulder plate mld and decorated with gold-trimmed collar and tie, six sew holes, leather arms, cloth body. Mark found on chest: "C.W. Leipold-307 8 St. New York" **$825-925**

18", Maker Unknown, Little Boy Parian. Cherubic face, blue glass eyes, short wavy blond hair, ears exposed, Parian limbs, cloth body **$795-895**

Plain Parian, 20", high-quality, all-original (including costume), D. Kay Crow collection, $275.

125

Highland Mary Parian, 14½", bisque forearms, kid body, $375.

18", Maker Unknown, Pink Turban Parian. Blond hair, pink mld turban, long slim face, blue ptd eyes, Parian limbs, body made of cloth **$495-595**

18", Maker Unknown, Rare Glass-Eyed Parian with Swivel Neck. Blond mld Civil War flattop hairdo, center part, feathered curls at sides and back, leather arms, cloth body **$1,200-1,500**

18½", English Worktable Companion Parian. Parian limbs, cloth body, original costume includes petticoat and drawers for pins, outer skirt has large pocket for needles, scissors, and thread, hat is a pincushion, rare . . . **$695-795**

18½", Maker Unknown, Necklace Parian. Blond hair styled with curls and braids decorated by blue ribbon, mld shirtwaist and necklace, PE, Parian limbs, body made of cloth **$795-895**

19", Emma Clear Gibson Girl Parian. Parian limbs, mld hat with flowers, high-heeled Parian boots, original Clear costume with a parasol **$695-795**

19", Maker Unknown, Bald-Head Parian. Blue ptd eyes, mohair wig, Parian limbs, cloth body **$795-895**

19", Maker Unknown, Lady Parian. Elaborate hairstyle consisting of looped braids and swirls, brush marks, cafe au lait colored hair, Parian limbs, body made of cloth **$695-795**

19", Maker Unknown, Marie Antoinette Parian. Elaborate blond hairstyle, PE, delicate fluting and pink rose, Parian limbs, cloth body **$1,000-1,200**

19", Maker Unknown, Round-Faced Common Hairdo Parian. Blue glass eyes, rare swivel neck with crossbar, leather arms, cloth body **$1,275-2,000**

19", Maker Unknown, Scarf Parian. Pink and blue glaze, blond hair, scarf with white fringe mld onto right shoulder, gold cockade on left side of head, Parian limbs, body made of cloth **$675-775**

19", Maker Unknown, Shirley Temple Parian. Blue glass fixed eyes, blue mld hair ribbon, clusters of fat blond curls piled high on head, Parian limbs, cloth body **$695-795**

19", Maker Unknown, Straw Hat Parian. Prim face, hat has pink feather and rosettes of blue and gold, blue ptd eyes, short eyebrows, ears exposed, brown hair brushed over ears and mld into bun, Parian limbs, body made of cloth **$495-595**

19½", Dresden Parian. Prim face, lt brown hair decorated with applied rosettes and braided severely over fully exposed PE, two fat black curls, rushing on shoulder plate, decorated bodice and pendant, Parian limbs, cloth body. **$1,000-1,200**

20", Dresden Parian. Applied pink roses, glass eyes, PE, fancy mld high collar, Parian limbs, cloth body. **$1,000-1,200**

20", Japanese Parian. Short blond hair, PE, blue ptd eyes, CM, Parian limbs, cloth body, quality doll. **$225-325**

20", Maker Unknown, Early Parian. Dead-white bisque and soapy texture, long black hair has snood over back, brush marks, blue ptd eyes, mld guimpe with glazed blue and white collar and tie, Parian limbs, cloth body, c. 1864. . . . . **$695-795**

20", Maker Unknown, Snood Parian. Rare black hair, stipple-painted temples, Parian limbs, cloth body. **$900-1,000**

20½", Emma Clear George and 19½", Martha Washington Parians. Fine Parian quality, Parian limbs, cloth body, dressed to type and period, c. 1940, pair **$895-995**

20½", Emma Clear George Washington and 19½" Martha Washington Parians. Fine Parian quality, Parian limbs, cloth body, dressed to period, c. 1940, pair. . . . **$895-995**

22", Borgfeldt Parian. Blond hair, mld collar, mld necktie, Parian limbs, PE, cloth body. Mark: "5M5." (This is one of many rather elaborate Parians handled by Borgfeldt, distinguished by elaborate hairstyles, decorations, necklaces, hats, glass and ptd eyes, pierced and unpierced ears, collars and ties, and tiaras. Other markings: "5E," "2K3," "5C5" and "G") **$395-695**

Parian, 16", upswept hairdo, ptd features, ears exposed, Jim and Sheila Olah Scheetz collection, $395.

22", Emma Clear Blue Scarf Parian. Blue fixed glass eyes, Parian limbs, cloth body, high quality, c. 1940................ **$295-395**

22", Maker Unknown, Child Parian. Quality bisque, round chubby face with fat cheeks, short curly blond hair, kid arms with stitched individual fingers, sturdy cloth body and legs, stitched toes.................. **$375-475**

22", Maker Unknown, Countess Dagmar. Dead-white soapy texture, protruding glazed eyes, mld guimpe with gold buttons, six sew holes, braids decorate back of hairdo, kid arms, cloth body............... **$595-695**

22", Maker Unknown, Parian Boy. Detailed blond hair, ptd features, cloth body, arms made of kid **$395-495**

22", Maker Unknown, Round-Face Parian. Short blond hair with tight mld curls, black ribbon and bow across front, blue ptd eyes, Parian limbs, cloth body........ **$450-495**

25", Maker Unknown, Solid-Dome Parian. Blue ptd eyes, HHW, Parian limbs, body made of cloth **$895-995**

27", Simon & Halbig Parian. Blond hair, PE, one-stroke thin brows, large blue ptd eyes, Cupid-bow mouth, round sloping shoulders, four sew holes, leather arms, body made of cloth **$675-775**

7
Wax Dolls

The term "wax doll" refers to a doll that is either poured with a hollow center or solid throughout. Signed or marked dolls are more desirable and costly than unsigned dolls simply because so few signed specimens are found today (although they were made by the leading wax modelers of the time). The wax dolls listed here are all in good condition and all original unless otherwise specified. Dolls that are extremely battered or broken cannot command these prices. All dolls are dressed in either original or old clothing.

7", Maker Unknown, Baby Girl in Papier-Mache Egg. Poured wax, blue inset glass eyes, mohair wig, poured wax arms crossed in front of chest, one leg fully exposed, the other leg ready to emerge (original material around thighs and upper body, pull string on side of egg for cry box), c. 1800......... **$395-495**

7½", Maker Unknown, Poured Wax Child. Black ptd eyes, CM, human hair inserted in slit on top of head, wax limbs, cloth body, old clothes, c. 1830-1840............. **$395-495**

8", Maker Unknown, Pink Wax Head. Poured, ptd hair, wax limbs, cloth body, ptd features, ptd boots, c. early 1800s.. **$495-595**

10", Maker Unknown, Baby Jesus. Poured wax head and limbs, cloth body, inset glass eyes, HHW..................... **$250-350**

10", Maker Unknown, Baby Jesus. All-wax, creche type, tiny blue glass inset eyes, CM, original mohair wig set in tiny ringlets, nude doll **$395-495**

10", Maker Unknown, Peddler. English, rare elderly man in original glass dome, carved wax head and hands, inset blue glass eyes, inset gray hair, cloth body and limbs, original costume and tray of wares **$2,000-3,000**

Poured Wax Baby, 15", inserted hair and lashes, glass eyes, original creation by Elva Weems, $125-150.

129

Rare Montanari Poured Wax Boy, 16", inset glass eyes, inset hair, wax hands, cloth body, old clothes, Jim and Sheila Olah Scheetz collection, $1,500-2,000.

10", Maker Unknown, Peddler. Rare young girl with a very pretty face, poured ptd features, brown mohair wig, lovely wax hands, well-sculpted bare feet, cloth body, wears original red cape, cap and dress, carries basket of old wares, all-original, the young face is very rare.............. **$2,500-3,500**

12", Maker Unknown, Fortune-Telling Doll. Black wax, pumpkin head type, pupil-less dark brown glass eyes, black wax arms, original costume consists of outer skirt and apron concealing petticoat, c. 1850. (Petticoat consists of two folded pleats of paper on which handwritten messages appear. The writing is in French)................... **$1,500-1,600**

12", Maker Unknown, Grandparent Dolls. In original wooden rockers, wax heads and hands, cloth body and limbs, dressed in original clothes, contemporary, Mexican, sold as a pair. **$165-195**

12", Maker Unknown, Lady Doll. Turned shoulder head, poured wax arms, cloth body and legs, ptd features, mohair wig, original clothes, c. early 1900s............ **$250-350**

12", Maker Unknown, Peddler. English, poured wax shoulder head, CM, blue ptd eyes, blond mohair wig, wooden limbs, cloth body, original peddler costume, stall and original wares...................... **$1,200-1,300**

12", Maker Unknown, Queen Victoria. Portrait type, beeswax head and limbs, cloth body, black wig, blue glass inset eyes, CM, dressed to period, c. mid-1800s. ... **$700-800**

13", Maker Unknown, Lady Doll. Poured, pipestem limbs covered with flesh-colored crepe paper, ptd features, mohair wig, cloth body, crepe-paper dress, c. 1920... **$225-325**

14", Maker Unknown, Little Girl Shoulder Head. Poured, CM, blue glass sleep eyes, embedded hair, muslin body, compo lower limbs **$450-550**

14", Maker Unknown, Two-Faced Solid Wax Head Doll. Papier-mache limbs, smile-cry faces, inset glass eyes, original mohair wig, cloth body pull string, pink wax .. **$345-445**

14", Montanari-Type Lady Doll. Poured,

CM, inset glass eyes, embedded blond hair, wax limbs, cloth body, bride **$595-695**

14½", Maker Unknown, Little Girl Shoulder Head. Wire-eyed wax type, CM, black pupil-less glass eyes, inset hair, poured wax lower limbs, cloth body, c. early 1800s... **$575-675**

16", Kinder-Kissen Packet Doll. Poured wax head and arms, blue glass fixed eyes, blond mohair wig, ribbon and lace swaddling clothes, pull string for cry box **$495-595**

16", Maker Unknown, Queen Victoria. Blue glass fixed eyes, CM, inset hair, poured wax shoulder head and limbs, cloth body, authentically dressed in original old coronation robes, c. mid-1800s **$1,000-1,200**

17", Maker Unknown, Baby Jesus. Solid beeswax, creche type, fixed blue glass eyes, embedded hair, CM, wistful expression, stationary limbs, beautiful hands and feet with toe and fingernail detail **$795-895**

17", Maker Unknown, French Twins. Laughing boy and crying boy, poured wax head, poured wax lower limbs, lovely hands and feet, straw-stuffed cloth body, brown HHW, brown fixed glass eyes, original early 1800s costume, mld teeth and tongue, sold as a pair **$1,500-1,600**

17", Maker Unknown, Little Girl Shoulder Head. Poured, CM, embedded hair, brown fixed glass eyes, poured wax limbs, body made of cloth **$525-625**

18", Maker Unknown, Lady Doll. Poured wax shoulder head and limbs, portrait face, CM, black ptd/mld hairstyle, fully exposed ears, long neck, large pupil-less glass eyes, cloth body, c. early 1800s **$800-900**

18", Maker Unknown, Little Girl Shoulder Head. Poured, brown glass sleep eyes, CM, mohair wig, wax-dipped compo limbs, muslin body **$400-500**

18", Pierotti Baby. Inset blue glass eyes, CM, poured limbs, cloth body stuffed with hair. Signed: "H. Pierotti" **$1,200-1,300**

19", Charles Marsh Lady Doll. Poured wax shoulder head and limbs, inset blue glass eyes, CM, embedded hair, PE, cloth body, fancy old clothes, shoes. Mark on body: "CHARLES MARSH" **$1,400-1,500**

19½", Maker Unknown, Beeswax Shoulder Head. Exposed ears, mld hair fashioned into bun, black bead eyes, CM, old clothes, cloth body, c. 1700s or early 1800s .. **$1,000-1,200**

20", Charles Marsh Little Girl Type. Shoulder head has four sew holes, angelic face, inset blue glass eyes, CM, blond hair in small tufts, wax lower limbs, cloth body. Mark on body under front shoulder plate: "From C. Gooch, Soho Bazaar, Chas. Marsh, Sole Manufacturers—London—Dolls Cleaned & Repaired" **$1,200-1,300**

20", Lucy Peck Child Doll. Poured wax shoulder head, arms and legs, CM, blue inset glass eyes, embedded blond hair. Cloth body labeled with Peck blue oval stamp reading: "M. Peck, London" **$900-1,000**

20", Maker Unknown, Little Girl Shoulder Head. Poured, CM, blue glass fixed eyes, wax-dripped compo arms, embedded hair, compo lower legs, mld boots, cloth body. (This doll has a Simon & Halbig look) **$450-550**

20", Maker Unknown, Stump Doll. Lady type, wax shoulder head, blue bulgy glass eyes, crimped mohair wig **$1,200-1,300**

20", H.J. Meech Poured Wax Girl. Brown fixed glass eyes, CM, embedded brown hair, poured wax limbs, turned head, cloth body, string at hips works "mamma" box. Body stamped: "H.J. Meech" **$1,500-1,600**

20", Pierotti Male Shoulder Head. Poured, CM, inset glass eyes, inset white hair, mustache, wavy white beard, wax forearms and lower legs, cloth body, depicts a high priest dressed in white robe and sandals, signed, c. 1860 .... **$1,200-1,300**

21", Maker Unknown, Little Girl Shoulder Head. Poured, turned head, mohair wig, CM, brown glass fixed eyes, leather fashion-type body, leather arms and hands with stitched fingers, leather legs with original sewed-on boots **$450-550**

22" (head cir), Maker Unknown, Male Bust. Beeswax, embedded hair, eyebrows, eyelashes, blue fixed glass eyes. French display item for hats (usually made into dolls by the collectors) **$750-850**

22", Maker Unknown, Poured Wax Shoulder Head and Arms. Little girl type, CM, blue glass fixed eyes, HHW, turned head, cloth body and legs. Body of doll stamped: "Holz Masse" **$695-795**

22", Montanari-Type Child. Poured, blue glass inset eyes, inset hair, wax limbs, cloth body, fat arms and legs **$750-850**

22½", Montanari Child. Inset glass eyes, CM, embedded brown hair, wax limbs, cloth body, Montanari roll of fat beneath chin and back of neck, fat limbs. Doll is signed on the foot: "Mty" **$1,500-1,600**

Poured Wax Doll, 17", creche type, c. 1880, lower limbs made of wax, cloth body, inset glass eyes, lamb's wool wig, old costume, Jim and Sheila Olah Scheetz collection, $1,200.

23", Maker Unknown, Lady Doll. Poured wax shoulder head and lower limbs, CM, inset eyes, embedded hair, cloth and hair-stuffed fashion body with small waist and wide hips, dressed to style. **$650-750**

23", H.J. Meech Poured Wax Girl. Inset brown HHW and eyelashes. CM, fixed glass eyes, turned head, poured wax limbs, cloth body. Mark on right thigh: "H.J. Meech, Kensington Rd., London, S.E." Mark on left thigh: "Dollmaker to the Royal Family" (in circle) **$1,800-1,900**

24", Maker Unknown, Baby. Poured wax, very heavy head, solid poured-wax limbs, CM, inset glass eyes, embedded hair, brows, lashes, heavy cloth body stuffed with hair (face appears almost human—probably a death mask type) **$800-900**

24", Maker Unknown, Little Girl Shoulder Head. Wired sleep eyes, HHW, OM with tongue, poured wax limbs, cloth body with lever at side (lever moves eyes and tongue), rare type **$795-895**

24", Maker Unknown, Queen Victoria. Poured wax shoulder head and limbs, CM, inset glass eyes, HHW, cloth body, blue velvet robe, crown, c. mid-1800s **$1,500-1,700**

25", Maker Unknown, Baby. Poured, turned shoulder head, yellow wax, CM, inset glass eyes, poured wax limbs (large realistic hands and feet), hair-stuffed cloth body, unmarked, embedded fine baby hair **$700-800**

25", Maker Unknown, Doll of Brittany. French, poured wax shoulder head and lower limbs, blue fixed glass eyes, embedded hair, cloth body, original old costume, c. late 1700s **$1,000-1,200**

27", Maker Unknown, German Lady Shoulder Head. Poured, ptd features, yellow flax wig, terra-cotta hands, cloth body and arms, wooden legs, elaborate 1700s costume, all original **$2,000-3,000**

27½", Lucy Peck Lady Doll. Poured wax head and limbs, CM, embedded HHW, inset glass eyes, cloth body with Luck Peck mark in purple ink, dressed in original bridal outfit and veil. **$1,200-1,300**

8
Wax-Over Dolls

The wax-over dolls comprise a large group of old dolls that are still with us, underpriced, but not as popular with contemporary doll collectors. Wax was used as a complexion improver and as a means of simulating the more expensive wax qualities for a cheaper, mass-produced doll. The wax-over dolls earned their chips and cracks by being genuine playthings for millions of children whose fathers could not afford to buy an expensive all-wax beauty. Thus, all kinds of cheaper grade dolls were waxed—papier-mache, composition, wood, tin, bisque, plaster, china—in short, anything durable enough for a wax adherence. Durability, then is the charm of these valuable old relics. When buying one of these dolls, a collector need not fear its perishable qualities. Should the thin wax coating chip or melt away, merely have it rewaxed. The value is retained, as is the original beauty.

The dolls in this chapter may have a few nose smudges, cracks or chips, but for the most part, they are in good condition. Damaged dolls cannot command these prices, however. All are dressed.

8", Maker Unknown, Bonnet Head. Blond mohair inserted beneath bonnet to simulate head of hair, dark pupil-less glass eyes, mld green and orange feathers on bonnet, waxed compo limbs, old muslin body, unusual size **$165-225**

10", Maker Unknown, Bonnet Head. Simulated straw bonnet, old coarse brown mohair inserted under edges, black pupil-less glass eyes, wooden limbs **$225-295**

11", Maker Unknown, Bonnet Head. Black ptd/mld hat and hair, inset glass eyes, compo limbs, muslin body **$195-295**

11", Maker Unknown, Interchangeable Wax-Head Doll. Wax-over-compo, fixed glass eyes, blond, brown and auburn HHW, CM, BJ compo body, pull string for voice box, original clothes, hat and box **$695-795**

Wax-Over-Compo, 17", black hair in waterfall style, all-original, D. Kay Crow collection, $875.

133

Wax-Over-Compo, 18", mld hat with plume, hair inserted, all-original, D. Kay Crow collection, $275-375.

11", Maker Unknown, Interchangeable Wax-Head Doll. Wax-over-compo, fixed glass eyes, blond, brown and auburn HHW, CM, BJ compo body, pull string for voice box, original clothes, hat, original box . **$695-795**

11½", Maker Unknown, Wax-Over-Compo Boy Doll. Compo lower limbs, waxed, dark brown pupil-less glass eyes, mld/ptd short black boy hairdo, muslin body and legs, pressure on upper chest works squawk box, pressure on lower chest moves head, well-dressed, unmarked **$395-450**

12", Maker Unknown, Pumpkin Head. Similar to the 14" Pumpkin Head, except this doll has brown ptd hair **$225-325**

12", Maker Unknown, Wax Slit-Head Kitchen Ornament. Brown pupil-less glass eyes, HHW inserted in slit, CM, cloth upper body and arms, compo lower arms, bell-shaped lower body covered with a skirt which opens to reveal miniature kitchen display, silk dress and parasol, matching silk bonnet, all original, English, c. 1840 . . . . . **$1,000-1,200**

14", Maker Unknown, Pumpkin Head. Inset black pupil-less glass eyes, mld hairdo type, ptd snood, blond mld hair, lt wax coating over wooden limbs, muslin body. **$225-325**

15", Maker Unknown, Wax-Over-Plaster. English, OM with teeth, fixed glass eyes, compo limbs, auburn hair wig, mld ankle-strap shoes and socks, straw-stuffed cloth body. Dampness is an enemy to these beautiful old dolls **$195-295**

16", Maker Unknown, Pink Wax-Over-Gesso Lady Doll. Solid-wax arms to shoulder joint, wax-over-compo lower legs, CM, blue glass fixed eyes, brown ptd/mld gloves, mld/ptd boots with black buttons and black heels, blond mohair wig, chambric body, dressed to period, rare. **$800-900**

16", Maker Unknown, Wax-Over-Mache Girl. Blue fixed glass eyes, mache lower limbs, mohair wig, kid body **$195-295**

16", Schmitt Wax-Over-Compo. Spherical-shaped neck adjusted to head socket, BJ compo body, CM, fixed glass eyes, HHW, French, christening dress. Body mark on doll: "Schmitt" **$1,500-2,000**

17", Maker Unknown, Wax-Over-Compo. Rare hairdo type, hair mld smooth over forehead and held with black ribbon, bunched into clusters of curls behind, hair ptd gray, exposed ears, wooden limbs, spoon hands and flat-soled shoes (similar to early Pumpkin Heads), fixed glass eyes, cloth body, dressed in original bridal outfit, bridal veil and pretty bouquet **$465-565**

17", Maker Unknown, Wax-Over-Compo Enigma Baby. Wire-eyed glass eyes (wire extends through hip), wooden limbs, cloth and card body, CM, heavier than the papier-mache type and more durable **$695-795**

17", Maker Unknown, Wax-Over-Compo Nanny. Lady type, inset brown HHW, blue fixed glass eyes, OM with two rows of teeth, compo limbs, muslin body, original costume, holds original 10" wax baby. Marked: "F. Aldis" **$1,275-1,400**

17", Maker Unknown, Wax-Over-Compo Shoulder Head. Original curly brown mohair wig, styled in high pompadour style, original gold paper band affixes hair in position, curls at back of neck, PI and earrings, compo lower limbs, muslin body, old clothes.... **$495-550**

17½", A & B Marked Wax-Over-Compo. Two faces, swivel head on shoulder plate, swivel hair wig, fixed glass eyes on one face, closed eyes on second face, compo limbs, muslin body.................... **$450-495**

18", Maker Unknown, Wax-Over-Wood Shoulder Head. Elaborately carved hairdo, black ptd hair, deep comb marks, rear section of hair braided in thick plaits and coiled high on top of head, fully exposed PE, lovely ptd features, wooden limbs, muslin body, c. 1860. At first glance, this doll appears to be a typical rare hairdo papier-mache type **$795-895**

18½", Maker Unknown, Bonnet Head. Three plumes sculpted on top of mld bonnet and hairdo, inset blue glass eyes, mohair wig inserted in slits beneath bonnet to simulate hair, compo limbs, muslin body... **$275-375**

19", Motschmann-Type Wax-Over-Mache Enigma Baby. Blue sleep glass eyes, OM with teeth, thin papier-mache shoulder head and limbs, cloth and card body, squawk box and string........................ **$450-550**

Wire-Wax Doll, 22", wax-over-mache, eyes operated by a wire protruding through midsection, hair inserted in slit on top of head, leather arms, c. 1840, D. Kay Crow collection, $450-550.

135

Wax-Over-Mache Boy, 16", rare, mld hat with plume, glass eyes, wooden limbs, straw-stuffed body with squawk box in tummy, Jim and Sheila Olah Scheetz collection, $375-475.

20", Fritz Bartenstein Two-Faced Doll. Laugh-cry faces, compo lower limbs, card torso, fixed blue glass eyes, permanent lace cap and mohair wig, string comes out of side of body dating this doll to 1881 patent. Mark: "BARTENSTEIN" (purple ink) . . . **$795-895**

20½", Maker Unknown, Wax-Over-Mache Baby. Shoulder head, wax-over limbs, glass sleep eyes with wire pull, OM with upper and lower teeth, covered card-type body contains mechanism which enables doll to kick and turn. Mark on body: "Maison Munnier of Paris" **$1,500-2,000**

21", Maker Unknown, Derby Head. Lady type, black derby-type hat with white plume sculpted over top, human hair inserted beneath derby, cobalt-blue bulging glass eyes, tiny pink mouth, PE, wooden limbs, muslin body, dressed to character. **$350-450**

21", Maker Unknown, Wax-Over-Compo Girl. Blue fixed glass eyes, CM, HHW, compo limbs, mld boots, body made of cloth, c. late 1800s **$165-265**

21½", Maker Unknown, Wax-Over-Compo Shoulder Head. Mohair wig, glass sleep eyes, wax-over-compo limbs, mld boots and mld stockings, squawk box, body made of muslin **$495-595**

22", Maker Unknown, Turned-Head Wax-Over-Compo. Blue fixed glass eyes, CM, mohair wig, voice box in muslin body, shoulder head, wax-over-compo lower limbs, black and gold high-heeled boots. . **$285-385**

22", William Webber Singing Doll. Sings a French ditty, Webber stamp on buttocks, large fixed blue glass bulging eyes, CM, blond mohair wig, leather arms, cloth body and legs. (This doll is found with German, French and British patents). **$1,000-1,100**

22½", Maker Unknown, Rare Hairdo Wax-Over-Compo Shoulder Head. Black ptd hair mld into rear bun with long orange comb decoration, head similar in appearance to china head doll, black pupil-less glass eyes, mld bosom, wooden limbs, ptd boots, muslin body **$475-575**

136

25", Maker Unknown, Slit Head. Wax-over-compo, dark blue inset glass eyes, wired for sleeping (wire comes through hip), often called wire-eyed wax, human hair inserted in slit, OM with teeth, detailed facial modeling, blue leather arms, muslin body and legs, sewed-on stockings and red leather boots, dressed to type, scarce. **$495-595**

25", Maker Unknown, Wax-Over-Mache Girl. Large bulgy glass eyes, compo limbs, HHW, muslin body. **$265-365**

25", Maker Unknown, Yellow Wax-Over-Compo Turned Head. Brown glass inset eyes, blond mohair wig, CM, compo limbs (not waxed), sawdust-filled muslin body with voice box, red mld boots with mld/ptd stockings and original gold garters, wears original corset and gown. These yellow wax-over dolls have layers so thick that they appear to be poured wax. The wax on the shoulder plate is thinner, revealing substance beneath **$395-495**

26", Maker Unknown, Chinese Baby Boy. Bald head has pigtail of human hair adhered through hole in back of head, slanted black pupil-less glass eyes, drooping closed lids, PE with gold earrings, pink fabric body, waxed limbs, voice box, bare feet have original embroidered Chinese shoes, original Chinese costume, detailed facial modeling makes this a very rare doll **$1,000-1,200**

26", Maker Unknown, English Slit-Top Wax. Wax-over-compo, black HHW, black pupil-less glass eyes, pink leather arms, muslin body and legs, doll is in excellent condition, 1830-1840 . . . . **$295-395**

27", Dressel Wax-Over-Compo. Lady doll, blue glass inset eyes, PE, OM with teeth, auburn HHW, waxed limbs, feet have mld orange ptd boots with blue tassels, horsehair-stuffed muslin body. Marked: "ERNST FRIEDRICH DRESSEL". **$500-600**

27", Maker Unknown, Wax-Over-Wood Shoulder Head. Long neck and rounded shoulders, prim little face with large ptd blue eyes and tiny pink mouth, rouge spots, old HHW, haircomb, mld earrings, thin wax coating on shoulder head only, wooden BJ body, dressed in ancient gown, gorgeous old relic, very rare, c. early 1800s . . **$2,000-3,000**

Wax-Over-Mache Pumpkin-Head Doll, 13", glass eyes, wooden limbs, straw-stuffed body with squawk box in tummy, Jim and Sheila Olah Scheetz collection, $225-325.

137

33", Maker Unknown, Bonnet Head. Lady type, mld bonnet covered with original old lace, mld blond hair, PE, blue glass eyes, wax-over-compo limbs, mld boots with heels, elaborately dressed in old clothes.. **$450-495**

Wax-Over-Compo, 32", bulging glass eyes, compo limbs on cloth body, Elva Weems collection, $225.

9

Old Papier-Mache and Composition Heads

Sometimes it is difficult to determine whether a doll's head is made of papier-mache or composition, especially if it has been painted and glazed. Most of the old papier-mache heads have a matt finish which distinguishes them instantly, while the hard shiny composition heads resemble a lush apple. The paint on the glazed mache heads seems to craze quicker than on the all-composition heads. Needless to say, whether the head is mache or composition both materials are similar enough to place the dolls in the same niche historically.

Unless otherwise stated, all dolls listed in this group are in excellent condition and have their original bodies, limbs, and wigs. All are dressed in either old or original clothing.

2" (head cir), Maker Unknown, Spinning Wheel Lady. Mache, swivel head, blue ptd eyes, mache body, wooden arms, mache legs, black ptd hair beneath black wig, black satin shoes with pink silk bows. This lady sits on a carved wooden chair before a black and tan wooden spinning wheel. Pull platform and doll's head and waist move from side to side while her foot presses treadle and turns spinning wheel **$1,500-1,700**

8", Milliners' Model. Black ptd hair, center part, long sausage curls concealing ears, wooden limbs, kid body......... **$410-510**

8", Milliners' Model Pincushion Doll. All original, c. 1820, made into a pincushion around 1863.................... **$495-595**

8½", Milliners' Model. Black vertical mld curls around back of head, center part, wooden limbs, kid body......... **$395-495**

9", Maker Unknown, Negro Baby in Mache Egg. Compo baby, black pupil-less glass eyes, bulging type, OM with teeth, black wool wig,

Russian Couple, 4¼", made in the Soviet Union, compo ptd faces, cloth and wire armature bodies, $100 pair.

French Fashion Papier-Mache, 13", c. 1815-1860, pink kid body, stiff limbs, blue ptd eyes, CM, black ptd pate with brush marks, nailed-on wig, old costume, Jim and Sheila Olah Scheetz collection, $1,000-1,200.

Unmarked Negro Baby, mache, Jim and Sheila Olah Scheetz collection, $125.

edges of upper thighs and neck trimmed with old lace, early cheaper example of the wax version **$350-450**

10", Maker Unknown, Country Bumpkin Character Boy. Black ptd hair, shaggy hairstyle, large blue ptd eyes, smiling watermelon mouth, squeeze him and he squeaks and tips his hat, wired arms, wooden legs, cloth body, red cord, hat, old shirt and overalls, all original.............. **$265-365**

11", Maker Unknown, Negro Character Boy. Compo shoulder head and limbs bulging black pupil-less glass eyes, skimpy black wig, straw-stuffed cloth black body, press his chest and he sticks out his tongue, all-original outfit................ **$325-425**

11", Milliners' Model. Black mld/ptd hair with twisted roll and dip at back of head, wooden limbs, kid body.......... **$425-525**

11½", Milliners' Model. Short wavy hairdo built high above exposed ears, wooden limbs, cloth body..................... **$425-525**

12", Enoch Morrison Autoperipatetikos. Mache head, leather arms, clockwork mechanism, original clothes, Pat USA 1962 by Enoch Morrison **$795-895**

12", Maker Unknown, Peddler Elderly Lady. Mache, original white mohair wig, inset glass eyes, cloth body and limbs, old wares with display case, old costume. **$750-850**

12½", Motschmann-Type Mache Enigma Baby. Inset brown glass eyes, compo and cloth body and limbs, nightgown....... **$350-450**

13", Greiner Child. Size 0, 1850 label, black hair, exposed ears, leather arms, body made of cloth **$245-345**

13", Maker Unknown, Solid-Dome Mache. Tonsure spot on head, peg-wooden body, blue ptd eyes, well-sculpted ears, lovely wooden hands **$550-650**

13", Milliners' Model. Cluster of heavy black ptd curls mld close to cheeks in 1840s style, center part, smooth top, back coil of braids wound into sleek bun (early Victorian type), deep shoulder modeling, mld bosom, wooden limbs, kid body **$450-550**

13¼", Milliners' Model. Fancy three-puff hairdo with double braid bun on top of head, wooden limbs, kid body **$450-550**

13¼", Milliners' model. Fancy three-puff hairdo with double braid bun on top of head, wooden limbs, kid body **$450-550**

13½", Greiner Child. Black ptd hair, 1858 label, ptd features, original china limbs, old cloth body, number 2 head size ... **$225-325**

13½", Maker Unknown, French Mache. Lady type, inset glass eyes, HHW, leather arms, cloth body **$695-795**

14", Manchurian Man and Woman. Ptd hair and features, cloth body and limbs, stitched fingers, original costume, c. 1920, sold as a pair **$350-450**

14½", Milliners' Model. Wide curl clusters at side of head, high braided topknot, braided bun, wooden limbs, kid body **$725-825**

15", Milliners' Model. Five long black mld curls hanging from back of neck, wooden limbs, cloth body **$525-625**

15½", Milliners' Model. Black ptd hair, round face similar to china head dolls of 1860s, kid body, wooden limbs **$525-625**

15½", Milliners' Model. Black ptd hair with center part, fat curls on each side of long slender face, braided bun at back of head, wooden limbs, kid body **$575-675**

16", Maker Unknown, Compo Shoulder Head. Bald head with HHW, bulging glass eyes, OCM with mld tongue, compo limbs, cloth body..................... **$185-285**

16", Maker Unknown, French Compo Shoulder Head Child. Bulgy blue glass eyes, CM, mohair wig, original bisque arms, kid-gusseted body.................. **$375-475**

16", Milliners' Shop. This rare and all-original hat shop is fully equipped with tiny mirrors, dressing tables, hats, hatboxes, lorgnettes, ribbon, jewelry, fans, plus the shopkeeper, complete with original old glass dome, French, c. 1830 .... **$2,000-2,500**

Chinese Scholar, 11", compo head, arms and feet, cloth body, $75.

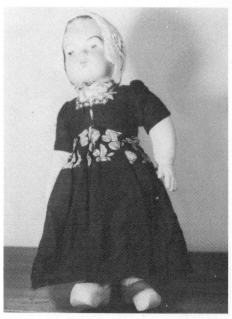

Dutch Doll, 15½", compo head and limbs, all-original, cloth body, marked "VOLLEN-DAM," $75.

Philippine Couple, 11½", Balintawak costume, Tag-a-log tribe, mache and cloth, marked "EDUCATIONAL DOLLS IDA B. MCCORY MANILLA, P.I.," $100 pair.

Traze Couple, 11½", Mestiza Philippines, mache and cloth, marked "EDUCATIONAL DOLLS IDA B. MC-CORY MANILLA, PHILIPPINES," $100 pair.

17", Cuno & Otto Dressel Compo Shoulder Head. Short black ptd hairstyle, brush marks, deeply mld shoulders with large sew holes, ribbon mld into hairdo at back, compo arms, cloth body. Mark inside back shoulder: "Patented Holz-Masse".......... **$350-450**

17", Milliners' Model. Black covered wagon hairdo, wooden limbs, kid body... **$650-750**

18", Greiner Child. Pre-Greiner, black pupilless glass eyes, leather arms, cloth body, wooden legs. Label reads: "PAT APPLIED FOR"....................... **$925-1,100**

18", M & S Superior 2015. Black ptd hair, common hairdo, old leather arms, cloth body, German....................... **$525-625**

18", Maker Unknown, Compo Shoulder Head. Weighted sleep glass eyes, OM with two lower teeth and tongue, blond mohair wig, compo limbs, pale pink cloth body, c. late 1800s........................ **$265-365**

18", Marion Kaulitz Doll. Mohair wig, compo head, ptd features, BJ compo body. Doll is stamped: "MUNCHNER KUNSTLER KAULITZPUPPEN"............ **$395-495**

19", Greiner Boy. Black flirty glass eyes that move from side to side, 1858 label, black mld/ptd hair, brush marks, leather arms, cloth body.................. **$1,000-1,200**

19", Maker Unknown, French Mache Lady. Slit crown for wig insertion, pupil-less blue glass eyes, pink kid body, old leather arms, c. 1850........................ **$695-795**

19", Maker Unknown, Negro Twin Boys. Mache head and arms, compo varnished legs, orange ptd CM, pupil-less glass eyes, black wool hair, excelsior-stuffed stiffened muslin body, dressed as twins.......... **$475-575**

19", Male Milliners' Model. Black ptd/mld hair, brush marks, rare black pupil-less glass eyes, wooden limbs, c. 1830 ...... **$895-995**

19", Milliners' Model. Black short curls cascading around head and sculpted into curly topknot, lovely face, old wooden limbs, kid body **$750-850**

142

19", Schilling-Marked Shoulder Head. Pale blue fixed glass eyes, compo head and limbs, CM, lamb's wool wig, straw-stuffed muslin body, deep shoulder modeling **$325-425**

19½", Greiner Child. Rare brown ptd hair, 1858 label, ptd features, leather arms, cloth body **$695-795**

20½", Gold Medal Compo Shoulder Head. Resembles M & S Superior, mld blond hair, exposed ears, ptd features, large blue glass eyes, leather arms, cloth body, Steuber legs, rare **$795-995**

22", Judge & Early Mache Shoulder Head. Head style similar to the 1870s chinas, cloth body, rare. Mark: "Judge & Early—N.2-Pat'd. July 27, 1875" **$895-1,095**

22", Maker Unknown, Early Mache. Made for French market, bamboo teeth, pupil-less glass eyes, pink kid body, HHW, old leather arms **$695-795**

22", Milliners' Model. Three-puff hairdo with braid bun, wooden limbs attached to kid body **$975-1,100**

22", Milliners' Model. Black ptd hair with center part, braided bun at back, long round face, startled facial expression, wooden limbs, kid body, c. 1830............. **$975-1,100**

22", Pre-Greiner Child. Severe black ptd hairdo, ptd features, ears exposed, dour expression, wooden limbs, cloth body. Label: "PAT APPLIED FOR"......... **$695-795**

23", Maker Unknown, German Portrait Man. Mache shoulder head, ptd brown hair, ptd brown eyes, sideburns, mustache on upper lip, rosy cheeks, red lips, cloth body and small waist, white kid arms, original costume (bicorne hat, velvet coat, linen shirt with ruffles, suspenders, trousers), Empire period doll **$895-1,095**

23", Maker Unknown, Mache Lady Doll. Blue glass fixed eyes, rare hairdo, small fashion waist, ptd shoes, PE, early type, cloth body, wooden spoon hands...... **$525-625**

24", Greiner Child. Black ptd hair, 1858 patent label, lower ears exposed, ptd features, leather arms and body. .... **$425-525** •

Chinese Empress and Emperor Dolls, c. 1937, Empress dowager Nora, Ching Dynasty, ptd mache head, arms and feet, paper decoration on cloth, **$200 pair.**

Dutch Doll, 14", compo head and arms, cloth body, all-original, marked "MARKEN, HOLLAND," $75.

143

French Mache, 13", marked "HP 3," original costume, Pat and Sunny Lupton collection, $125.

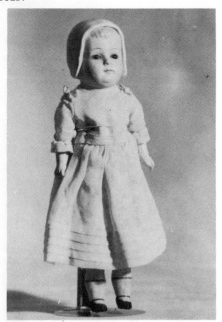

Papier-Mache Bonnet-Head Doll, 14", glass eyes, mache limbs, cloth body, old costume, Jim and Sheila Olah Scheetz collection, $300.

24", Greiner Child. Black hair, 1858 label, ears exposed, black pupil-less glass eyes, leather arms, cloth body **$795-895**

24", Maker Unknown, Compo Shoulder Head. Muslin body, blue sleep glass eyes, compo lower limbs, blond mohair wig. Stamped on right leg: "Winged Angel" and "Fabrik-Mark deponit" **$395-495**

24", Maker Unknown, German Mache Shoulder Head. Rare brown ptd and mld curly hairdo, exposed ears, blue ptd eyes, brooding facial expression, sullen CM (Does she resent being so old?), old muslin body, wooden arms **$475-575**

24", Milliners' Model. Black center-parted hair, forehead brush marks, clusters of curls emanate from center part to top of ears (ears partly covered), back hair coiled into braids, brown ptd eyes, prim features, long neck and sloping shoulders, wooden limbs, kid body, c. 1830 . . . . **$1,500-2,000**

25", Learch & Klagg Compo Shoulder Head. Black ptd hair, ptd features, exposed ears, old worn leather arms, cloth body and legs, resembles Greiner. Paper label on shoulder plate reads: "Learch and Klagg Manufacturers, Philadelphia, Pa" **$650-750**

25", Maker Unknown, Compo and Mache Shoulder Head. Cobalt-blue glass eyes, old mohair wig, compo limbs, body made of cloth **$265-365**

25", Maker Unknown, Compo Shoulder Head Boy. Black ptd hair, mld black ptd helmet and red mld plume, ptd features, compo limbs, straw-stuffed muslin body, original Rifle Corps Volunteer uniform of 1860 . . . . **$375-475**

25", Yamato Ningyo Japanese Boy Doll. Dark brown glass eyes, compo covered with layers of gofum for porcelain-like finish, OM, articulated body, genital detail, old original costume, bare well-modeled feet, exquisite hands, black HHW, c. late 1800s . . **$695-795**

26", Maker Unknown, Baby Clown. French mache, 19½" head cir, blue glass fixed eyes, black ptd hair with spit curl in front of each exposed ear, OM with two upper teeth and tongue, mouth ptd bright red, dead-white ptd face, surprised curved eyebrows, mache bent limb baby body, crepe de chine clown costume and ptd clown hat, silk shoes **$695-795**

26", Maker Unknown, Compo Shoulder Head. Face resembles early Jumeau, bulging brown glass eyes, pink cloth straw-filled body, compo limbs, HHW **$285-385**

26", Maker Unknown, German Shoulder Head. Glass pupil-less eyes, black ptd hair in 1840s style, exposed ears, hair is center-parted and draped in front of ears, long sausage curls mld onto shoulders, serene facial expression, leather arms, cloth body **$695-795**

26", Maker Unknown, Japanese Anatomical Doll. Head and limbs modeled in one with body, ptd black hair, ptd features, OCM (inner cavity ptd red), entire figure ptd in ivory white, large hands with long separated fingers, nervous system vividly mapped on doll's body outlining the 660 spots that control nerves and muscles, nude, rare **$2,000-3,000**

26", P.D. Smith Compo Shoulder Head. Compo limbs, cloth body, HHW, pretty ptd face, blue ptd eyes to the side, dressed, c.1916. These rare old dolls were made in the state of California **$495-595**

27", Adolph Wislizenus Child. Mache shoulder head, paper sticker intact, blond sculpted wavy hair, center part, baby face, cup and saucer neck, deep shoulders, striated effect on brows and mouth, large blue ptd eyes, lower lashes only (similar to china heads of 1860s), china limbs **$1,000-1,200**

27", Greiner Child. Severe black ptd hairdo, 1858 label, exposed ears, rare brown ptd eyes and upper eyelashes, leather arms, body made of cloth **$725-825**

27", Maker Unknown, Early Compo and Mache Shoulder Head Doll. Inset dark pupil-less glass eyes, well-sculpted blond hairstyle with fancy curls and rolls, red ribbon, exposed ears, leather arms, cloth body **$495-595**

27", Maker Unknown, Mache Shoulder Head Lady. Long neck, deep sloping shoulders, top of bosom modeling, well-sculpted ears, black hair in classic hairdo (tiers of braids wound into high chignon and held by black comb),

French Fashion, 30", mache, upper and lower bamboo teeth, black pupil-less eyes, nostril holes, ptd hair under wig, pink kid body, fashion-type with stitched fingers and toes, Jim and Sheila Olah Scheetz collection, $975.

Greiner 9, 24", leather body and arms, Jim and Sheila Olah Scheetz collection, $425-525.

Papier-Mache Mechanical Clown, 15", c. 1890, all-original, mld mache top hat (mld onto head), OCM with ptd teeth, wooden limbs, wires for arms and legs, squeeze tummy and he clangs cymbals, Jim and Sheila Olah Scheetz collection, $900.

sensitive facial expression, leather arms, kid body, dressed in Empire style... **$995-1,095**

27", Unmarked Pre-Greiner Type. Flirty movable eyes, leather arms, body made of cloth **$975-1,075**

27", Waschecht-Marked Shoulder Head. Hard mld/ptd compo, mld/ptd black curly hair, lower ears exposed, lt brown brows, large blue ptd eyes, CM, wooden arms, cloth body and legs. (These dolls were advertised as washable. Consequently, few are found in mint condition. Most look faded and washed! This one is better than most.) "A0/50" written inside head **$950-1,150**

28", Maker Unknown, Victoria-Type Papier-Mache. Pupil-less glass eyes, exposed ears, hair braided and looped in front of ears, extended back and coiled into bun, leather arms, cloth body and legs **$2,000-2,500**

28", Milliners' Model. Black ptd hair mld into curls at side of head with coils of braids at back, held by mld comb, exposed ears, brown ptd eyes, old wooden limbs and kid body, c. 1830 .... **$2,000-2,500**

30", Greiner Child. Black hair, 1872 label, cloth limbs, cloth body **$495-595**

31", Maker Unknown, German Mache. Made for French market, compo and mache, OM with bamboo teeth, black pupil-less glass eyes, HHW nailed to head, kid-gusseted body, kid arms, c. mid-1800s **$975-1,075**

31", Maker Unknown, German Mache Lady. Black short curly hair, exposed ears, well-modeled bosom, wooden limbs, kid body, wire armature within sawdust-filled body (for posing), blue bands at elbows and knees, red ptd shoes and flat heels, inset black pupil-less glass eyes, c. early 1800s **$950-1,200**

32", Greiner Child. Blond hair, 1872 label, ptd features, head almost mint, leather arms, cloth body **$525-625**

33", Early Pre-Greiner Type. Flirty glass eyes that actually move, short black ptd hair, exposed ears, leather arms, body made of cloth **$1,200-1,300**

33", Maker Unknown, French Mache Lady. Long oval expressive portrait face, black pupil-less glass eyes, finely modeled nose, OM with bamboo teeth, one-stroke thin curved brows, black tonsure spot beneath HHW, leather arms, stitched fingers, kid fashion body. This doll is not a typical example of the type with bamboo teeth **$1,200-1,300**

34", Milliners' Model. Dark brown pupil-less glass eyes, exposed ears, black hair mld smooth from center part, braided behind ears, long sausage curls mld onto shoulders, stiff kid body, wooden limbs, flat-soled shoes ptd red **$2,300-2,800**

37", Milliners' Model. Black pupil-less porcelain eyes, PN, very short mld hairstyle popular during early 1800s, wooden limbs, kid body. **$3,000-3,300**

Greiner Child, 26½", marked "Pat. 1858-1872," rare hairdo, kid body and limbs, D. Kay Crow collection, $495.

Papier-Mache Man Doll, 16", French look, all-original, D. Kay Crow collection, $895.

M & S Superior, 18", marked, rare head with ears exposed and brush marks, looks like a child, either boy or girl, D. Kay Crow collection, $700.

147

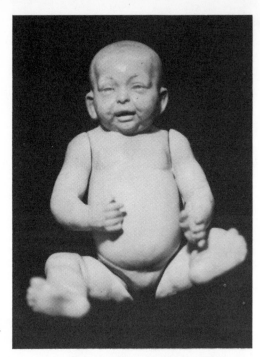

All-Compo Baby, 13", called Prince Otto or Kaiser Baby, D. Kay Crow collection, $250.

Papier-Mache Milliners' Model Twins, 6½", rare size, waterfall hairdo, colored bands join limbs, D. Kay Crow collection $350-450 each.

Compo-Head Baby, 15½", grumpy expression, marked "ACME TOY CO.," old cloth body and limbs, original clothes and cap, Herron collection, $85.

10
Wooden Dolls

The wooden doll, both primitive and sophisticated, is one of the oldest doll types. The ancient examples are almost extinct. Termites, decay, and mouse nibblings have always been a bane of these old dolls. Consequently, one rarely finds a wooden doll in mint condition. The ones listed here are in good condition, considering their age, are dressed, wigged, and in some cases, marked.

4", Schoenhut Felix the Cat. **$125-225**

6", Russian Matryushkas. All-wood nest dolls, largest doll holds four smaller dolls, older set **$35-65**

6½", Schoenhut Barney Google. Wooden hat, nailed-on clothes **$195-295**

7", Hopi Kachina Doll. Carved from cottonwood, God of the Pueblo Indians, decorated with feathers, brightly ptd and designed, contemporary **$45-65**

7", Schoenhut Elephant. Decal eyes, kid ears, rubber at end of trunk **$95-225**

7", Schoenhut Jiggs. Delightful comic strip character......................... **$495**

7½", Maker Unknown, Pointed-Bottom Wooden. Head carved, gesso-covered, pupil-less enameled glass eyes decorated with dots, wig tie holes at rear of head, arm tie holes, straight back, c. 1700 .... **$1,000-1,200**

8", Schoenhut Circus Donkey. All-wood, leather ears, rope tail **$95-225**

8", Schoenhut Rolly Dolly. Papier-mache (these round-bottomed dolls came in several characters). Label: "ROLLY DOLLY" **$225-325**

Schoenhut Girl, 15", carved hair, blue bow on back of head, blue intaglio eyes, c. 1911, Jim and Sheila Olah Scheetz collection, $895-995.

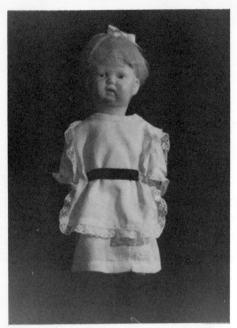

Schoenhut Walker, 17" ptd features, blond wig, original clothes including special walking shoes, D. Kay Crow collection, $500-600.

Schoenhut Boy, 14", ptd features and hair, jtd hips and knees, clothes not original, D. Kay Crow collection, $400-500.

9¼", Maker Unknown, Queen Anne. All-wood, dressed, c. 1700 . . . . **$1,000-1,200**

9¼", Maker Unknown, Queen Ane. All-wood, dressed, c. 1700 . . . . **$1,000-1,200**

9½", Schoenhut Happy Hooligan. Tin can on head, boxed. Box reads: "Geo. Borgfeldt & Co. New York. Sole Licencees & Distributors. A. Schoenhut Mfgrs. Phila. Pa" . . **$250-350**

9½", Schoenhut Maggie. Another delightful comic strip character **$495**

10", Avis Lee All-Wood Man. Old sea-salt with peg leg, holds knife in one hand and piece of whittling wood in the other, long carved beard **$95-225**

10½", Maker Unknown, Door of Hope Chinaman. Carved-wood head and arms, ptd features, black ptd hair, cloth body, well-carved hands, handmade clothes . . **$145-165**

11", Maker Unknown, Peg-Wooden. Black ptd spit curls in front of ears **$650-750**

11", Maker Unknown, Peg-Wooden. Yellow tuck comb (Victoria type), earrings, brown ptd eyes **$875-975**

11¾", Maker Unknown, Peg-Wooden. Costume made entirely of tiny seashells, flat-heeled red slippers, well-carved head, black ptd/mld hairstyle, head covered with gesso and paint, could have been dressed in France, c. 1830 . . . . **$950-1,050**

12", Maker Unknown, Carved-Wood Court Lady. Creche, inset glass eyes, white wool wig (each curl separately sewn), CM, leather body, wooden legs, rather crude oversized wooden hands, old and original costume, c. mid-1700s **$2,500-3,000**

12", Maker Unknown, Eskimo Woman. Carved and ptd features, wood and sealskin, Baffin Island **$250-350**

12", Maker Unknown, French Fashion Lady. Carved wooden shoulder plate, crude work, gesso-covered, ptd HHW, thin stick arms, long wooden body, stick legs nailed to wooden stand, original costume made of orange paper and black gauze, primitive art at its best, c. 1700s **$2,000-2,500**

12", Maker Unknown, Peg-Jointed Man. Rare 1830s peg-wooden type, mortise and tenon joints, ptd features, dark mustache, mld hat (these peg-woodens appear to have been watercolored, then varnished for permanance; the enameled types came later), torso, upper arms and upper legs ptd brown possibly to denote underwear, brown ptd/mld shoes, dressed **$1,000-1,500**

12", Mason & Taylor Child. Popular wooden body and limbs, compo head, pewter hands, blond mld hairdo, blue ptd eyes... **$595-795**

12", Schoenhut Mechanical Girl. Blue ptd eyes, CM, brown mohair wig, metal hands and feet, holds guitar, does the hula, clockwork in body, wind key on back, ptd shoes, workable, rare, unmarked **$795-895**

12½", Schoenhut Clo-Pin Dolly. Tagged, body construction similar to Schoenhut circus clowns, held together with elastic, clothespin limbs, cute ptd face, yarn hair, nailed-on clothes, c. 1935 .... **$185-285**

(L. to R.) Schoenhut Toddler Boy, 14", $400-500. Boy with wig, 16", pouty-type, Jim and Sheila Olah Scheetz collection, $550-650.

13½", Maker Unknown, Queen Anne. All-wood, pupil-less glass eyes, HHW, 1-pc body, legs jtd at hips, old clothes **$1,250-1,500**

14", Maker Unknown, Creche Man. Carved-wood portrait face with intricately carved hat and hair, beautifully carved hands and feet, glass inset eyes, OCM, very expressive face, body made of moss and tow... **$1,300-1,500**

14½", Schoenhut Girl. Carved bonnet, blue intaglio eyes, spring-jointed..... **$925-1,025**

14½", Schoenhut Girl. Brown intaglio eyes, CM, carved brown ptd hair with blue hair band, spring-jointed **$895-995**

14½", Schoenhut Pouty Boy. Brown intaglio eyes, CM, spring-jointed, original mohair boy wig........................... **$525-625**

15", Joel Ellis Lady. Black-haired shoulder plate reminiscent of 1870s china heads, brown ptd eyes, tiny red mouth, the head is compo mld over wooden base, wood-jointed body, metal hands and feet **$650-850**

15", Maker Unknown, Hermaphrodite. French Court doll, shoulder head of carved wood, wooden lower pelvic section and lower

Modern Woodens, 17", Beatrice Kelsh, $180 pair.

151

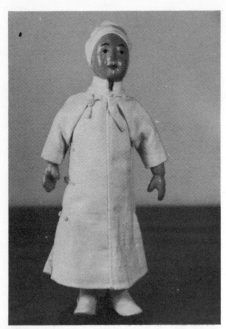

Chinese Mourner Doll, 10", wooden limbs and head, cloth body, Sing Mission, c. 1940, $100.

Old Clothespin Peddler Doll, 4½", holds basket of 1" wooden dolls, all-original, $75.

limbs, upper limbs cloth, wound as in upper torso, face has the features of both sexes, heavy ptd brows, carved hair, CM, ptd brown eyes, carved bosom. This doll has the carved reproductive organs of both sexes, no underwear, dressed as female, original elaborate court attire **$3,000-3,500**

15", Schoenhut Character Girl. Blue intaglio eyes, CM, carved and mld hair. Incised: "Schoenhut Doll-Pat. Jan. 17. 1911—U.S.A. and Foreign Countries" **$895-995**

15", Schoenhut Pouty Baby. Blue ptd eyes, ptd hair, spring-jointed, has a bent limb baby body **$400-500**

15", Schoenhut Toddler. Spring-jointed toddler body, ptd hair and features, OCM. Mark: "H.E. Schoenhut 1913" **$400-500**

15½", Schoenhut Laughing Boy. Blue intaglio squinting eyes, OCM with two upper and two lower teeth, black ptd/mld hair, body is spring-jointed................. **$950-1,050**

15½", Schoenhut Tootsie-Wootsie. Blue intaglio eyes, OM with teeth, mld/ptd hair, spring-jointed, original outfit (blue cotton jacket, knickers, white linen dickey, brown cotton stockings, brown leather shoes with two holes on the bottom for the posing stand) **$1,000-1,200**

15½", Schoenhut Walking Doll. Brown ptd eyes, brown mohair wig, arms jtd at shoulders, OCM with teeth, elbows and wrists, legs set to metal joints under torso.......... **$500-600**

16", Maker Unknown, Peg-Wooden Peddler. Original wares, peg-jointed, original peddler outfit, English **$1,350-1,500**

16", Schoenhut Doll-Face Boy. Decal eyes, OCM with teeth, blond mohair wig, spring-jointed.................. **$400-500**

17", Maker Unknown, Creche Lady. Pensive face tipped to the right side, downcast ptd eyes, mld lids, CM, HHW, all-wood, original old clothes **$895-995**

17", Schoenhut Boy. Carved hair, CM, blue intaglio eyes, spring-jointed....... **$895-995**

18", Joel Ellis Negro Lady. Similar to the 15" Joel Ellis Lady Doll, rare **$975-1,075**

18", Maker Unknown, Negro Wooden Man. Carved head, inset pupil-less glass eyes, curly hair wig, carved wooden lower limbs, hollow body, mouth moves by wire lever, doll is dressed **$495-595**

18", Schoenhut All-Compo Girl. Blond mld hair, blue ptd eyes, CM, jtd at neck, shoulders and hips, bent arms, straight legs, rare, c. 1930. Label on back reads: "SCHOENHUT TOYS MADE IN USA" **$795-595**

18", Schoenhut Pouty Girl. Blue intaglio eyes, CM, spring-jointed, mohair wig . . . **$495-595**

18½", Maker Unknown, Man Doll. All-wood, glass pupil-less eyes, 1-pc body, doweled hands, gesso-covered, hand-stitched, original clothes. **$1,500-2,000**

19", Schoenhut Farmer. Mannequin type, lay figure (same model sold as baseball player), original costume (overalls, shirt, hat, tie, shoes, and socks) **$950-1,050**

20", Maker Unknown, Ugly Wooden. Large blue glass eyes set close giving her the appearance of being cross-eyed, tiny dots accentuate depth of eyes and thin brows, carved nose (thin at top, wide at bottom), bow-shaped mouth with straight lines extending upward, garish rouge spots on round cheeks, very high forehead, gesso covers head, square-bottom torso, cloth arms nailed to shoulders, carved wooden hands, cloth legs nailed to bottom, wooden feet covered with blue leather shoes **$2,795-3,795**

21", Maker Unknown, Religious Figurine Doll. All-wood, cage-type body, inset glass eyes, dressed, gold base **$795-895**

21", Schoenhut Girl. Spring-jointed, mld teeth in OCM, blue intaglio eyes, auburn mohair wig. **$475-575**

21", Schoenhut Girl. Brown intaglio eyes, OCM with two teeth, HHW, spring-jointed. **$500-600**

Kokeshi Wooden Japanese Doll, 9", revolving music box plays a Japanese lullaby, marked "SK" in diamond shape, c. 1958, $100.

Creche Wooden Lady, 15", glass eyes, expressively carved face, realistic detail, old clothes, D. Kay Crow collection, $1,200.

22", Schoenhut Girl. Rare brown sleep eyes, OCM with teeth, mohair wig, body spring-jointed. (These are the late Schoenhuts made in imitation of the bisque and compo dolls popular at the time) **$525-625**

22", Schoenhut Girl. Simulated glass eyes, CM, mohair wig, spring-jointed . . . **$600-700**

25", Maker Unknown, Queen Anne. All-wood, brown glass eyes, dotted brows and lashes, red cheek spots, hemp wig, 1-pc head and torso, fork fingers, usual age scratches, dressed, c. 1700 . . . . **$2,500-3,500**

25", Schoenhut Adult Lady Doll. Brown sleep eyes, OCM with teeth, thick brown HHW, torso has small waist, wide hips and bosom, spring-jointed, original clothes, shoes, stockings, rare **$1,250-1,500**

27½", Maker Unknown, Empire-Period Wooden. Portrait face with exposed and well-carved ears, Titus coiffure, BJ wooden body varnished and gesso-covered, red ptd flat-soled shoes, Empire costume, lovely work of art, rare **$3,500-4,000**

32", Maker Unknown, Carved-Wooden Portrait Lady Shoulder Head. Long oval face, 1830s hairstyle, blue ptd eyes, long neck, sloping shoulders with some top-of-bosom modeling, head glued to kid body, leather arms and legs, gesso over wood, possibly Swiss **$1,400-1,700**

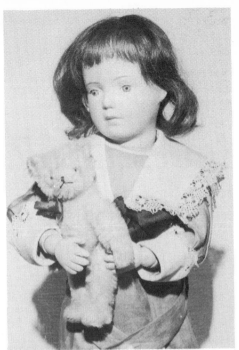

*Exquisite Schoenhut Boy and his teddy, 21½",
dressed similarly to picture in Eleanor St.
George's Dolls of Yesterday, pique collar with
lace, $600-700.*

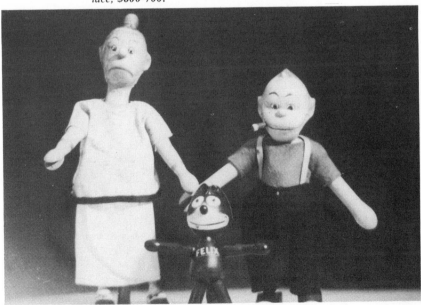

*Maggie, 9", and Jiggs, 7", Schoenhut, **$495 each.** Felix the Cat, 4", Schoenhut, Jim and
Olah Scheetz collection, **$125-225.***

11
Fabric Dolls

The fabric or rag dolls listed here are all in mint condition and dressed in their original or old clothing and accessories. Others have their "clothing" on their bodies. Fabric dolls that are faded, worn, bald, undressed, or in poor condition cannot command these prices.

Fabric Doll, 6½", Italy, Lenci-type, all-original, $50-60.

7½", Palmer Cox Brownies. Cloth, twelve different characters, printed, sold individually, Arnold Print Works **$50-100**

9", Dean's Peggy and Teddy. Drayton-inspired, legs separate, hands printed on stuffed-cloth bodies, costume, Peggy holds her baby doll, sold as a pair **$200-250**

9", Lenci Candy Box. Felt head and bust on top of box, ptd eyes looking upward, OCM, bee-stung lips, brown curly mohair wig, green silk shoulder cover held by two felt roses, lace-trimmed, blue velvet box trimmed with gold braid, labeled, mint **$250-350**

9", Lenci Farm Girl. All-original condition, tag **$125-225**

9", Norah Wellings Soldier Boy. Broad ptd smile, ptd blue eyes to the side, felt face, broad-brimmed hat, boots, soldier uniform, brown label, early type **$45-55**

10", Autoperipatetikos. Patented by Enoch Rice Morrison, cloth head, ptd brown eyes to the side, designed to resemble china version, black ptd hair, leather arms, all original, including original box. Mark on bottom of doll: "Patented July 15th, 1862"... **$750-850**

10", Lenci Shirley Temple. Pink and white felt dress, matching beret, blond short mohair curls, dimples, good likeness...... **$450-550**

10", Norah Wellings Mounty. Stockinet face, original hat and uniform, white label, early type **$50-60**

10½", Chad Valley Boy. Paste-stuffed fabric face, blue ptd eyes to the side, sewed-on large ears, paper label on plush or velvet body, jtd at neck, shoulders and hips, original sailor suit and hat, was possibly designed by Norah Wellings **$125-145**

10½", Maker Unknown, Little Bo Peep. Dolly Dingle, stuffed pillow doll **$85-95**

10¾", Dean's Wounded WWI Soldier. Blue hospital uniform, red handkerchief, printed face and features, arms separate from body, bandaged arm held by white bandage around shoulder, cap, mint. Foot mark: "SPECIALLY MADE FOR BOOTS THE CHEMIST BY DEAN'S RAG BOOK CO. HYGENIC STUFFING" **$125-145**

10¾", Maker Unknown, Little Red Riding Hood. Dolly Dingle, printed and stuffed cloth doll, legs apart **$85-95**

10¾", Maker Unknown, Mary and Her Lamb. Dolly Dingle, printed and stuffed pillow doll **$85-95**

11", Averill Chocolate Drop. Negro Drayton-type doll, all-cloth, ptd features, three black yarn pigtails, movable limbs, common old dress, c. 1923 .... **$135-165**

11", Grace Drayton Two-Faced Rag Doll. Dolly Dingle (pleasant face) and Dolly Dingle (cry baby), old bonnet and nightie, features are ptd **$125-145**

11", Maker Unknown, Baby Dolly Dingle Rag Doll. One face, dressed in bonnet and short dress **$95-125**

11", Maker Unknown, Hug-Me-Tight Rag Doll. Boy Campbell Kid hugs girl Campbell Kid, printed together, pillow doll ... **$85-115**

11", Norah Wellings Black African Girl. Lamb's wool wig, velvet, original **$55-65**

11¼" Chase Hospital Baby. Stockinet and cloth, oil ptd, completely dressed in original, signed old clothes, c. 1891-1930 ... **$325-425**

Fabric Shoulder-Head Doll, 26", fabric head reinforced with wire around the shoulder edge, ptd and mld hair and features, vertical eyelashes, old cloth and leather body, rare item, museum quality, Jim and Sheila Olah Scheetz collection, $1,000-1,200.

157

Rag Doll, 12", Godey-type, made by Louise W. Stevens, $75-85.

11½", Dean's Charlie Chaplin. Printed on one piece of cloth, stuffed, has mld Tru-to-Life face, rare **$175-275**

11½", Dean's Little Betty Oxo. Mask face, ptd features, giveaway rag doll (in exchange for Oxo tokens), mint............... **$125-145**

12", Arnold Print Works Pickaninny Baby. Rag doll in long dress sewn to round base for standing, arms ptd onto body, one hand holds hat, printed 5th July 1892 and 4th October 1892.......................... **$125-165**

12", Chase Little Girl. Dutch-cut hairdo, rare size **$395-495**

12", Cobo Alice Rag Doll. Round head, brown ptd hair, brown ptd features, red lips, two red dots for nostrils, needle-sculpted nose (head very hard), cloth body and limbs, a later version **$125-225**

12", Dean's Miss Sue. Printed on cloth, c. 1903-1925, advertisement for Sue Flakes Beef Suet, black stockings on separate legs, white shoes with bows, black 1920s bobbed hair, hands printed on printed clothes, one hand holds spoon, apron printed on uniform. Baking cup marked: "Miss Sue" ... **$95-125**

12", Georgene Teardrop Baby. Madame Hendren pressed cloth head, ptd features (very tearful and sad!), cloth body and limbs, mitten-type hands. Tag on nightie: "Georgene Dolls—Teardrop Baby—Georgene Novelties, N.Y.".......................... **$125-145**

12", Hanff Diana. Aunt Jemima's little girl, fabric, legs separate from body, arms ptd onto body, flowered dress, designed by M.M. Hanff, c. 1902 .... **$95-125**

12", Knickerbocker Buster Brown and Tige. Printed, cloth-stuffed, designed by R.F. Outcault, c. early 1900s, pair **$125-165**

12", Maker Unknown, Dolly Double and Topsy Turvy. Rag doll with white head and dark head on each end, wears wig, red print dress **$45-65**

12", Maker Unknown, Orphan Annie and Sandy. Stiff cloth, c. 1932, pair ... **$150-200**

12½", Aunt Jemima. Premium for Aunt Jemima Pancake Flour, oil cloth, stuffed, ptd features, clothes in one with body .. **$95-125**

13", Chase Boy. Stockinet and cloth, oil ptd, rare **$400-500**

13", Lenci Little Girl. Brown ptd eyes to the side, original green organdy dress with felt flowers on skirt, felt coat, shoes, yellow felt hat, blond mohair wig **$250-350**

13", Mollye Goldman Little Louisa. Yarn hair, ptd features, mask face, all original, c. 1930 .... **$95-125**

13½", Albert Bruckner Rag Doll. Little girl, hard mask face, printed features, cloth body and limbs (limbs separate from body), dressed in old clothes, bonnet. Front shoulder mark: "PAT'D July 8th 1901" **$125-150**

14", Dean's Dolly Dips. Wears 1920s style swimsuit, skirt separate, flat ptd face, ptd hair and bow, arms and legs separate .. **$125-145**

14", Kathe Kruse Early Girl. Blond HHW, mld/ptd muslin head, jtd muslin body, gray ptd eyes, foot mark, old clothes... **$400-500**

14", Lutheran World Services Rag Doll. Made in Hong Kong, contemporary, designed for export fund-raising projects, black wool wig decorated with flowers, embroidered features, mitten hands, dressed in traditional Chinese brocade costume, original wicker wardrobe trunk filled with additional costumes and shoes **$45-65**

14", Madame Alexander Alice in Wonderland. Mask face with raised hand-painted features, blue ptd eyes to the side, yellow yarn hair, pink muslin body, cloth limbs, original clothes, c. 1923 .... **$350-400**

14", Maker Unknown, Punch and Judy Rag Dolls. Costume printed onto body in reds and blues, flesh-colored face and hands, old English creations, sold as a pair... **$125-145**

14", Mignionne Rag Doll. Autographed (facsimile autographed by Paul Guilbert), printed little girl holding elf, long gown and hat, ptd roses in ptd hair, arms ptd in one with body, c. 1912 .... **$95-125**

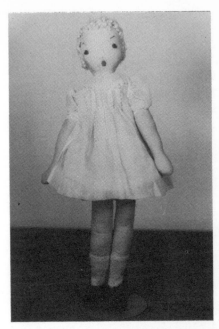

Fabric Doll, 12", made for "Bundles for Britain," c. 1940, all-original, $100-110.

Korean Grandpa Doll, 9", all-fabric, $75-85.

14½", Dean's George Robey Rag Doll. From Tru-to-Life series, pressed face, separated arms and legs, costume, c. 1923 ... **$135-125**

14½", Dean's Joan and Peter Dancing Dolls. Mohair wig, ptd features, costume, seem to dance when joined together, not mechanical, all fabric-stuffed, sold as a pair ... **$250-300**

15", Chase Alice in Wonderland. Stockinet and cloth, mld/ptd short blond hair, original clothes. (This rare set includes Frog Footman, the Duchess and Baby, the Mad Hatter, Tweedledee and Tweedledum, the Rabbit, Tish Footman, and the Cheshire Cat, **$600-700** each doll) **$675-775**

15", Farnell Alpha Toys. These dolls have a Lenci look and may confuse the collector. Felt head, velvet limbs, cloth body, mohair wig, swivel neck, 4-pc BJ body, original clothes, c. 1930 (eyes ptd to the side). Foot label reads: "FARNELL'S ALPHA TOYS MADE IN ENGLAND" **$185-225**

15½", North Western Consolidated Lithographed Rag Doll. Advertising doll, printed. Marked: "Ceresota" **$95-125**

16", Chad Valley Girl. Stiffened felt head, inset blue glass eyes, velvet body, jtd at neck, shoulders and hips, auburn mohair wig, dressed as baby flapper in cloche and costume, c. 1924 .... **$225-300**

16", Chase George Washington. Stockinet and cloth, oil ptd, clothing **$500-600**

16", Chase Little Girl. Rare hairdo type, Dutch-cut with bangs, ptd facial features, round rosy cheeks, old clothes, shoes, socks, signed, c. 1880 .... **$425-525**

16", Chase Negro Mammy. Stockinet and cloth, oil ptd, original clothes **$500-600**

16", Effanbee Popeye. Stuffed cloth doll, originally came with pipe and crate of spinach, c. 1933 .... **$65-75**

16", Hanff Sunny Jim. Premium for Force Wheat Flakes, designed by M.M. Hanff, rag doll, legs separate, c. 1902 .... **$65-125**

16", Ida A. Gutsell Boy Rag Doll. Consists of

,six pieces of printed fabric blank for 3-D effect, old tan suit, uncut......... **$125-225**

16", Kathe Kruse Early-Type Boy. Well-stuffed jtd cloth body, mld/ptd muslin head, Kruse stamp on foot, old clothes.. **$425-525**

16", Lenci Sailor Boy. Brown eyes ptd to the side, brown mohair wig, felt head, stiff cloth body, original outfit and shoes.... **$350-450**

16", Maker Unknown, Russian Tea Cozy. Stockinet, HHW, well-modeled face, holds a bowl of tea in her hand, mouth is puckered as though doll is blowing. **$125-145**

16", Norah Wellings Nightcase Doll. Also made by Chad Valley and Dean, ptd features, broad smiling mouth, mohair wig, dressed as gypsy with bead bracelet and beads around neck, flowered cap matches bodice of gown, underclothes, wears a pair of shoes and stockings, c. 1920 .... **$150-195**

16", Steiff Lady. Felt face with seam down center, button eyes, ptd features, HHW, all-felt body, metal button in ear, thumb separate from stitched fingers, costume **$265-365**

17½", Dean's Little Girl. Mask face, big blue ptd eyes to the side, red smiling mouth, black mohair wig, rivets secure arms to body, movable limbs, dressed in blue velvet and imitation fur, hat, all original. Rivets marked: "DEAN'S A-1" **$250-300**

17½", Lenci Christopher Robin. Felt. Stamp on foot: "LENCI".............. **$350-400**

17½", Maker Unknown, London Rag Baby. Cloth body and limbs, mld wax mask face covered with tinted muslin, ptd features (some facial mars and scratches) **$600-700**

18", Ada Lum Hong Farmer and Wife. Modern rag dolls, embroidered features, yarn hair, traditionally dressed, pair...... **$65-75**

18", Dean's Master Puck. A 4-pc rag doll. c. 1912 .... **$100-125**

18", Horsman Babyland Rag Doll. Flat face with printed features, all-cloth, mohair wig, later version.................... **$95-145**

Fabric Doll, 12", made by Albert Bruckner, patented July 8, 1901, all-original, D. Kay Crow collection, $125-150.

161

Albert Bruckner Doll, 13", marked "Pat'd July 8th, 1901," all-original, D. Kay Crow collection, $125-150.

18", Horsman Gee-Gee Dolly. Grace Drayton designer, mask face, ptd hair and features, cloth body and limbs, wears original pink dress and bonnet, bonnet has large white bow, original pink box, c. 1912-1914 ... **$225-265**

18", Madame Alexander Tippy Toe. Round blue ptd eyes, tiny mld nose, little red mouth, hair wig, dressed, c. 1925 .... **$150-200**

18", Mother's Congress Rag Doll. Realistic round contours to body shape, 7-pc rag doll design, single-piece head is lithographed with flat features, dressed **$350-550**

18", Wimpy. Popeye's good friend, all-original, tag **$125-145**

19", Art Fabric Mills Negro Girl. Similar to the 24" Art Fabric Mills Girl, wears old clothes, rare **$145-245**

19", Horsman Bye-Bye Kiddie. Cloth, mld mask face, ptd features, blond mohair wig, muslin body, well-shaped limbs, fingers are separate, foot is marked, homely old doll, c. 1917 .... **$125-145**

19", Louise R. Kampes Little Girl. Blue ptd eyes looking straight ahead, mld mask face, ptd features, blond hair wig, cloth body and limbs, original dress, shoes, coat, and hat. Red paper heart on chest reads: "KAMKINS A DOLLY MADE TO LOVE. PATENTED FROM L.R. KAMPES, ATLANTIC CITY, N.J." **$400-500**

19", Trilby Flapper Doll. Cloth face, ptd features, hair wig, cloth body, felt clothes and slippers, c. 1924, often mistaken for Lenci, eyes ptd straight ahead, American Stuffed Novelty Co. **$125-145**

20", Chase Hospital Baby **$285-385**

20", Dean's Big Baby. Improved version of Dean's 22" Big Baby, has seam under chin for realism **$125-145**

20", Eugenie Poir. All-fabric, mld and hand-painted face, blue eyes to the side, curly mohair wig, jtd at shoulders and hips, lovely costume, socks, shoes, c. 1920 .... **$200-300**

20", Kathe Kruse Sleeping Baby. Sand-filled, early, foot mark, old clothes.... **$800-1,000**

20", Lenci Little Girl. Blue glass eyes, green felt dress with flowers of various colors, yellow trim, matching hat and shoes, all original, tagged **$750-850**

21", Izannah F. Walker Child. Stockinet, hand-painted pressed head, large ptd blue eyes, prim red CM, applied ears, muslin body, treated limbs, black ptd hair with corkscrew curls (some have plain hairdos), c. 1873. Other sizes: 15, 17, 18½, 20, 24. Prices range from **$600** to **2,500** **$1,600-2,600**

21", Lenci Marlene Dietrich. Felt tuxedo and top hat, all original. **$700-800**

21", Sheppard Philadelphia Baby. All-cloth, hard-modeled head, ptd features and hair, treated lower limbs, stocking body, applied ears, c. 1900 . . . . **$595-695**

22", Carl Wiegand Shoulder Head. Looks mache, hand-painted, mld of fabric and paper (resembles M & S Superior), leather arms, cloth body, black ptd hair and ptd features, signed **$850-1,050**

22", Dean's Big Baby. Arms and legs sewn separate from body, flat ptd face and features, artistically designed to give depth to flatness of cloth, detailed underclothes **$135-165**

22", Lenci Little Girl. Original **$350-450**

22", Maker Unknown, Mary Pickford. Possibly untagged Lenci, felt head and limbs, cloth body, blue ptd eyes to the side, red mouth, long blond curly HHW, swivel neck, jtd at shoulders and hips, wears huge original hair bow at back of head, original green silk dress and underclothes, silk socks and leather shoes **$500-600**

22", Maker Unknown, Shirley Temple. Possibly untagged Norah Wellings or Richards Sons & Allwin, beautifully hand-painted features and dimples, lovely blond curly mohair wig, original bonnet, dress, undies, socks, shoes **$300-400**

22½", Ella Smith Alabama Indestructible Doll. All-cloth, mld face, ptd features, ptd black hair (later dolls had hair wigs), applied ears, movable cloth limbs, cloth body, ptd stockings and shoes, c. 1904 . . . . . . **$595-695**

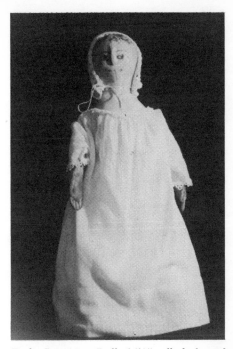

Early Primitive Doll, 16½", all-cloth, ptd face, leather arms, D. Kay Crow collection, $500-600.

163

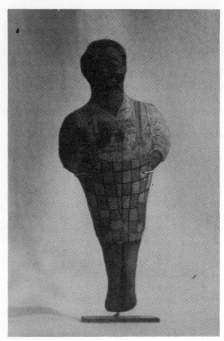

Wade Davis Aunt Jemima, 10", D. Kay Crow collection, $95-125.

23", Beecher Rag Baby. Stockinet, yarn wig, hand-painted and stitched features, rare type **$600-700**

24", Art Fabric Mills Girl. Printed face, undies, shoes, socks, dressed in old clothes. Foot mark: "ART FABRIC MILLS FEB 13 1900" **$125-165**

24", Lenci Pierrette. Partner to Lenci Pierrot, brown ptd eyes to the side, short blond mohair wig, all-felt, original pink felt short dress and sewed-on top, black felt ruffle around neck, pink felt cap, twelve black felt buttons decorate costume, beautiful legs, silk stockings, black felt high heels with pink wool pompons, jtd at shoulders and hips, gorgeous doll, c. 1920 . . . . **$1,000-1,200**

24", Mollye Goldman Baby Joan. Hand-painted face mask, cloth body and limbs, costume and bonnet, c. 1930 . . . . . . **$145-165**

24", Mollye Goldman Dilly. Cloth, hand-painted features, yarn hair, original bonnet and dress, c. 1930 . . . . **$145-165**

24", Mollye Goldman Muffin and Raggi. Yarn hair, girl has large hair bow, boy wears cap, hand-painted mask face, all original, c. 1931, sold as a pair **$225-245**

25", Lenci Spanish Dancing Girl. Boudoir type, all original **$500-700**

25", Maker Unknown, Boudoir Doll. Plastic lower limbs, compo shoulder head, black ptd high-heeled slippers, cloth body and limbs, pink satin long gown and bonnet, undies, blond mohair wig around front of head only, inserted lashes over ptd eyes, slip sewn to dress, cheap lace trim, c. 1947 . . . . . . **$25-35**

26", Emma and Marietta Adams Columbian Doll. All-cloth, crude, homemade type, hand-painted hair and features, treated arms and legs, soft cloth body, dressed. Mark: "COLUMBIAN DOLL EMMA E. ADAMS OSWEGO CENTRE N.Y." **$650-750**

26", Maker Unknown, Stockinet Cloth Shoulder Head. Reinforced with metal around edges, black ptd hair, one-stroke brows, almond-shaped eyes with tiny upper and lower lashes, black pupil-less ptd eyes, prim little mouth, leather arms, cloth body and legs **$795-995**

28", Lenci Lady. Boudoir type. ptd blue eyes to the side, long blond curly mohair wig, long arms and legs, one arm bent at the elbow, gorgeour clothes, with high heels and silk stockings...................... **$600-800**

28", Mary Hortence Webster Flapper Doll. Mohair wig, ptd features, all-cloth, original old clothes, c. 1921. Doll is signed: "American Made"........................ **$125-145**

29", Maker Unknown, Boudoir Doll. Auburn mohair wig, ptd mask face, pink cloth body, long thin limbs, silk stockings and leatherette high-heeled slippers with ties, compo hands and wrists, original green 2-pc satin pajama suit, lace-trimmed, c. 1925.......... **$45-65**

29", Maker Unknown, French Boudoir Doll. Hand-painted mld face mask, brown mohair wig, original French outfit including silk hose and satin high-heeled slippers with buckles, unmarked. (These dolls were also made in New York, Italy, and England, so be careful when calling them French) **$95-125**

29", Maker Unknown, Pierrette Boudoir Doll. Pressed mask face, ptd features, inserted lashes, platinum wig, white satin Pierrette suit with ruffle around neck, white pompon at waist, pink muslin body and limbs, leatherette high-heeled slippers **$65-85**

29", Mollye Goldman Sunny Girl. Hand-painted, mask face, all-cloth, sateen arms, mitten hands, outfit and hat **$135-155**

30", Consuelo Fould Posing Flapper. French, ptd silk face, body wired for realistic posing, mohair wig, dressed elaborately, came in various sizes, c. 1919. Mark: "CONSUELO FOULD BREVETE" **$300-400**

30", Lenci Pierrot, Brown ptd eyes to the side, felt and cloth body, black felt sewed-on cap, black silk 2-pc Pierrot suit, purple chiffon neck ruffles, six purple buttons on costume, felt slippers with pompons, one of the slippers is missing **$1,000-1,200**

Flapper Boudoir Doll, all-original, pressed mask face, Pat and Sunny Lupton collection, $65-95.

Kathe Kruse Mannequin, 32", all-original, c. 1914, signed, $1,500-2,000.

32", Kathe Kruse Little Girl Mannequin. Long HHW, ptd features, muslin, jtd at shoulders and hips, dressed **$1,500-2,000**

33", Norah Wellings Britannia Girl. Same as the 33" Norah Wellings Bo Peep, felt head, swivel neck, ptd features, coy smile, all-original costume, rare **$350-400**

33", Norah Wellings Little Bo Peep. Pink felt bonnet, pink felt shoes, white organdy dress, ptd features with eyes to the side, blond mohair wig, quality creation **$265-365**

34", Norah Wellings Maori Boy. Inset brown glass eyes, velvet face, limbs and body, dressed in sewed-on bib trousers with buttons, broad smiling mouth, swivel head **$350-400**

35", Dean's Dutch Boy and Girl Twins. Display type, well-made, ptd features, felt face, black mohair wig, exquisite costume, stockings, Dutch wooden shoes, rare, sold as a pair **$1,000-1,200**

(L. to R.) Boudoir Doll, 18", $65-85 (this doll once belonged to Mae West). Boudoir Doll, 23". Both dolls were made in the 1920s and are from the Herron collection.

12
Odd-Material Dolls

The odd-material doll is usually a primitive or folk type and most often handwrought, although commercially made dolls and the dolls of rubber, celluloid, brass, and pewter will also fall into this rather precarious class. Originally, these dolls were considered an alternative to the more expensive breakable bisque, china, and wax dolls. Perhaps this is true, as so many have survived unscathed. Unfortunately these are the least popular and most difficult dolls to sell regardless of age or rarity or obvious museum quality. Yet they remain invaluable treasures conceived in an era when things were made to last a lifetime. Dolls listed in this chapter are all in good condition and dressed in original or old clothes. Inferior examples cannot command these top prices.

4", Bernard Ravca Elderly French Couple. Man and woman, bread crumbs, c. 1930, good condition, dressed, pair **$225-245**

6", Kestner Little Girl 201. Head, arms and legs of celluloid, fine leather jtd body, sleep glass eyes, mohair wig **$150-175**

6", Minerva Celluloid Baby Doll in Wicker Basket. Wind key on side of basket, wheels beneath basket move baby forward and backward, all-original including nightgown, pillow and coverlet. Doll is clearly marked: "MINERVA HELMET" **$95-125**

7½", Bruckner Baby. Compo head, hands and feet, c. 1921. Metal body impressed: "Made in Switzerland Patents Applied For" .. **$95-125**

8", Maker Unknown, Acrobat Man. Bisque head, ptd features, black ptd/mld hair and mustache, jtd wooden body, elastic cord holds joints, red and green costume trimmed with gold braid...................... **$95-125**

9", Egyptian All-Sugar Doll. Decorated with brilliantly colored sugar and paper, sold on

Old Cornhusk Indian Doll, 8", faceless, leather and cloth with bead trim, $50-60.

Old Cornhusk Indian Doll, 8", ptd. face, made from trade cloth, Onondaga tribe (the United States Government had a treaty with the Iroquois nation for trade goods), $75-100.

Pincushion Doll, 4", made in the Soviet Union, $50-60.

Egyptian streets the first day of the birth of the Prophet Mahomet **$15-20**

10", Maker Unknown, Celluloid Boy. Celluloid limbs, blue ptd eyes, cloth body. Mark: "American" **$85-95**

10" (head cir), Putnam Bye-Lo Baby. Rubber, signed Grace Storey Putnam, cloth body, celluloid hands, original labeled box, original clothes.................... **$1,000-1,200**

10½", Parsons-Jackson Baby Doll. All-celluloid, spring-strung, blue ptd eyes, smiling OCM, bent limbs **$160-200**

11", Maker Unknown, Celluloid Girl. Original Norway costume, CM, blue ptd eyes, blond mld hair, bisque hands, cloth body and limbs, German.................. **$95-125**

12", Goebel Hummel. Hard rubber, original clothes, c. 1950 .... **$85-100**

12", Goebel Hummel. Vinyl **$25-35**

12", Maker Unknown, French Negro Baby. Celluloid, swivel neck, jtd at shoulders and hips, CM, inset glass eyes. Mark on doll reads: "France"....................... **$145-165**

12", Maker Unknown, Pewter-Head Doll. Wooden body with movable arms and fixed legs, lovely face, ptd features, hair detail, peg-jointed at elbows, lower arms and hands made of pewter **$350-450**

12", Minerva Music Box with Protruding Celluloid Boy Shoulder Head. Twirl stick and hear the music, box covered with wine-colored figured silk, trimmed with old gold braid, shoulder head enhanced by wide tulle ruffle. Shoulder mark: "2." Mark on front of doll: "MINERVA"................... **$285-300**

12", Sun Rubber Baby Doll. All-rubber, blue ptd eyes, brown mld hair, CM, bent limbs, jtd at hips and shoulders. Mark on doll reads: "SUN RUBBER CO., BARBETON, O, USA, Patent 2118682" **$35-45**

12½", Maker Unknown, Negro Man. Black ptd leather face, body and limbs, old clothes, folk type, c. mid-1800s.......... **$250-300**

Dutch Girl, Heubach head on tea cozy, coral necklace, D. Kay Crow collection, $200-300.

17", Metal Head, deep mld hair, brown glass eyes, kid body, bisque arms and legs, dressed in white muslin and with black shoes, D. Kay Crow collection, $125-150.

9", All Bisque, stationary glass eyes, OCM, jtd limbs, fine bisque quality, mld high-heeled shoes in gold with black gussets, toes, and heels, ribbed white socks, D. Kay Crow collection, marked "164/13," $300-400.

17", Wax-over-Papier-Mache, black mld waterfall hairdo, all original, D. Kay Crow collection, $200-225.

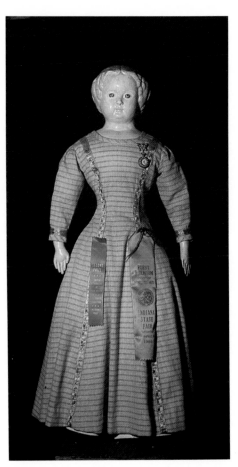

7", Bisque Girl, compo body, bisque arms, long brown wig (new), straw hat, D. Kay Crow collection, **$200-225.**

34", M & S Superior, ptd features, mld hair, cloth body, leather arms, D. Kay Crow collection, **$595-695.**

15", K Star R 121 Toddler, mint, in original box, D. Kay Crow collection, $475-575.

5", Pincushion Half Doll, doll holds mirror, arms away, original blonde wig, marked "14495 Germany," D. Kay Crow collection, $150-175.

16", Kestner Hilda, bald, D. Kay Crow collection, $1,500-1,800.

11", K Star R 122, OCM with two teeth, mohair wig, D. Kay Crow collection, $350-450.

6", Heubach Baby, all original, mint, marked "HEU" in a square, D. Kay Crow collection, $235-335.

French Bisque Mechanicals, 9¹/₂", Steiner Lady, $2,000-2,500. 12¹/₂", Schmitt & Fils Jester, D. Kay Crow collection, $3,000-3,500.

18", Unmarked French Fashion, new body, costume, D. Kay Crow collection, $600-700.

12", Unmarked French Fashion, all original, D. Kay Crow collection, $900-1,000.

11½", French Fashion, all original, marked "FG," D. Kay Crow collection, $1,000-1,200.

17", French Bisque Bru Jne, all original, authentically marked, D. Kay Crow collection, $6,000-7,000.

13", Eskimo Man and Woman. Carved stone heads, man on stone base, woman on wicker base, original costume, tagged, Canada, sold as a pair **$125-135**

13", Maker Unknown, French Powder Box Doll. Plaster of paris half-doll, white mohair wig, ptd features, plaster arms, attached to lid of powder box covered with old taffeta and lace, c. 1921, Paris **$65-85**

13½", Madame Hendren Celluloid Shoulder Head Girl. Bobbed mld hair, exposed ears, blue ptd eyes, OCM with teeth, compo limbs, cloth body, c. 1920. Mark on doll reads: "Genuine Madame Hendren Doll-1714-Made in Germany" **$225-265**

13½", Minerva Tin Shoulder Head 5. Short blond mld hair, exposed ears, can be either a boy or girl, blue ptd eyes, CM, compo lower arms, kid body **$95-125**

14", K Star R Character Baby. Rare rubber head, compo jtd body, mohair wig, blue ptd eyes, CM **$295-395**

14", Maker Unknown, Baby Doll. Earthenware, English, jtd at shoulders, hips, and head, ptd features and mld hair, c. WWI....................... **$95-125**

14", Petitcollin Little Girl. French, celluloid, fixed blue glass eyes, CM, mohair wig, lovely serene facial expression, celluloid jtd arms and legs, celluloid body, white ptd socks, red strap slippers, dressed in original costume, Petitcollin mark (Tete d'Aigle) **$215-245**

14½", Diamond Pottery-Head Baby Doll. Shoulder head, blue ptd eyes, CM, head almost bald, pipe clay legs and arms, cloth body, English, c. 1908-1925. Mark: "Regd. 654738 DP Co." **$95-125**

15", Maker Unknown, Leather Pixie. Dressed in old pixie gear, c. 1890 .... **$200-250**

16", Kathe Kruse Boy. Celluloid, turtle mark on head and body, costume **$200-250**

16", Minerva Tin Shoulder Head. Blue ptd eyes, blond mld hair, CM, bisque lower arms, kid body....................... **$125-145**

Cornhusk and Cotton Doll, 8½", labeled "SINKING VALLEY CRAFTS, WEST VA," $50-60.

Old Chinese Actor Dolls, 10", Hwaiking Mission School, Hunan, China, embroidered clothing, plaster heads, mld and ptd hair with mld and ptd ornate headress, $100-125 pair.

177

Micki and Mecki, 7", German Steiff mark, latex, wood, cotton, $100-125 pair.

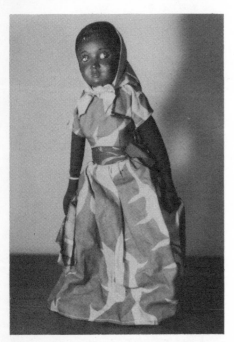

West Indies Doll, 14", plaster of paris head, cloth body and limbs, $75–85.

16", New York Rubber Co. Shoulder Head. Black ptd hair mld into short sausage curls resting on neck, round sloping shoulders, blue ptd eyes, one-stroke brows, lower lashes only, CM, brown leather arms, old cloth body and legs, facial and hair flaking, rare. Marked: "NEW YORK RUBBER CO. GOODYEAR'S PAT 444" $695-795

16½", Petitcollin Celluloid Boy. French, brown mld hair, jtd shoulders only, blue sleep lashed eyes. Mark: eagle head $225-245

17½", Maker Unknown, Celluloid Boy. Turtle mark, blue glass eyes, compo limbs, cloth body. Mark: "Germany" $175-195

18", Darrow Rawhide Lady Shoulder Head. Hairstyle and facial modeling resemble early mache-china type (although her features are not as precisely painted), cloth body and legs, leather arms $695-795

18", Goodyear Rubber Co. Child. Blond hair mld in deep waves sweeping away from forehead in wide wings, blue ptd deep-set eyes, fat little cheeks, tiny nose and mouth, twill body, compo hands, c. 1850. Mark: "G" (in a small circle) $650-750

18", Madame Hendren Celluloid Baby Shoulder Head. Flange neck, mld and ptd lt brown hair, OCM with two lower teeth, blue ptd eyes, celluloid hands, cloth body with bent cloth legs $250-275

18", Maker Unknown, All-Leather Rawhide Girl. Well-sculpted, lovely leather head fits into a socket enabling movement, body, arms and legs stuffed leather, rare jtd wrists, large blue ptd eyes fringed with inserted human hair eyelashes, bald head with HHW, dressed, possibly English $850-950

18", Maker Unknown, French Brass Shoulder Head Girl. Large blue glass eyes, OCM with ptd teeth, lovely red mld hair with deep swirls and waves, bisque lower arms, kid body. Impressed: "Deponert".......... $350-400

18", Maker Unknown, Little Girl. Kid-over-compo shoulder head, kid body and limbs, HHW, CM, lovely ptd features, applied ears, possibly late 1800s, English, old clothes, rare and charming.................. $675-775

18", Schutz Marke Negro Celluloid Boy. Heavy quality, CM, white ptd teeth, red ptd trousers, bare feet, jtd arms only, doll is made in Germany **$200-225**

19", Juno Embossed Tin Shoulder Head Girl. Blond mld/ptd hair, CM, blue ptd eyes, wood lower limbs, muslin body **$145-165**

20", Darrow Rawhide Man. Very rare, black center-parted smooth hairstyle with exposed ears, leather arms, muslin body and legs, dressed as a gentleman, facial scuffs. Doll is marked: "F.E. DARROW—PATENT—MAY 1st, 1866" **$895-995**

20", K Star R Celluloid Baby with Crier. Blue flirty glass eyes, cloth body, celluloid limbs. Mark: "K Star R W 351-4" **$145-165**

20", Kammer & Reinhardt Celluloid Girl. Celluloid head open at crown, OM with teeth, blue sleep eyes, celluloid body and limbs, jtd at shoulders and hips, turtle mark, HHW **$285-300**

20", Maker Unknown, Leather-Head Lady Doll. English, leather head swivels on leather shoulder plate (leather stretched over mache or wooden base), brown inset glass eyes, OM with mld teeth, HHW, leather limbs, cloth body, ugly doll, c. 1820 .... **$795-895**

21", Maker Unknown, Glazed Earthenware Shoulder Head Girl. Exposed ears, 1850s hairdo, black ptd hair, resembles china heads of this period, hair center-parted and smooth on sides and back, curls around edges, leather arms, cloth body, rare **$795-895**

22", Lucretia E. Sallee Shoulder Head. Fine leather stretched taut over a plastic compound base, firmly glued and mld to shape, black hair, exposed ears, ptd features (at first glance this doll might pass for an 1860s mache doll), thick eyebrows, brown leather arms, cloth body and legs, old clothes. Incised in dark brown ink under the shoulder plate: "Lucretia Sallee 1865" **$985-1085**

22", Maker Unknown, Little Girl. Sleep glass eyes, OM with teeth, HHW, celluloid shoulder head, kid body and arms, cloth legs and feet, unmarked, early 1900s **$250-300**

K Star R 255, 20½", celluloid shoulder head, kid body, turtle mark, D. Kay Crow collection, $285-300.

Carved Ivory-Head Doll, 6½", all-original, D. Kay Crow collection.

179

Creche Figures, 13", made of terra-cotta, all-original, D. Kay Crow collection, $1,000-1,200 each.

22", Marks Brothers of Boston Celluloid Girl Shoulder Head. Blue ptd eyes, OCM with ptd teeth, HHW, compo limbs **$125-165**

22", Metal Doll Co. All-Steel Doll. Blue glass fixed eyes, OCM with teeth, interchangeable wigs adherred by snaps on head, spring-jointed, c. 1902 .... **$385-445**

22½", Goodyear Rubber Co. Shoulder Head. Dark green rubber, blond ptd hair, blue ptd eyes, deep shoulder plate, six sew holes, leather arms, muslin body and legs, paint is flaking on the face. Doll is marked and dated: "1861"......................... **$795-895**

23", Rubber Comb Co. (India Rubber Comb Co.) Shoulder Head. Blond mld/ptd hair, dark red rubber, some paint flaking on face, leather arms, cloth body and legs, rare. Mark: "I.R. Comb Co.".............. **$795-895**

24", K Star R Celluloid Head. Flirty eyes, OM with teeth, HHW, BJ body **$300-350**

25", Giebeler-Falk Child. Aluminum head, hands and feet, wooden body and limbs (most of these dolls are found with aluminum heads on BJ compo bodies), blue ptd sleep eyes with eyelashes, HHW **$350-400**

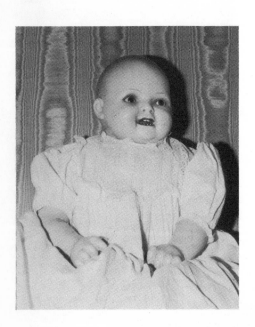

Baby Doll, 20", enameled red clay, flanged head on cloth body, compo bent arms and legs, brown glass sleep eyes with lashes, OM with six teeth (two on top, four on bottom), movable tongue, ptd. lt. brown hair, marked "GERMANY" (appears to be the work of J. I. Orsini), Pat and Sunny Lupton collection, $800-1,000.

Mutt, 6", and Jeff, 8", all-original, bisque head, hands and feet, metal BJ body, rare, Jim and Sheila Olah Scheetz collection. $1,000 pair.

Baby Doll, 22", pressed card, ptd. features and hair, lovely old clothes, Elva Weems collection, $350.

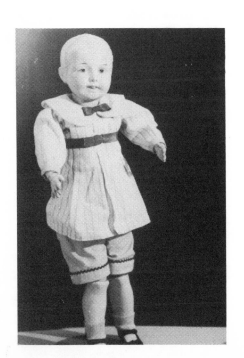

Celluloid Minerva Doll, 24", c. 1889–1930, blue intaglio eyes, OCM, swivel head on BJ compo body, all-original, Jim and Sheila Olah Scheetz collection, $250–350.

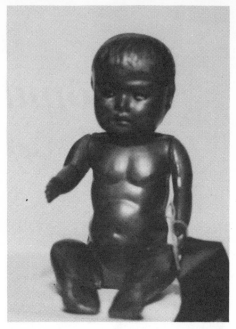

(L. to R.) O'Neill Kewpie, 5", celluloid, movable arms, c. 1920, **$25**. Celluloid Carnival Doll, 5¾", c. 1940, **$15**. Both dolls from the Herron collection.

All-Brass Baby, 12", D. Kay Crow collection, **$200-300**.

(L. to R.) Chalk Sheba Doll, 13", c. 1927, **$35-45**. Flapper Bathing Doll, 11½", chalk, c. 1922, **$45-65**. Chalk Sit-Me Doll, 6½", **$35**. All dolls from the Herron collection.

13
Popular 20th Century Dolls

Personality Dolls

All of the dolls listed here are in mint, near mint, or good condition and are all-original (wig, clothes, and so on). Dolls in poor condition cannot command these prices.

3", Maker Unknown, Baby Peggy. All-bisque, jtd arms, mld hair, ptd features . . . **$150-200**

4", Maker Unknown, Baby Peggy. All-bisque, ptd pink, jtd at shoulders and hips, mld hair, ptd features, chest label **$200-300**

4", Maker Unknown, Roy Rogers and Dale Evans. Celluloid, mld hair, ptd features, dressed. Mark: "Japan" **$15-20**

5½", Maker Unknown, Jackie Coogan. Celluloid body and limbs **$25-35**

6", Mattel Buffy. This doll has her own plastic and cloth Mrs. Beasley, boxed **$15-20**

9", Maker Unknown, Pinky Lee Pull-String Toy. Tag **$65-75**

9½", Maker Unknown, Betty Boop. Vinyl, fully jointed, c. 1968 . . . . **$12-15**

10", Maker Unknown, Little Orphan Annie. All-compo, unmarked Patsy-type body, mld/ptd hair, ptd features, original Annie dress, shoes, c. 1930 . . . . **$125-145**

10½", Maker Unknown, Annette Funicello. Vinyl, movable limbs, sleep eyes, rooted acetate hair, original clothes (felt skirt, turtleneck sweater, lace-trimmed panties, high heels), additional wardrobe (three party dresses, taffeta petticoats, full-length rayon

Plaster of Paris Half-Doll, pincushion base, c. 1920.

183

Porcelain Pincushion, 5", German legs, original wig and cushion base, $350.

cape with hood, nylon stockings, and extra pair of high heels) **$25-35**

10½", Maker Unknown, Miss Gigi (Gigi Perreau). Teen doll, all-vinyl, fully jointed with swivel body, rooted hair (plastic high heels; twelve additional dresses purchased separately) **$27-30**

10½", Maker Unknown, Pollyanna (Hayley Mills). Plastic, sleep eyes, blond rooted hair, fully jointed, dressed, trunk **$25-30**

11", Maker Unknown, Blondie. All-original in original box, tag **$200-225**

11¾", Horsman Elizabeth Taylor. Plastic and vinyl, rooted hair, ptd features, completely original with box and clothes **$18-22**

12", American Character Doll Co. Puggy. Possibly Jackie Cooper, mld/ptd hair, blue ptd eyes to the side, frowning brows, pug nose, CM, jtd at neck, shoulders, and hips, original old clothes, c. 1931. Doll is marked: "A PETITE DOLL" **$265-275**

12", Aviatrix Amy Johnson. Possibly British, compo head, ptd features, cloth body and limbs, mitten-type hands, dressed in felt suit and hat **$95-110**

12", Baby Berry Daisy Mae. Vinyl, blond rooted hair, blue sleep eyes, mld bosom, CM, dressed, c. 1957 .... **$50-60**

12", Cameo Doll Products Betty Boop. Compo and wood, ptd black hair and features, molded-on bathing suit **$385-400**

12", Horsman Billiken. Compo head with mld peak on top, slanted eyes and brows, smiling CM, velvet (or plush) body. Cloth body label: "BILLIKEN" (right foot) **$225-300**

12", Ideal Baby Snooks. Compo head, body, hands and feet, limbs made of metal cable for posing, mld hair, OCM, ptd features. Mark: "IDEAL" (head) and "Flexy—an Ideal Doll Fanny Brice's Baby Snooks" **$195-225**

12", Ideal Superman Doll. Articulated biceps, c. 1939 .... **$265-275**

12", Maker Unknown, Darlene Gillespie Mouseketeer. Vinyl, fully jointed **$15-20**

12", Maker Unknown, Skeezix. Compo, mld brown hair, large ptd eyes, squirrel jaws, freckles, jtd at neck, shoulders and hips, original clothes, rare............ **$265-300**

12", Ralph Freundlich Baby Sandy (Henville). All-compo, mld/ptd hair, sleep eyes, jtd at neck, shoulders and hips, c. 1939. Pin reads: "THE WONDER BABY genuine BABY SANDY doll mfg. RALPH FREUNDLICH Doll Baby Sandy" (back) **$165-185**

12", Uneeda Patty Duke. "Go-Go" teen doll, c. 1965, bendable vinyl plastic, rooted hair with bangs, dressed in lounging pajamas **$27-30**

13", Baby Berry Lil' Abner. Vinyl, ptd eyes to the side, black mld hair, OCM with teeth, large feet, shoes, dressed, c. 1957 .... **$50-60**

13", Baby Berry Mammy Yokum. Vinyl, mld hair, ptd features, mld bosom....... **$50-60**

13", Baby Berry Pappy Yokum. Vinyl, ptd features, dressed **$50-60**

13", Ideal Marilyn Knowlden. Movie star, c. 1935, OM with teeth, blue sleep eyes, auburn mohair wig, jtd at head, shoulders and hips, all-compo, mint. Mark: "U.S.A./13" (back) and "Ideal Doll/Made in U.S.A.".. **$350-400**

13", Maker Unknown, Jackie Robinson. Negro, all-compo, black mld hair, ptd brown eyes with whites to the side, CM, jtd body, original cap and Dodgers outfit, shoes, socks, boxed, unmarked **$185-200**

14", Madame Alexander Brigitta *(Sound of Music)*. Soft vinyl rooted hair, wears Alpine Austria costume **$65-75**

14", Maker Unknown, Dagwood. All-original in original box, compo, tag, wears 2-pc dark suit, shirt, bow tie.............. **$200-225**

14", Natural Doll Co. Angela Cartwright. Made of plastic **$32-35**

14", Plastic Molded Arts Linda Williams. General Foods premium, plastic. Mark: "Linda Williams" (back of head) **$45-65**

14½", Amberg Charlie Chaplin. Portrait face,

Sparkle Plenty, 15", Pat and Sunny Lupton collection, $65-75.

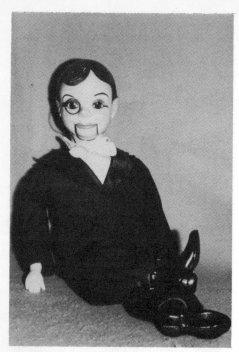

Charlie McCarthy, 32", c. 1930, marked "K & S," compo head and hands, mld shoes, satin body stuffed with straw, original costume, Pat and Sunny Lupton collection, $300.

ptd features, mld black hair and mustache, OCM, original old clothes with a label on the shirt sleeve **$295-315**

14½", Maker Unknown, Little Orphan Annie. Compo shoulder head and arms, cloth body and legs, mld/ptd hair, ptd features, red cloth dress with white trim, knee-length stockings, leatherette shoes, no mark **$185-200**

15½", Horsman Jackie Coogan. Compo head and hands, cloth body with shoulders and hip joints, gray ptd eyes, HHW, CM, original red jersey turtleneck sweater, gray flannel trousers. Mark: "E.I.H. Co. 1921" (copyright circle center of date). Metal button reads: "HORSMAN DOLL-JACKIE COOGAN KID-PATENTED" **$250-300**

16", Madame Alexander Baby Jane Quigley. Compo, sleep eyes, OM with teeth, blond mohair wig (wigs come in both blond and brown), jtd at head, shoulders and hips, original pink dress with white lace and tiny pink flowers, undies and slip attached, shoes, socks. Mark: "BABY JANE, REG. MME. ALEXANDER" (head). Dress label: "UNIVERSAL STARLET, BABY JANE, MADAME ALEXANDER" **$400-450**

16", Madame Alexander Carmen Miranda. All-compo, CM, sleep eyes, black mohair wig, jtd at head, shoulders and hips, original turban, earrings, outfit. Mark: "MADAME ALEXANDER" (head). Dress tag: "Carmen—Madame Alexander, N.Y. U.S.A.—All Rights Reserved" **$185-200**

16", Maker Unknown, Honey West. Comes with a box, c. 1965 .... **$20-25**

16", Terri Lee Gene Autry. Terri Lee-type face of hard plastic, ptd features, decal eyes, OCM, all-original cowboy outfit and hat. Mark: "Terri Lee. Pat. Pending" **$350-400**

17", Maker Unknown, Pollyanna (Hayley Mills). Plastic, sleep blue eyes, rooted blond hair, wears gingham-checked cotton dress with matching lace-trimmed pantalettes and straw hat, shoes, stockings **$35-40**

18", Arranbee Sonja Henie. **$95-110**

18", Ideal Judy Garland. All-compo, OM with teeth, sleep eyes, HHW in pigtails, jtd at neck,

shoulders and hips, original dress, c. 1939.
Mark: "IDEAL DOLL" (on head and body).
Judy Garland, 16", **$625-675** **$650-700**

18", Madame Alexander Jane Withers. This
doll is personally autographed on the arm by
Jane Withers, all original **$850-900**

18", Madame Alexander Margaret O'Brien.
Plastic, c. 1948, tag, brunette wig in pigtails,
matching bows, dressed from the film *Our
Vines Have Tender Grapes,* **$175-195**

18", Reliable Doll Co. Charlie McCarthy.
Compo and cloth, pull-strings for mouth,
original old clothes **$65-85**

18", Vinyl Elvis Presley. Original clothes,
mld/ptd black hair and sideburns, ptd
features, OCM. Mark: "ELVIS PRESLEY
ENTERPRISES, 1957" **$225-300**

19", Ideal Deanna Durbin. All-compo, OM
with teeth, sleep eyes, HHW (or mohair), jtd at
neck, shoulders and hips, c. 1938. Mark:
"DEANNA DURBIN IDEAL DOLL, USA"
(metal picture button). Deanna Durbin, 18",
$185-210; Deanna Durbin, 20" and 21",
$200-225 . . . . **$195-225**

20", Amberg Baby Peggy. Bisque shoulder
head, brown glass eyes, CM, black HHW,
bisque lower arms, kid body, c. 1923. Mark on
doll reads: "192 (in circle) 24 N-Y, Germany-
50-982/2, Amberg" **$1,000-1,200**

20", Amberg Baby Peggy. Bisque shoulder
head, brown glass eyes, smiling CM, black
HHW, bisque lower arms, kid body, c. 1923.
Mark: "192 (in circle) 24 N-Y, Germany-50-
983/2, Amberg" **$1,000-1,200**

20", Effanbee Charlie McCarthy. Compo and
cloth, original costume. Mark: "EDGAR
BERGEN'S CHARLIE MCCARTHY, AN
EFFANBEE PRODUCT." (If personally
autographed by Edgar Bergen add $200 to the
price. If once personally owned by Mr. Bergen
add $500 to price) **$175-195**

20", Madame Alexander Jane Withers. All-
compo, OM with teeth, sleep eyes, mohair
wig, swivel neck, jtd at shoulders and hips,
original clothes, c. 1937. Mark on doll reads:
"Jane Withers All Rights Reserved Madame

*Composition Ballerina, 22", disk-jointed
compo arms, compo legs to just above the
knees, bent arms and slanted feet, cloth body,
blond mohair wig, blue glassine sleep eyes
with lashes, original clothes, unmarked, c.
1930, Pat and Sunny Lupton collection,* **$150.**

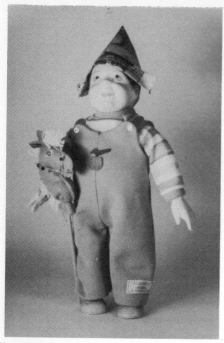

Little Apple, 12", Faith Wick creation, souvenir doll, $125.

Alexander, N.Y." Jane Withers, 13 15", $400-500 .... $650-700

21", Amberg Baby Peggy. Bisque socket head, CM, brown glass sleep eyes, mohair wig, BJ body, c. 1924. Mark: "19 copyright (c) 24 LA&S NY GERMANY-50-982/2." Baby Peggy, 18-20", $900-1,000 ..... $1,200-1,400

21" Arranbee Sonja Henie. All-compo, CM, sleep eyes, HHW, jtd at neck, shoulders, and hips, original skating outfit, c. 1939. Mark: "R & B (ARRANBEE)" $125-135

21", Baby Berry Mammy Yokum. Stuffed vinyl, ptd eyes and mouth, yarn wig, pipe, large hands, cloth body and limbs, felt clothes, c. 1952 .... $65-75

21", Madame Alexander Margaret O'Brien. All-compo, CM, sleep eyes, dark mohair wig in pigtails, jtd at neck, shoulders and hips. Mark: "ALEXANDER" (on the head) and "Madame Alexander Margaret O'Brien" (on dress tag). Margaret O'Brien, 18", $325-350 .... $375-400

21", Maker Unknown, Judy Garland Teen Doll. All-original clothes, compo (this doll also has a photograph of Judy Garland holding the doll, a gift of the *Los Angeles Examiner,* should you subscribe to their newspaper), rare item $700-800

22", Maker Unknown, Dennis the Menace. Soft stuffed vinyl, swivel head, mld hard vinyl body, shirt, trousers, shoes, socks. Head mark: "DENNIS THE MENACE" .. $22-25

22½", Mattel Mr. Doolittle. All-original clothes, hat, c. 1967 .... $25-30

24", American Character Doll Co. Annie Oakley. Hard plastic, yellow satin blouse with green cuffs, green fringed skirt, guns on belt. Doll is marked: "ANNIE OAKLEY" (in yellow script) $65-75

30", Maker Unknown, Jackie or Buster Brown. Unmarked, mld cap on top of mld hair, ptd features, pottery shoulder head with blue intaglio eyes, CM, tiny gauntlet hands, straw-stuffed cloth body, original clothes in old Coogan style (perhaps an unauthorized Coogan doll that has been commercially made), c. 1920 .... $375-400

36", Uneeda Pollyanna (Hayley Mills). Lightweight washable plastic, rooted blond hair, sleep eyes, dressed **$65-70**

48", Maker Unknown, Spanky McFarland Doll Figure. Wood-jointed, ptd, dressed as Spanky in *Our Gang* **$1,000-1,200**

Mollye Dolls
International Doll Company
Philadelphia, Pennsylvania

9", Martha Washington. Hard plastic, hand-painted face, white mohair wig, dressed in original costume **$25-35**

14", Judy Garland. All-compo, CM, sleep tin eyes, mohair wig in pigtails with bows, unmarked. Dress tag reads: "A MOLLYE PRODUCT/AMERICAN MADE." Judy Garland, 16", **$225-240**; Judy Garland, 21", **$300-325** **$175-195**

15", Ginger Rogers. Sleep eyes, CM, HHW in pageboy style, original costume ... **$300-350**

17", Business Girl. Hard plastic, sleep eyes, blond wig, dressed in original Mollye business outfit, unmarked **$125-135**

19", Betty Grable. Hard plastic and vinyl, white wig (also known as Dancing Deb), original gown and music box **$300-350**

19", Olivia de Havilland (Melanie). Hard plastic and vinyl, sleep eyes, OCM, wig, original costume. Mark on head reads: "X" (in a circle) **$265-300**

19", Princess Elizabeth Rose. Hard plastic and vinyl, OCM, sleep eyes, white wig, original bridal outfit. Mark on head reads: "X" (in a circle) **$265-300**

20", Mamie Eisenhower. Hard plastic and vinyl, dark brown wig, sleep eyes, OCM, original gown and music box. Mark on head: "X" (in a circle) **$300-350**

21", Baby Joan. Hard plastic head, latex limbs, cloth body, sleep eyes, OM with teeth, synthetic wig, original bonnet and dress. Mark on head: "450" **$65-75**

Salvation Army Couple, 8", original clothes, unmarked, plastic and cloth, $25–35.

189

Bambol, 15½", made in Italy, compo, all-jointed, including waist, flirty eyes, all-original, $175.

27", Jeanette McDonald. All-compo, long neck, long body, long limbs, OM with four teeth, blond wig, unmarked, original long gown, shoes, socks **$350-400**

36", Pollyanna. Plastic and vinyl, sleep eyes, white rooted hair, wears an old and original Mollye outfit **$85-95**

The Old Reliables

3½", China Pincushion Half-Doll. Bonnet and hands mld toward hat, china legs beneath rayon pincushion skirt, c. 1940. Mark on doll reads: "Japan" **$15-20**

4½", Maker Unknown, Mechanical Dancing Couple. Celluloid, has a windup spring motor, c. 1940 .... **$95-110**

5½", Maker Unknown, Nancy Ann Storybook Doll. Dressed as Little Red Riding Hood, ptd bisque, all original....... **$20-30**

6", O'Neill Kewpie Planter. The Thinker. Mark: "U.S.A." **$150-175**

6½", Maker Unknown, Nancy Ann Storybook Doll. All-plastic, original picture hat and long dress **$12-15**

6¾", Maker Unknown, Celluloid Hula Dancer. Brown ptd celluloid, metal legs, windup spring makes her hula, rayon fringe skirt, c. 1940 .... **$95-110**

6¾", Maker Unknown, Shirley Temple Statuette. Plaster of paris, ptd, stands on plaster base, holds blue skirt outward at sides, c. 1935 .... **$25-35**

6¾", Maker Unknown, Sit-Me Doll. Plaster of paris, ptd features, mohair wig, blue ptd dress, seated position with elbows on knees and hands under chin, c. 1920, also known as The Thinker.................... **$65-75**

6¾", Maker Unknown, Sit-Me Doll. Plaster of paris, ptd black hair, large ptd lashed eyes, yellow ptd dress with black dots, yellow shoes, c. 1927, also The Thinker.......... **$55-65**

7", Fortune Toys Pam. All hard plastic and vinyl, walker **$12-18**

7", Maker Unknown, Coquette Pincushion. China, stuffed silk body is bound with braid, c. 1924 . . . . **$125-135**

7", Maker Unknown, Feather-Dressed Celluloid Doll. Wavy silver ptd hair, large ptd eyes to the side, gold glass beads around neck, gold glass earrings, metallic hat, feather dress, celluloid cane, c. 1940. Doll is marked: "MADE IN JAPAN" **$15-20**

7", Maker Unknown, Topsy Turvy Doll. Compo white body with arms, black body and arms, dressed **$35-45**

7", Maker Unknown, Yellow Kid. All-compo, large protruding ears, black ptd hair, ptd features, wide OCM with upper teeth, jtd at shoulders and hips, old and ugly, c. 1897 (original tissue-paper clothes) **$145-185**

7½", Maker Unknown, Baseball Doll. Possibly patented by Estelle Allison, New York, on April 22, 1924, unmarked, baseball head with large side-ptd blue eyes, upper lashes only, tiny Cupid-bow mouth, baseball-type body with double row of stitches across front, all-compo, wears a bow on the side of the head **$150-200**

7½", Sun Rubber Co. Little Natalia. Rubber, no joints, blond mld curls, OCM with teeth (a Shirley Temple type). Mark: "Little Natalia/Sun Rubber Co." **$20-30**

7½", Terri Lee Ginger. All hard plastic, walker, straight legs, wears original old clothes, mint **$15-20**

8", Maker Unknown, Betsy McCall. All-original, green dress, barrette **$23-28**

8", Maker Unknown, China Half-Doll Brush. Hands touching bonnet, similar to the 1920s type, c. 1940. Stamped: "JAPAN" . . . **$12-18**

8", Maker Unknown, Ginger. Hard plastic and vinyl, original clothes, mint **$12-15**

8", Maker Unknown, Hanging Pincushion. Small bisque doll sitting on top, heart-shaped bottom covered with silk ribbon, ribbon loop and bow, c. 1924 . . . . **$125-135**

8", Maker Unknown, Hollywood Doll.

Old Japanese Lady Doll, 18½", rare bisque head on mache body, inset glass eyes, HHW, original costume, $200-300.

Madame Alexander's Little Nell, 16", c. 1923-1930, all-original, paper wrist tag, felt face, blue ptd eyes, CM, original mohair wig, pink cloth body, original costume, Jim and Sheila Olah Scheetz collection, $300-400.

Valentine costume, compo jtd body, mohair wig, ptd features, mld/ptd shoes and socks, all-original, c. 1945. Mark on doll reads: "HOLLYWOOD DOLL" **$18-25**

8", Terri Lee Ginger. All-original clothes, round hatbox trunk, wardrobe......**$35-45**

8", Terri Lee Ginger Scout Doll.....**$18-23**

8½", Maker Unknown, Cowboy, Indian, Sailor, and Popeye. Plastic composition (plaster of paris), carnival items, ptd and decorated in bright colors, c. 1940, dolls are sold separately...................**$10-20**

8½", Maker Unknown, Dolly Dingle's Pretty Kittie. White stuffed fabric.......**$125-135**

9", Lesney Negro Teenage Girl. Vinyl, England Miss Matchbox Disco Girl.**$18-23**

9", Maker Unknown, Doll Pincushion. Standing china doll with movable arms, doll dressed in silk on top of silk-covered pincushion, braid-trimmed, c. 1926...**$145-165**

9", Maker Unknown, Dolly Dingle's Doggie. All-fabric **$125-135**

9", Maker Unknown, Negro Topsy Doll. All-compo, movable head and limbs, three mohair pigtails, original cloth diaper and safety pins, c. 1940 ....**$25-35**

9", O'Neill Kewpie. All-compo, heart label on chest, foot label................**$200-225**

10", Horsman HEbee-SHEbee Twins. All-compo, dressed in original playsuits, dolls sold as a pair **$500-550**

10", Kallus Margie. Compo and wooden segmented, mld blond hair, side ptd eyes, OCM with ptd teeth. A red label on the chest reads: "MARGIE—DES. & COPYRIGHT by JOS. KALLUS" **$145-165**

10", Maker Unknown, Buster Brown. Can't Break 'Em head and lower limbs, unmarked, inset blue glass eyes, mld blond hair, cloth body, wears green velvet suit with black bow and velvet cap, white shirt, clothes lovely but not original (Buster Brown items are coveted and rare), possibly made by Non-Breakable Doll Co. **$225-250**

10", Maker Unknown, Chenille Mannequin. Compo ptd head, silk cord on head for carrying, soft chenille body, chenille limbs, c. 1940 . . . . **$25-35**

10", Maker Unknown, Half-Dolls on top of Dresser Set. Lusterware, two perfume bottles, powder jar, imported, c. 1926 . . . . . **$200-225**

10", Maker Unknown, Happifat. Compo head and limbs, cloth body, happy ptd features, ptd hair (one lock down middle of bald head), some crazing, old clothes **$265-300**

10", Maker Unknown, Patsy/Campbell Kid Look-Alike. Blue ptd eyes to the side, ptd features, jtd at shoulders and hips, lower body has an unusual swivel attachment (hook strung to arms), lower hips and legs in one piece, c. 1920. Doll embossed on the back: "Pat/
Applied" **$195-225**

10", Terri Lee Baby. Soft vinyl, features are ptd, dressed **$100-115**

10", Tiny Jerri Lee. Same characteristics as the 10" Tiny Terri Lee, except this particular doll is a boy **$65-85**

10", Tiny Terri Lee. Celanese hard plastic, inset eyes, lashes, jtd at neck, shoulders and hips, brown wig, original clothes **$65-85**

10½", Kallus Joy 1932. All-wood segmented, mld/ptd hair, mld loop for hair ribbon, ptd features. (There were two versions of this doll. The earlier version had bare feet and different features; the later version had a pair of pink painted-on shoes) **$145-165**

10½", O'Neill Kewpie. Bisque head, brown glass eyes, compo body, Rose O'Neill personal autograph on back **$5,000-6,000**

11", Horsman HEbee-SHEbee. All-compo, dressed as cowboy with original hat, hat has Horsman mark on hatband **$265-275**

11", Kallus-Ideal Pinocchio. Segmented wooden parts, red suit with three yellow buttons, yellow hat with feather . . . **$285-300**

11", Maker Unknown, Carmen Miranda. Plaster of paris head, ptd features, black mohair wig, gold earrings, wire-armature

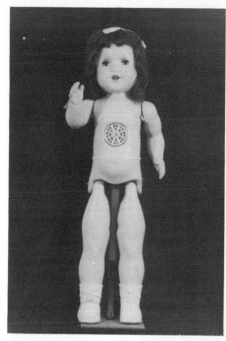

Debutante Walker, 28", compo, D. Kay Crow collection, $95-125.

193

Three-Faced Trudy, 14", unmarked, original pink and blue felt outfit, Pat and Sunny Lupton collection, $200-250.

body stuffed and padded on wooden base, beautifully designed turban and matching dress, c. 1937 . . . . **$25-35**

11", Maker Unknown, Sally. All-compo, jtd at shoulders and hips, mld Patsy bob, ptd features, original old dress, shoes and socks (Patsy look-alike), marked **$65**

11", O'Neill Kewpie Baby. Compo head and hands, cloth body (stuffed with straw), cloth feet, no wings, Tag reads: "KEWPIE REG. U.S. PAT. OFF. ROSE O'NEILL. MAR. 1913 C., J.L.K." **$285-300**

11", Wondercraft Bobbi-Mae. Swing and sway doll **$135-145**

11½" (head cir), Averill Allie Dog. Bisque head, brown sleep eyes, OM, movable bisque tongue, plush body **$3,500-4,000**

11½", Maker Unknown, Feather-Dressed Celluloid Doll. Wavy gold hair, gold glass beads at neck, ears, wrists, feather dress, all-celluloid, c. 1937 . . . . **$20-25**

12", Amberg Edwina. Shoulder head, mld blond bobbed hair, sleep eyes, CM, all-compo, jtd at shoulders and hips, swivel waist, original clothes and dog on leash. Mark: "LA&S C (in circle) 1928" **$350-375**

12", Arranbee Nancy. All-compo, CM, blue ptd eyes, mld hair, dressed. Mark on body: "ARRANBEE" and "NANCY" **$55-65**

12", Barney Google. Hand puppet, mld hat, ptd features, costume **$45-65**

12", Effanbee Little Red Riding Hood Set. Wolf, Grandma, and Patsy-type Little Red Riding Hood, doll is costumed (for the Patsy collectors) **$300-350**

12", Horsman Baby Bumps. Negro, labeled on romper, ptd hair and eyes, OCM, well-modeled large ears, movable limbs, cloth body and limbs, face resembles the K Star R Baby, c. 1912 . . . . **$225-250**

12", Horsman Jo-Jo. All-compo, CM, green tin sleep eyes, jtd at shoulders and hips, bent arms, straight legs with a slight bend at the knee, dressed, c. 1937. Mark on doll reads: "c (in a circle) 1937 Horsman" **$85-95**

12", Horsman Poor Pitiful Pearl. All-original, c. 1963 . . . . $35-40

12", Ideal Betsy Wetsy. Compo head, rubber body, sleep eyes, jtd at neck, shoulders and hips, drinks and wets, original clothes. Mark: "IDEAL." (Later versions include hard plastic head and rubber body, $35-40; hard plastic head and vinyl body, $25-30; vinyl head and vinyl body, $10-15) $45-65

12", Ideal Mortimer Snerd. Compo head, hands, feet, arms and legs, flexible metal, wire-mesh type body, original clothes. Embossed: "IDEAL DOLL". $185-195

12", Ideal Snoozie. Compo baby boy, compo head and limbs, cloth body, original clothes, emblem, c. 1933 . . . . $125-145

12", Kallus Bandmaster. An advertising doll for the General Electric Company, wooden, c. 1935 . . . . $225-250

12", Kallus Crownie. This doll is segmented for posing. $165-185

12", Kallus Mickey Mouse. $300-350

12", Laxture Products, Inc. Marianne Fashion Designing Set. Plastic doll boxed with pattern, dress material, wooden stand, and booklet listing other patterns, mld hair, ptd blu eyes, jtd arms. $38-48

12", Maker Unknown, Bonnie Braids. Soft stuffed vinyl, ptd features, mld ears, OCM, two hair wisps, jtd at shoulders $27-38

12", Maker Unknown, Clara Bow-Type Flapper. Plaster of paris, lt brown mohair wig, ptd features, red rouge spots on cheeks, yellow ptd bathing suit with gilt, red rouge spots on knees, arms and legs in one with body, stands on yellow ptd round plaster base $65-75

12", Maker Unknown, Little Orphan Annie and Sandy. All-compo, mld/ptd hair, ptd features; original dress, slip, shoes, socks, includes Annie storybook and the original box, c. 1940 . . . . $250-300

12", Maker Unknown, Mickey & Minnie Mouse. Weighted feet, marked, c. 1930, sold as a pair $265-285

Three-Faced Trudy, 14", D. Kay Crow collection, $250-300.

Marlene Dietrich Portrait Doll, 28", plaster of paris head, hand-painted, original by Paul Crees, $700.

12", Maker Unknown, Popeye. Plastic composition (plaster of paris), ptd in bright colors, wooden pipe in mouth, arms and legs mld in one with body, c. 1940 . . . . **$45-55**

12", Maker Unknown, Snookums. Can't Break 'Em mld head, OCM, one large tooth, mld blond hair, plush body. This is an ugly old doll **$300-400**

12", Maker Unknown, Snow White & the Seven Dwarfs. Compo, set **$500-600**

12", O'Neill Negro Scootles. This doll is all-compo **$285-300**

12", O'Neill Scootles. All-compo, mld hair, ptd features, CM, jtd at neck, shoulders and at the hips **$185-215**

12", Putnam Fly-Lo. Compo head, CM, celluloid hands, pink rayon front cloth body, reversible wings. Incised: "Copr. by Grace Storey Putnam" **$900-1,000**

12", Putnam Fly-Lo. Bisque head, blue sleep eyes (some have ptd eyes), green rayon front cloth body, hands are made of celluloid, CM, doll is marked **$1,200-1,500**

12½", Ideal Soldier Boy. Compo shoulder head and hands, wire legs and wooden feet, doll is dressed **$125-150**

12½", Lil' Sis. Compo, ptd blue eyes, mld/ptd hair, CM, original clothes (Patsy look-alike). Mark on doll reads: "Lil' Sis/A/Toy Product, c. 1933" **$95-125**

12½", Vogue WAC Doll. Compo, blond mohair wig, original dress, coat, hat, bag, shoes and socks **$95-125**

13", Krueger Kewpie. All-fabric, Pat. #1785800, fabric body sewn in one seam, ptd mask face, cloth limbs **$95-125**

13", Lee Co. Buddy Lee. All-compo, original cowboy outfit and hat, ptd features, ptd hair, movable arms, c. 1920. Mark: "BUDDY LEE" (on shoulders) **$135-145**

13", Lee Co. Buddy Lee. Hard plastic, original outfit and cap, c. 1949-1962 . . . . **$95-125**

13", Madame Alexander Snow White. Sleep eyes, CM, black mohair wig, all-compo, jtd at neck, shoulders and hips, original costume. Mark on head: "PRINCESS ELIZABETH ALEXANDER DOLL CO." Dress tag reads: "SNOW WHITE".............. **$150-200**

13", Madame Alexander Wendy-Ann. Sleep blue eyes, CM, blond wig, all-compo, jtd arms and legs, swivel waist, original clothes, c. 1938. Mark on body reads: "WENDY-ANN— MADAME ALEXANDER" **$135-165**

13", Maker Unknown, Doll Lamp. Plaster of paris, ptd features, hand covers nude breasts, mohair wig, wire bottom with cord and plug, covered with orchid rayon taffeta, somewhat faded, c. 1927 .... **$25-45**

13", Maker Unknown, Doll Lamp Bed Light. Plaster of paris, ptd features, mohair wig, wire base with usual cord and plug covered with silk and braid, mint, c. 1928 .... **$45-65**

13", Maker Unknown, Mae West. Plaster of paris, brightly ptd, V for Victory on skirt, carnival item, c. 1942 .... **$25-35**

13", Maker Unknown, WWI Doughboy. Unmarked, deeply mld blond hair, compo shoulder head and hands, cloth body, legs and arms made of cloth, ptd features, original hat and uniform................... **$185-200**

13", O'Neill Kewpie. All-compo, movable limbs, dark flesh color **$165-175**

13", O'Neill Kewpie on Blue Base. All-compo, blue wings, paper label **$175-185**

13", Vogue WAVE Doll. Compo, ptd features, brown mohair wig, original coat, hat and bag, paper label on dress .. **$95-125**

13½", Amberg Peter Pan. Girl version, hard smooth compo, jtd at neck, shoulders and hips, swivel waist, short lt brown hair, brown ptd eyes, brown Peter Pan costume, brown cap with feather, black shoes, white socks, high-quality compo, all original. Tag: "An Amberg Doll With A Body-Twist All Its Own. Pat. Pend. #320018" **$275-300**

13½", Kallus Merry Widow Kewpie. Wood pulp, original wig, original black dress with jet

Marlene Dietrich, 28", top hat and tails, plaster of paris head, hand-painted, original by Paul Crees, $700.

Agatha Christie Portrait Doll, 7", by Ann Parker of England, $125.

beads, c. 1915, a Joseph Kallus doll for George Borgfeldt **$600-700**

13¾", Amberg Sunny Orange Blossom. Compo head and limbs, cloth body squeaks when squeezed, CM, blue ptd eyes, mld and ptd "orange" head, original clothes including shoes and orange dress with name on ribbon. Mark on head: "c (in circle) LA&S 1924 Pat. Louis Amberg & Sons, Distr" **$195-225**

13¾", Effanbee Patsy. All-compo, jtd at neck, shoulders and hips, bent right arm, brown ptd eyes (eyes ptd looking straight ahead, no eyelashes or brows). This rare doll is embossed with the words: "EFFANBEE PATSY PAT. PEND. DOLL" **$195-225**

13¾", Maker Unknown, Kewpie. Plaster of paris, movable arms, stands on round plaster base, original green satin dress decorated with satin braid and rosettes, c. 1917 ... **$125-145**

14", Arranbee Nancy Lee. All-compo, CM, sleep eyes, blond mohair wig, jtd at neck, shoulders and hips, original dress, hat. Dress tag reads: "R&B" **$85-110**

14", Effanbee Catherine. Compo, mld red Patsy bob, ptd eyes glancing to the side, a Patsy-type body, bent right arm, original clothes, c. 1927 (even Effanbee made some Patsy look-alikes!) **$125-135**

14", Effanbee Negro Doll. All-compo, jtd at shoulders, hips and knees, black ptd eyes with whites, black mld hair. Mark: "Emily Ann V. Austin, Effanbee" **$265-300**

14", Horsman Gene Carr Character Boy. Compo head and hands, mld/ptd hair, round ptd eyes to the side, smiling OCM with two upper teeth, large ears, cloth body, original old clothes **$265-300**

14", Ideal Betsy McCall. This doll is one of Ideal's P-90 line, all-original **$55-65**

14", Ideal Harriet Hubbard Ayer. Ideal's P-90 line, the cosmetic "doll of beauty" with accessories, original clothes **$95-110**

14", Ideal Mary Hartline. Ideal's P-90 line, same characteristics as the Toni doll, dressed in original red outfit, white boots, baton, blond wig, heart-shaped wrist tag ... **$75-85**

14", Ideal Miss Curity. Same characteristics as the Toni doll, dressed as "Miss Curity – the Famous Nurse Doll," all-original clothes, accessories and box $95-110

14", Ideal Sparkle Plenty. "Magic skin" vinyl, long blond hair, has original sacque and diaper, c. 1947 .... $65-75

14", Kallus Giggles. Compo mld/ptd hair with bangs, ptd features, CM, all-compo, original clothes and box, c. 1949 .... $265-300

14", Madame Hendren Patsy Type. All-compo, Patsy mld bob, ptd features, jtd at shoulders and hips, rare ball-jointed waist (ball made of wood), Hendren clothes (for Patsy and Hendren collectors) $225-245

14", Maker Unknown, Denny Dimwit. Mint, box, swing and sway doll $125-135

14", Maker Unknown, Patsy. All-compo, mld Patsy bob, jtd at shoulders and hips, original percale dress and matching slip, original shoes, socks, c. 1940 .... $85-115

14", Maker Unknown, Polish Doll. Plastic mask face, blue ptd eyes to the side, CM, blond wig on front of head only, cloth body and limbs, kerchief on head, original Polish costume, white cloth shoes. Stamped on back of leg: "POLAND" $20-25

14", Maker Unknown, Shirley Temple. Plaster of paris, carnival item, stands on green plaster base, holds pink skirt outward at sides, c. 1937 .... $65-85

14", Maker Unknown, Tiny Tears. Early version, hard plastic head, rubber body, tight curly mohair wig, playsuit has "Tiny Tears" sewn on front $55-65

14", Mary Hoyer Child. All-compo, CM, sleep eyes, mohair wig, swivel neck, jtd at shoulders and hips, dressed $95-110

14", Mary Hoyer Girl. Hard plastic, CM, sleep eyes, HHW, swivel neck, jtd at shoulders and hips, dressed. (Boy doll this size, mint, all original and dressed, $100-125) $75-85

14", Old Mexican Doll. All-compo, ptd features, black mohair wig, jtd at shoulders and hips, original India Xochiimilco costume,

(L. to R.) All-Composition Doll, 15", made and dressed in old Mexico, c. 1930, original costume and wig. Mexican Doll, 20½", all-original, made in old Mexico, c. 1930, cloth body and limbs, compo head, body stuffed with straw, Herron collection, $45-65.

Flapper Trinket Box, 11", c. 1925, Herron collection. $150-200.

red leatherette shoes and white socks (looks like Shirley Temple), c. 1930-1940 ... **$65-75**

14", Reliable Eskimo Boy. Brown compo, brown ptd eyes, dressed in fur-trimmed Eskimo costume **$85-95**

14½", Famous Artists Little Orphan Annie. Compo shoulder head and arms, straw-stuffed cloth body and legs, mld/ptd hair, ptd features, original clothes. Mark: "FAMOUS ARTISTS SYND" **$225-300**

14½", Maker Unknown, Snow White. Plaster of paris, ptd in bright colors, a carnival item, c. 1939 .... **$35-40**

15", Clodray Little Brother. Vinyl, in original marked box. Mark: "CLODRAY 7324. MADE IN FRANCE" **$100-115**

15", Effanbee Baby Grumpy. Negro, all-compo, three black wool pigtails in black mld hair, side-glancing eyes, CM, original flowered dress **$265-285**

15", Effanbee Ice Queen. Dewees Cochran design, sleep eyes, HHW, OM with teeth, all-compo, fully jointed, original costume (white taffeta dress with marabou trim, long white hose, high shoe skates, hat with marabou trim) rare doll, c. 1938. Mark: "FB 37" (on head) and "FB 31" (on body) **$350-400**

15", Maker Unknown, GI Joe. Molded-on cap, service uniform. Label reads: "PRAISE THE LORD AND PASS THE AMMUNI-TION, WW II" **$85-95**

15", Maker Unknown, Gob-Ette. Plastic composition (plaster of paris), ptd in bright colors, cigarette in mouth, cap, dressed in mannish clothes, tough, c. 1940 ..... **$20-25**

15", Maker Unknown, Negro Baby. All-compo, brown glass sleep eyes, bent limb baby body. Mark: "H.W. 4" **$200-225**

15", O'Neill Scootles. Rare sleep eyes, wooden pulp and compo, c. 1931 .... **$400-500**

15", Putnam Bye-Lo. Vinyl, c. 1950, plastic limbs, cloth body, voice box in body, ptd blue eyes and upper lashes, CM, dressed. Doll is incised on head: "c (in a circle) GRACE STOREY PUTNAM" **$35-45**

15", Walt Disney Snow White. All-compo, brown ptd eyes to the side, black mld hair, original dress has dwarf trim **$225-245**

15", Washington State Apples Indian Doll. Advertising item, compo head and hands, cloth body and feet, ptd features, doll wears original outfit **$45-65**

15½", Hasbro Little Miss No Name. All-plastic, inset brown eyes (large and round), rooted blond hair, burlap dress with red and orange patch, c. 1965 .... **$35-40**

15½", Kallus The Selling Fool. Elastic-strung, mache head and coat, wooden BJ body, radio tube hat, made for RCA radio, Harrison, N.J.,by J. L. Kallus, c. 1926. One foot marked on bottom: "Art Quality Mfg. Co. Cameo Doll Co. N.Y." **$195-215**

15½", Maker Unknown, G.O.B. Molded-on cap, service uniform, WW II. Label reads: "PRAISE THE LORD AND PASS THE AMMUNITION" **$85-95**

(L. to R.) Boudoir Table-Lamp Doll, 17", all-original, c. 1920, $65. Boudoir Bed-Lamp Doll, 15½", c. 1920, $65. Both dolls have mohair wigs and plaster of paris half bodies, Herron collection.

15½", Maker Unknown, WAVES. Molded-on cap, service uniform **$85-95**

15½", Old Mexican Doll. Compo shoulder head and limbs, soft black yarn-type wig, ptd features, cloth body, young woman type, original Mexican costume, gold ptd shoes with heels, white socks, c. 1950 ..... **$25-35**

15½", Three-In-One Trudy the Toddler. Three-faced doll, compo head and limbs, kapok-stuffed body (pink muslin), head rotates from wooden peg in a wooden collar (concealed by ribbon and dress), tufts of hair under bonnet (some dolls have no hair), mint, all original. Printed on Trudy's dress: "SMI-LY TRUDY, WEEPY TRUDY, SLEEPY TRUDY. PAT. OBTAINED MAY 21, 1946 by THREE-IN-ONE-DOLL CORP. OF N.Y. N.Y." **$200-250**

16", Amberg Mibs. Compo shoulder head, compo limbs, cloth body, blond mld hair, blue ptd eyes, CM, dressed, designed by Helen Drucker, c. 1921. Paper label on the doll reads: "AMBERG DOLLS, PLEASE LOVE ME, I'M MIBS" **$350-400**

16", Amberg Victory Doll. All-compo, blue

(L. to R.) Buster Brown, 10", inset glass eyes, mld hair, cloth body and Can't Break 'Em head, rare doll, $300. Rare Campbell Kid, 10½", marked "DD" on back shoulder plate, original old clothes, Can't Break 'Em head, Herron collection, $225-325.

metal sleep eyes, OM with teeth, BJ compo body, HHW, dressed **$165-175**

16", Dora Petzold Doll. Compo shoulder head, ptd features, auburn wig, CM, cloth body and limbs, mitten-type hands, old costume, c. 1920, Germany. Mark: "DORA PETZOLD-REGISTERED-TRADEMARK -DOLL-GERMANY" **$300-350**

16", Famlee Doll. Twelve compo heads (Dutch girl, Dutch boy, Chinaman, Clown, Negro boy, French girl, Indian girl, Susie Bumps, Pierrette, Dolly Dimple, Little-Sweet-Face, Sailor boy), mld hair and wigs, ptd eyes, closed eyes, metal eyes, OCM or CM, costumed to character. Chinaman marked: "Pat. Apr. 12-21." Mark also on screw attaching head to body **$795-895**

16", Five-Faced Moo-Vee Doll. Moo-V Doll Mfg. Co., 1919-1920, Bridgeport, little girl type, compo head and lower limbs, dark brown mohair wig, ptd features, push nose and doll's face tqrns to reveal five different facial expressions or "movie" moods, original yellow lace-trimmed organdy dress, slip, pants, shoes, socks, yellow organdy bonnet, mint. Mark on back of shoulders: "MVD CO." Original box marked: "MOO-VEE DOLL" (assignee of a U.S. patent by Michael Johndruff of Bridgeport) **$500-600**

16", Horsman Jeanne. Compo head and limbs, cloth body, mld hair, exposed ears, blue tin sleep eyes, tiny round mouth, original clothes, c. 1937. Mark on doll's head reads: "Jeanne/Horsman" **$115-125**

16", Ideal-Uneeda Biscuit Boy. Compo head, arms and legs, CM, mld brown hair, blue ptd eyes, cloth body, mld black boots, old clothes (some versions have a mld hat) ... **$245-300**

16", Jerri Lee Boy. All-original **$95-125**

16", Kallus Marcia. All-compo, mld blond hair, ptd eyes to the side, CM, jtd at neck, shoulders and hips, ptd shoes and socks, wears original French outfit and cap. This is the largest size, c. 1933 .... **$265-300**

16", Maker Unknown, WW I Soldier Boy. Compo head and limbs, cloth body, ptd/mld hair, ptd features, well-tailored army outfit, mld black boots, removable cap, portrait face (looks like Wallace Reid) **$295-300**

16", Metropolitan Doll Co. Compo Shoulder Head. Cloth body, mld orange-colored hair and mld hairbow, ptd features, compo limbs, dressed in old clothes **$95-125**

16", Old Mexican Doll. Compo shoulder head, ptd features, black mohair wig, CM, straw-stuffed cloth body, pink cloth limbs, jtd at shoulders and hips, original old costume, red shoes, socks, c. 1930 .... **$65-75**

16", Terri Lee Black Child. **$150-200**

16", Terri Lee Child. Celanese hard plastic, CM, ptd features, blond wig, jtd at neck, shoulders, and hips, clothes **$85-115**

16", Vogue Brickett. All-plastic, sleep green eyes, orange rooted hair, smiling CM, jtd at neck, shoulders, and hips, swivel body, original clothes, c. 1960 .... **$37-48**

16½", Black Snow White. From original Snow White mold, OM with teeth, brown ptd eyes, black ptd hair with red bow, original costume, c. 1939 .... **$285-300**

16½", Maker Unknown, Compo Flange Head Girl. Pink cloth body and limbs, blond wig, original dress and bonnet, made in England, c. 1947 .... **$95-115**

17", Horsman Poor Pitiful Pearl. All-original, c. 1963 .... **$45-65**

17", Horsman Poor Pitiful Pearl. All-original, c. 1976 .... **$25-35**

17", Hummel. Rare compo head-type, original tagged costume **$150-160**

17", Maker Unknown, Peter Rabbit. Stuffed body, unbreakable head, jtd limbs, dressed in original coat, vest, trousers, shoes and neck bow, c. 1917 .... **$95**

17", Monica Child. All-compo, unmarked, CM, blue ptd eyes and eye shadow, long legs and arms, HHW. Monica Child, 15", **$95-110;** Monica Child, 20", **$200-215;** Monica Child, 22", **$225-240** **$185-195**

Greta Garbo as Camille, 27", by Paul Crees, rare one-of-a-kind original doll, $900-1,200.

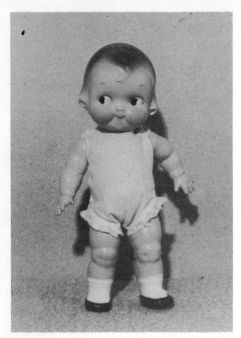

Campbell Kid, 12½", toddler body, compo, $125-150.

18", Arranbee Nancy. Compo swivel head on compo shoulder plate, compo limbs, cloth body, sleep eyes, OM with teeth, wears a mohair wig, and original clothes, c. 1930. Mark: "ARRANBEE" **$85-110**

18", Bonomi of Italy Doll. Made for Neiman-Marcus, c. 1950, hard plastic, jtd, 2-pc blue and white check dress, white blouse, red leather shoes, large straw hat with red ribbons. Dress tag: "BONOMI (ITALY) PUPPE ORIGIALE BONOMI" **$85-95**

18", Horsman Bisque Swivel Head (on wooden ring socket). Compo limbs, cloth body, fixed glass eyes, OM. Incised: "E.I.H. Co., Inc." **$350-400**

18", Horsman Ella Cinders. Compo head and limbs, cloth body, flange head (like the Bye-Lo), black ptd hair (I believe this doll was patterned after flapper Colleen Moore), surprised round blue ptd eyes, OCM, freckles, original clothes, comic-strip character doll, c. 1925. Embossed: "1925 MNS c (in circle) 1919" **$295-325**

18", Horsman-Nippon Bisque Shoulder Head. Blue sleep glass eyes, OM, mohair wig, compo limbs and cloth body. Doll is incised: "1 HORSMAN/NIPPON" **$325-350**

18", Ideal Flossie Flirt. Compo shoulder head, flirty eyes move from side to side as doll walks, cloth body, rubber arms, original clothes, paper label **$200-225**

18", Ideal Toni Doll. Hard plastic, CM, sleep eyes, auburn nylon wig, jtd at neck, shoulders and hips, all-original clothes. Mark: "Ideal Doll-P-90-Made in U.S.A." Wrist tag reads: "Genuine Toni Doll" **$65-75**

18", Kallus Baby Blossom. Blue sleep eyes, blond mld hair, OM with two teeth, cloth body, compo head and arms, Bye-Lo type body, c. 1927, dressed. Embossed: "Copy-Right J.L. Kallus, U.S.A." **$225-250**

18", Madame Raleigh Doll. High-quality compo head, hands and feet, cloth body, spring-strung, deeply mld short hair, ptd eyes, intaglio style, OCM, two upper teeth, little girl portrait face, old clothes, c. 1919 . . **$200-225**

18", Maker Unknown, Cheerful Cherub. Compo shoulder head, compo limbs, cloth body, kewpie face **$145-165**

18", Maker Unknown, Doll Lamp. Plaster of paris upper body, head and arms, mohair wig, ptd features, wire bottom covered with rose rayon taffeta, gold lace, ribbon trim, c. 1927 . . . . **$65-75**

18", Maker Unknown, Negro Girl. Compo shoulder head and limbs, cloth body, rolling eyes, hair on top of head and sides, dressed **$65-85**

18", RT WWI Doughboy, Compo head, brown mld/ptd hair, blue ptd eyes, red CM, baby face, compo body to elbows, cloth lower body, tiny hands, original doughboy uniform. Incised: "RT. MFG CO." **$225-300**

18", Tony Sarg Mammy Doll. Plastic and compo head, ptd features, broad smiling mouth, white mld teeth, mohair wig, earrings, brown cloth body, compo limbs, molded-on black shoes, original clothes, red handkerchief in hair, tag **$225-245**

19", Arranbee Rosie. Compo shoulder head with swivel neck, compo limbs, cloth body, brown sleep eyes, mld Patsy bob, OM, original clothes (another Patsy look-alike). Mark: "ARRANBEE" **$125-135**

19", Averill Yawn Baby. Compo head and limbs, cloth body. Tag on dress: "Georgene's Baby Yawn—True to Life—Georgenes Novelties, N.Y." Head embossed: "Georgene 1946 Y". **$145-165**

19", Freundlich General MacArthur. All-compo, lead hat, ptd features, jtd at shoulders and hips, original uniform. Paper label reads "GENERAL MACARTHUR—THE MAN OF THE HOUR, FREUNDLICH NOVEL-TY COMPANY 1942" (on pin) . . . **$165-185**

19", Maker Unknown, Eva. All-compo, marked (Patsy look-alike) **$95-115**

19", Maker Unknown, Mortimer Snerd. All-compo, dressed as sheriff. **$195-210**

20", Amberg Walking Boy. Compo shoulder head and limbs, blue ptd eyes, OCM, two upper teeth, brown ptd hair, straw-filled cloth body, hinged walking legs, dimpled cheeks, original old clothes. Embossed: "LA&S 1919". **$235-245**

20", Gem Toy Co. Baby Doll. Compo shoulder head, CM, celluloid and metal blue sleep eyes, hair eyelashes, compo bent limbs, cloth body, original old dress and bonnet, good condition. Tag reads: "GEM—WALKING AND TALKING DOLL—BABY'S VOICE-MOTHER'S CHOICE" **$135-165**

20", Hendren Baby Georgene. Compo head and limbs, cloth body, sleep blue tin eyes, 16½" head cir, marked, dressed **$85-95**

20", Horsman Rosebud. Compo head and limbs, cloth body, brown ptd eyes, HHW, old clothes. **$95-115**

20", Mattel Chatty Cathy. Negro version, all-original **$65-75**

21", Coleman Dolly Walker. Compo shoulder head, wooden limbs, original Chinese outfit and cap, painted-on shoes **$285-300**

21", Maker Unknown, Educational Domino Doll. Bisque shoulder head and lower limbs, ptd shoes, garters, hair and features, muslin body stamped and printed with domino, numeral, birds, fruits, animals, pictures, and names of items for the young child's education, undressed, c. 1914 . . . . **$195-210**

22", Mattel Scooba Doo. Vinyl head, sleep blue eyes, blond rooted hair, cloth body and limbs, CM, pull-string voice box, original dress, c. 1964 . . . . **$35-40**

22", Sheba Carnival Doll. Plaster of paris, 1920s type, mohair curls over ears, large side-ptd eyes, feather plumes in assorted colors encircle doll, mint, c. 1940 . . . . **$45-65**

22", Skookum Indian Doll. Mary McAboy, U.S.A., H.H. Tammen Co., and Arrow Novelty Co., compo ptd head and features, wooden legs, mohair braided wig, arms mld into blanket, c. 1913. . . . . **$25-35**

23", Morimura Bisque Shoulder Head. Japanese Import House, N.Y., c. 1915-1922, OM with teeth, inset glass eyes, mohair wig, bisque lower arms, imitation kid body, dressed, lovely doll **$235-245**

23", Old Mexican Doll. Compo shoulder head, arms and legs, jtd at shoulders and hips with wire, cloth straw-stuffed body, mld hair under soft black mohair braided wig, ptd features, c. 1920 . . . . **$95-110**

24", Maker Unknown, Sun Maid. Advertising doll, black hair, brown sleep eyes, soft vinyl, wears advertising dress and bonnet printed with boxes of raisins, c. 1974 . . . . **$25-35**

25", Maker Unknown, Advertising Doll. Black top hat with hatband marked: "I. & E. Fisher Theatrical Hat Makers, New York," compo shoulder head, hands and feet, ptd eyes, CM, mohair wig, cloth body, all-original clothes and boots **$500-550**

25", Maker Unknown, Bellhop Boy Doll. Compo head, ptd features, ptd hair, cloth body and limbs, dressed in original broadcloth bellhop uniform and hat, c. 1940 . . . . **$65-75**

25", Maker Unknown, Boudoir Doll. Compo shoulder head, compo limbs, cloth body, blond mohair wig, blue ptd eyes with inserted hair eyelashes, original Red Cross nurse outfit, cape, c. 1930 . . . . **$65-75**

26", Ideal Walker. Compo shoulder head, compo limbs, cloth body, metal device for leg movement, blue tin-celluloid sleep eyes, OCM, HHW, c. 1918 . . . . **$225-275**

26", Yamato Ningyo. Black HHW, glass eyes, large hands and feet, hard ptd mache head, hands and feet, cloth body and limbs, old kimono, Japanese, c. 1931 . . . . **$350-400**

29", Maker Unknown, Flapper Chair or Boudoir Doll. Pressed sateen face, ptd features, sateen body and long limbs, white hair, undressed, some had composition ptd faces, c. 1927. These dolls could be tied by their limbs to bedposts **$35-45**

30", Ideal Giggles. Display doll, rooted blond hair, all-original clothes **$95-110**

32", Walt Disney Dopey. Pelham puppet, England, all-compo **$225-245**

34", Dagmar (of Mama TV Fame). All-original, c. 1950 . . . . **$95-115**

60", Sasha Lady Doll. Compo under netting material, black cord hair, jtd limbs, swivel neck, glass eyes, CM, Sasha Morgenthaler, Germany, rare **$1,500-1,600**

Life-Size, Kallus Kewpie. Compo head and flange neck, straw-stuffed cloth body and limbs, blue wings, mint **$300-350**

Fulper Dolls
Fulper Pottery Company
Flemington, N.J.

All dolls listed below are in good condition, dressed and marked.

11", Kewpie. All-bisque, ptd features, wings and Fulper mark on back **$500-550**

14", Fulper Girl. Bisque shoulder head, blue tin sleep eyes, OM with seven upper teeth, mohair wig, BJ toddler body. Marked: "E.I. Horsman" **$275-325**

17", Fulper Girl. Bisque shoulder head, OM with two teeth, short mld blond hair, intaglio blue eyes, no eyelashes, eyelid line, Fulper brows, fine bisque quality **$400-450**

18", Fulper Girl. Blue glass eyes, CM, ptd upper and lower lashes, Fulper brows, bisque shoulder head and compo limbs, imitation kid body, HHW **$425-475**

18", Fulper Toddler. Sleep glass eyes, OM, Dutch-cut mohair wig **$350-400**

21", Fulper S-10. Bisque shoulder head and lower arms, OM with two teeth, blue glass eyes, mohair wig, kid body **$300-350**

23", Fulper Baby Girl. Bisque shoulder head, OM with two upper teeth, fixed glass eyes, BJ bent limb body, HHW **$385-425**

Grace Drayton Dolls

All of the dolls listed below are in good condition, wearing old or original clothes, and marked. Damaged specimens cannot command these prices. Dolls do not have to be marked to be considered Campbell Kids.

5½", Design Pat. Mfg. September Morn. All-bisque, jtd at shoulders and hips, mld hair, large ptd eyes to the side, tiny round mouth. Chest label reads: "September Morning, Germany-Drayton." Back label reads: "Design Pat. Mfg. in Germany" ... **$500-600**

7½", Horsman Peek-A-Boo Drayton Doll. Campbell Kid, compo head, arms and legs, cloth upper body, mld hair, ptd features, original striped playsuit with "Peek-A-Boo" label, originally called "Gee-Gee," lower body and legs of this doll are compo and in one piece, barefoot **$225-300**

8", Ideal Campbell Kid. Plastic, original Scottish outfit, hat, c. 1952 .... **$35-45**

10½", Campbell Kid. Can't Break 'Em-type head and lower limbs, cloth body, mld hair, brown eyes ptd to the side, original blouse, jacket, long blue skirt, undies, bare feet, rare early type. Mark: "10/DD—M" ... **$225-325**

12", Amberg Bobby Blake. Compo head and hands, some had cloth hands, pink sateen cork-stqffed body, unusual head design (wide, with tongue curling up from corner of mouth in a "yummy" expression), mld hair, old clothes, c. 1911 .... **$265-300**

12", Bobby Bounce. Campbell Kid-type, all-compo, jtd at shoulders and hips, mld hair, ptd features, original clothes (white blouse, checked short pants, ptd brown shoes, blue socks), round tag on suit **$250-300**

12", Dolly Dingle. Stuffed rubber or early vinyl, mld hair, ptd features, swivel neck, jtd arms, original pink playsuit, beautiful likeness, shoes, socks, unmarked .. **$125-145**

12", Horsman Campbell Kids. All-compo, boy and girl, jtd at shoulders and hips, mld hair, ptd features, black ptd shoes and white socks, wears original baker's cap and short suit, c. 1948, sold as a pair **$250-300**

12", Indian Campbell Kid. Brown color to compo head and hands, mld hair, brown eyes, cloth body and limbs, original Indian costume with shoes and socks **$200-225**

12", Puppy Pippin and Pussy Pippin. Can't Break 'Em heads, ptd features, plush bodies, sold as a pair **$500-550**

12½", American Character Doll Co. Dolly Dingle. All-compo, swivel neck, mld hair, ptd features, jtd at shoulders and hips, original dress, hat, shoes and socks, c. 1923. Mark: "A PETITE DOLL" **$195-215**

13½", Horsman Negro Campbell Kid. Compo head and limbs, cloth body with squeak mechanism, bent arms, straight legs, c. 1925. Mark: "E.I.H. Co., Inc." **$265-300**

15½", Horsman Campbell Kids. Can't Break 'Em heads, mld hair, flange neck, cloth body and limbs, cloth label sewn to sleeve of original playsuit, c. 1910 (some of these dolls have compo hands) **$165-185**

16", Horsman Campbell Kids. Compo head and limbs, cloth body, mld hair, ptd features **$145-165**

Grace Drayton Banks

Drayton Doggie Iron Bank. Signed, dog has a bee on his back **$195-250**

Little Bo Peep. Iron bank **$195-250**

Pussy Pippin Glass Bank. Jar-type with tin lid **$45-55**

Pussy Pippin Iron Bank. Signed, large bow around neck **$195-250**

September Morn with Apologies. Drayton chalk statuette. **$40-60**

Miscellaneous Collectible Moderns

7½", Vogue Ginny. Hard plastic, original clothes, c. 1949. Mark on head: "Vogue." Mark on back: "Vogue Doll" **$35-45**

8", Vogue Toodles. All-compo, blue ptd eyes, hair, dressed. Mark on head: "Vogue." Mark on body: "Doll Co." **$40-50**

8", Vogue Toodles Baby. All-compo, jtd at shoulders and hips, wig, ptd features. Mark: "Vogue" **$60-70**

8", Vogue Toodles Boy and Girl. All-compo, wardrobe trunk and original clothes. Mark: "Vogue" **$125-145**

8", Vogue, Toodles Mexican Girl. All-compo, blue ptd eyes to the side, black wig, original Mexican costume, c. 1940 .... **$40-50**

8", Vogue Toodles Sailor Boy. All-compo, blue ptd eyes to the side, mld hair, original sailor outfit. Mark on head: "Vogue." Mark on body: "Doll Co" **$40-50**

10", Vogue Jill. Original skating costume, hair, c. 1958 .... **$30-40**

10", Vogue Miss Ginny. Plastic and vinyl. Head mark: "Vogue Dolls Inc" **$30-40**

12", Vogue Betty Jane. All-compo, blue sleep eyes. Original tagged costume: "Vogue Dolls, Inc. 1947 (Ideal for Vogue)" **$85-95**

12", Vogue Black Ginny Baby. Vinyl head and limbs, CM, cloth body, sleep eyes, original clothes, c. 1964. Mark: "Vogue Doll/1964" **$15-20**

12", Vogue Bunny-Hug Baby. Vinyl head, CM, sleep eyes, ptd hair, body and limbs pink plush, c. 1964. Mark: "Vogue Doll/1964" **$15-20**

12", Vogue Little Miss Ginny. Plastic and vinyl toddler, original clothes, c. 1970. Mark on head: "Vogue" **$18-23**

15", Vogue Little Miss Ginny Bride. Sleep eyes, hair, all-vinyl, no marks on doll, bridal outfit, tagged **$35-45**

16", Vogue Character Baby. All-vinyl, OM with tongue, dimples, sleep eyes, ptd/mld hair, original clothes. Mark on head: "Vogue Dolls Inc/1966." Mark on back: "VOGUE DOLL" **$25-35**

18", Vogue Baby Dear. Vinyl head and limbs, cloth body, original clothes, c. 1960. Head mark: "Vogue Dolls." Back of leg marked: "1960/E. Wilkins"................. **$35-45**

20", Vogue Mary Ann. All-compo, blue sleep eyes, mohair wig, CM, unmarked. Original costume tagged: "Vogue/Medford, Mass. (Ideal Doll)" **$85-95**

Beatrice Wright Dolls

Modern plastic and vinyl doll prices are based on the more popular and scarce types within groups and on the degree of originality, not on actual age or true value.

16", Alfie Cowboy and Florie Cowgirl. White dolls, plastic and vinyl, CM, sleep blue eyes, feet built into bottom of suit, c. 1967, sold as a pair **$125-135**

18", Brenda, Patricia, and Jacqueline. Plastic with vinyl wigs, black, mint, original costumes, c. 1967 .... **$50-60**

19", Christine, Alfie, Christopher, and Juanita. Plastic and vinyl wigs, c. 1967............................. **$50-60**

Madame Alexander Dolls

The Alexander doll has always been popular with collectors. Except for some of the earlier composition dolls which cracked and crazed easily, the modern Alexander doll is well made, artistically designed and costumed, and sports a stylish wig is the latest fashion. The long-term popularity of this doll has almost taken her out of the precarious "fad" class and placed her in the more stable price bracket, which means that when you sell your Alexander doll, you will more than likely get what you paid for her plus a little bit more.

The Alexander dolls listed in this section are mint and original in every way. Damaged, undressed, or bald versions cannot command these prices.

7", Alexander Tinies. Also 9", compo head stationary on body, CM, ptd features, mohair wig, movable limbs, tagged clothes. This series represented Doll of the World and Storybook Characters, original costume (larger size had jtd neck). Mark on doll reads: "Mme Alexander" (back)..................... **$55-75**

7½", Dionne Quints Toddlers. All-compo, mld dark curls, ptd features, CM, dressed in original organdy dresses and bonnets, lockets around necks inscribed with names, original wicker basket, signed, mint, set ... **$600-700**

7½", Dionne Quints Toddlers. All-compo, mld dark curls, ptd features, CM, dressed in original organdy dresses and bonnets, lockets around necks inscribed with names, original cradles, signed, mint, set **$600-700**

8", Dionne Quints. All-compo, mld hair, ptd eyes, CM, swivel necks, jtd at shoulders and hips, original dresses, tag, c. 1935, dolls are sold separately................... **$95-125**

10½", Dionne Quints. Toddlers, all-compo, brown sleep eyes, brown mohair wigs, signed, original clothes, sold separately ... **$125-135**

10½", Dionne Quints. All-compo, mld straight dark hair, brown sleep eyes, OCM, bent legs, white organdy dresses and bibs, dresses marked "Alexander" with the name of each Dionne, complete with original basket and blanket, sold as a set **$750-850**

12", Butch. Sleep eyes, CM, mohair wig, cloth body, compo head, hands and legs, original clothes, c. 1940 .... **$95-115**

12", Little Women. Hard plastic, CM, sleep eyes, synthetic hair, jtd at neck, shoulders and hips. Mark on head: "ALEXANDER." "Meg," "Jo," "Beth," "Amy," "Marmie" on tags. Lissy face in this size, sold separately (14" and 15" dolls, **$125-150**) **$100-125**

14", Bride and Bridesmaids. All-compo, CM, sleep eyes, mohair wigs, jtd at neck, shoulders and hips, c. 1940. Mark: "MME ALEXANDER" (head) and "MADAME ALEXANDER" (dress). 18" doll, **$150-160**; 21" doll, **$175-185** **$125-135**

14", Jenny Walker. All-compo, CM, sleep eyes, mohair or HHW, jtd at neck, shoulders and hips. Mark: "ALEXANDER PAT. NO. 2171281 Jenny Walker—Madame Alexander, N.Y., U.S.A. All rights reserved".. **$165-175**

14", Little Colonel. All-compo, CM, sleep eyes, dimples, swivel head, jtd at shoulders and hips, mohair wig, original bonnet, dress, c. 1935 .... **$375-475**

16", Alexander Fabric Character Dolls. Mask face, flocked with felt, hand-painted features, eyes ptd to the side, mohair wigs, cloth body and limbs, original clothes have tag of character represented (these dolls have often been mistaken for Lenci dolls) **$225-240**

16", Alice in Wonderland. Trademark #304488, mask face, ptd features, yellow worsted hair, cloth body and limbs, red or blue print dress, white organdy apron, black shoes, white socks (an earlier 1923 version of the cloth Alexander Alice had a flat face, hand-painted features, yellow yarn hair, pink muslin body, cloth limbs; after 1948, the Alice dolls were made of plastic and vinyl) ... **$150-200**

16", Little Shaver. Mask face, ptd eyes to the side, CM, floss wig, cloth body and limbs (body actually pink stocking type), original costume, mint, c. 1927. Mark on doll reads: "Little Shaver Madame Alexander New York All Rights Reserved" **$165-175**

18", Baby Genius. Sleep eyes, CM, mld hair, compo head and legs, wears original clothes, c. 1938 .... **$125-135**

18", Betty. All-compo, CM, mld hair with wig, sleep eyes, swivel neck, jtd at shoulders and hips, bent right arm (Patsy look alike), all-original clothes, unmarked doll, c. 1935. Dress tag: "Betty Madame Alex".. **$185-195**

18", Flora McFlimsey. All-compo, OM, sleep eyes, jtd at neck, shoulders and hips, freckles, HHW with bangs, c. 1938. Mark: "PRINCESS ELIZABETH, ALEXANDER DOLL CO" (head) and "Flora McFlimsey of Madison Square" (dress) **$185-200**

18", Karen Ballerina. All-compo, CM, sleep eyes, blond braids coiled with flowers, jtd at neck, shoulders and hips, original costume, c. 1946. Mark: "Alexander" (head) and "Madame Alexander" (dress tag) .. **$165-185**

18", Kate Greenaway. All-compo, OM, sleep eyes, mohair wig, swivel neck, jtd at shoulders and hips, c. 1938. Mark: "PRINCESS ELIZABETH ALEXANDER DOLL CO" and "KATE GREENAWAY"..... **$185-200**

18", Scarlet O'Hara. All-compo, CM, green sleep eyes, black wig, jtd at neck, shoulders and hips, all-original outfit, c. 1937. Mark: "SCARLET O'HARA MADAME ALEXANDER N.Y. U.S.A., ALL RIGHTS RESERVED" (dress tag)........ **$285-300**

20", McGuffey Ana. All-compo, sleep eyes, human hair pigtails, jtd at neck, shoulders and hips, original costume and hat, c. 1937. Mark on doll reads: "PRINCESS ELIZABETH-Alexander" (head) and "McGuffey Ana" (dress tag)..................... **$250-300**

20", Princess Elizabeth. All-compo, OM, sleep eyes, mohair wig, jtd at neck, shoulders and hips, c. 1937. Mark on doll reads: "PRINCESS ELIZABETH ALEXANDER DOLL CO" (head) and "Princess Elizabeth" (dress tag)..................... **$165-185**

21", Alice in Wonderland. All-compo, CM, sleep eyes, mohair wig, jtd at neck, shoulders and hips, c. 1947. Mark on doll reads: "Alexander" (head) and "Alice in Wonderland" (dress tag) **$225-245**

21", Fairy Princess. All-compo, CM, sleep eyes, mohair wig, jtd at neck, shoulders and hips, original costume includes necklace, tiara, shoes and socks, c. 1942. Mark on head reads: "Madame Alexander." Mark on dress: "Fairy Princess" **$225-325**

21", Portrait Dolls. All-compo, CM, sleep eyes, human hair or mohair wigs, jtd at neck, shoulders and hips, ptd fingernails, unmarked, long dress, wrist tag. Dress label reads: "Madame Alexander"...... **$325-350**

Contemporary Alexander Dolls

The following Alexander dolls are among the most popular of the modern dolls. All are mint and in original condition. Lesser examples cannot command these high prices. Again, popularity governs doll prices. The Mary Ann head was used on many of these dolls.

8", Little Genius. Hard plastic and vinyl, c. 1956-1962 .... **$55-60**

8", Sound of Music Tinies. (10" doll, **$85**; 12" doll, **$137.50**) **$70**

10", Cissette. Hard plastic, c. 1957 .. **$65-70**

10", Jacqueline. Cissette head..... **$185-190**

10", Queen. Cissette head **$135-140**

10", Scarlet. Cissette head **$135-140**

10", Southern Belle. **$135-140**

11", Sound of Music Dolls. (14" doll, **$135**; 17" doll, **$147.50**) **$97.50**

14", Gidget. c. 1966 .... **$135-140**

14", Grandma Jane. c. 1970 ...... **$115-128**

14", Jenny Lind. c. 1970 .... **$225-240**

14", Jenny Lind & Cat. c. 1969 ... **$185-225**

14", Little Granny. c. 1966 ...... **$125-135**

14", Little Orphan Annie. Mary Ann head, c. 1965 .... **$135-145**

14", Madame. c. 1967-1975........ **$75-80**

14", Mary Ann. Vinyl and hard plastic, c. 1965 .... **$165-175**

14", McGuffey Ana 1450. .... **$135-145**

14", Peter Pan. c. 1969 .... **$125-135**

14", Renoir Girl 1474. c. 1967 .... **$165-175**

14", Renoir Girl 1476. c. 1967 .... **$165-175**

14", Renoir Girl 1477. c. 1967 .... **$165-175**

14", Riley's Little Annie. c. 1967 .. **$147-155**

14", Scarlet 1495. c. 1968 .... **$135-145**

14", Wendy. c. 1969 .... **$125-135**

15", Maggie. c. 1948-1953 .... **$85-95**

21", Cissy. Hard plastic and vinyl, c. 1955-1959 .... **$87-93**

Collectible
English Bisque Dolls

The English bisque doll somehow never managed to reach the high degree of perfection accomplished by the more experienced German and French doll manufacturers. Consequently, the rather scarce examples found today in collections and museums are the least impressive of the 20th Century doll output. Somehow they appeal more to the doll connoisseur than to the average collector. Nonetheless they are worthwhile and should be collected and treasured. The examples listed here are all in good condition and are dressed in old clothing.

11½", Maker Unknown, Toddler Girl. Bisque shoulder head, CM, blue ptd eyes, mld blond hair, straight bisque limbs, cloth body, poor bisque quality. Mark on doll reads: "S. Classic England" **$250-300**

12½", Hancock Bisque Shoulder Head. Hancock & Sons, Cauldon, Staffordshire, bisque lower limbs, fixed blue glass eyes, HHW, kid body, poor bisque quality. Mark: "3½ English Make. Hancocks".... **$285-300**

12½", Mayer and Sherratt Lady Doll. Bisque shoulder head and lower arms, cloth body and legs, blue ptd eyes, CM, mohair wig, poor bisque quality. Mark: "M & S" ... **$300-350**

16", Mayer and Sherratt Bisque Shoulder Head. Bisque lower limbs, OM with teeth, inset glass eyes, mohair wig, kid body with pin-rivet joints at hips and gusset joints at elbows and knees, made by Mayer and Sherratt, Clifton Works, c. 1900. Mark on doll reads: "MELBA" **$300-350**

18", Goss Bisque Shoulder Head. Blue glass sleep eyes, dark red OCM, HHW, pottery-type limbs, pink cambric body (stuffed with wool fibers). Mark: "Goss" **$350-400**

18", Hancock Bisque Shoulder Head Girl. Blue fixed glass eyes, CM, HHW, bisque lower limbs, cloth body. Mark on doll reads: "S.H. & S." **$395-425**

22", Maker Unknown, Ceramic. Ceramic limbs, fixed glass eyes, CM, mohair wig, a rather poor quality doll, rare type, c. 1920. Head incised on rear shoulder plate: "Dorothy-9082-made in England". . **$295-325**

Snow White, 17", glass sleep eyes, original wig, costume, $250. Dwarfs, 12", ptd eyes, all-original, Jim and Sheila Olah Scheetz collection, $250 each.

(L. to R.) Mache Flapper Head, 7½", marked "GERMANY," $25. Wax Lady Head and Bust, 5", white mohair wig, marked "PARIS," $65. Bisque Flapper Doll Head, 6", slit at top for coins (called a bank doll when attached to body, wig covered slit in head), $25. All dolls from the Herron collection.

14
The Shirley Temples

Composition Shirley Temples

The composition Shirley Temple doll, manufactured from 1934 until the late 1930s by the Ideal Toy & Novelty Company, has become the most popular of all the 20th Century fad dolls. This means that a rather cheaply made composition doll is commanding prices comparable to the better quality china, parian, papier-mache, bisque, and metal dolls of antiquity. Consequently, when one pays these outlandish prices, one must expect to find a doll that is in mint condition and original in every way, including the wig, costume, shoes, socks, and pin. Nude, cracked, crazed, rewigged, repainted, restored, and redressed Shirleys cannot command top prices.

Some characteristics of the old dolls are: mohair and human hair wigs in golden blond, ash blond, dark ash blond, black, and reddish strawberry blond; brown, hazel, green and blue flirty or painted eyes; open and closed mouths; gray eyeshadow or no eyeshadow at all; red felt or molded tongue; realistic-looking teeth or teeth outlined on a white celluloid base; indented dimples and dimples outlined by a circle and a dot; fat and slim face shapes; chubby or slender bodies; chubby legs and slender legs; variations on head markings and genuine unmarked Shirleys; dolls painted either a pale matt flesh tone or a rosy gloss shade; sleeping eyes; varied arm and hand shapes; two types of dress pins; and two different dress labels.

Old Shirleys were made of wood pulp composition which shrank with age, causing the paint to craze and crack. An 8" Ideal Shirley has been reported, as has a 36" composition version. In 1934, the Los Angeles Doll Company made a Shirley from the Baby Burlesk series. Special Shirleys were designed for promotional purposes. Many unmarked Shirleys were made (some with cloth bodies, some with vinyl; some were Negro versions) to dupe the buyer into thinking they were bona fide Ideal Shirleys. Unmarked or not, they *are* Shirley Temple dolls. Some actually look more like Shirley than the popular Ideal version. However, one pays top dollar only for *marked* specimens and that means *Ideal* Shirleys only.

The Shirley Temple dolls listed here are mint and original in every way. They are described merely as pricing examples for dolls in similar sizes.

All-original Shirley Temple Doll, Pat and Sunny Lupton collection, $750-800.

11", Shirley. Rare size, dressed in Scotty dress from "Our Little Girl" **$450-500**

11", Shirley. In all-original rangerette or cowboy outfit **$650-700**

13", Marama, the Hurricane Doll. Dark Shirley (often called the Negro Shirley when found undressed), all-compo, dark ptd flirty eyes, black yarn wig, OM with teeth (CM and sleep-eyed versions found in this dark Shirley type), white shoes, grass skirt, mint, c. 1937. Mark on head: "SHIRLEY TEMPLE." This rare doll came in three sizes **$600-700**

13", Shirley. In crisp pink taffeta dress from "The Little Princess" **$300-350**

13", Shirley. In all-original rangerette or cowboy outfit **$700-750**

16", Shirley. In white organdy dress with red dots and edging of blue and red from "Stand Up And Cheer" (in all-original rangerette or cowboy outfit) **$750-800**

17", Shirley. Dressed in Tyrolean costume from "Heidi" **$375-475**

17", Shirley. This size in all-original rangerette or cowboy outfit **$750-800**

18", Shirley. Dressed in Little Miss Broadway outfit, dainty blouse with a Peter Pan collar and puffed sleeves, pleated jumper in contrasting color with painted cross-stitch that gives an embroidery effect, two bows in hair to match color of jumper **$400-450**

18", Shirley. Dressed as Snow White, all-compo, OM, sleep eyes, black mohair wig, this doll wears original outfit consisting of velvet bodice and cape, rayon skirt (decorated with dwarf figures), c. 1939. Dress mark: "AN IDEAL DOLL" **$500-600**

18", Shirley Toddler. All-compo, swivel head, jtd at shoulders and hips, flirty eyes, mld hair, chubby straight legs, chubby body, bent arms, body, head and dress marked **$400-500**

Author's note: Wardrobe trunks complete with labeled dresses were sold with the 13", 16", and 18" Shirleys. Finding an all-original Shirley with her original trunk and clothes adds to the value of the doll, often as much as $300-500.

(L. to R.) All-Bisque Shirley Temple, 7¼", made in Japan, $125-150. Rare Compo Shirley Temple, 7¾", unmarked, $200. All-Bisque Shirley Temple, 6½", made in Japan, original dress and pants, $150-175. All dolls from the Herron collection.

20", Shirley. Dressed in Captain January 2-pc blue (or white) sailor suit, matching hat with contrasting tie **$425-450**

22", Shirley. Dressed as Wee Willie Winkie, jacket dress with striped trim **$450-500**

25", Shirley. Dressed in familiar original sailboat dress **$475-525**

25", Shirley Temple Baby. Compo swivel head on shoulder plate, compo limbs, cloth body, OM, sleep eyes, mohair wig, wears original clothes (some Shirley babies have mld hair), c. 1934 .... **$525-625**

27", Shirley. Dressed as the Little Colonel, bonnet, ruffles **$500-600**

27", Shirley. In all-original rangerette or cowboy outfit **$800-850**

29", Madame Alexander Little Princess. This beautiful high-quality doll looks more like Shirley than the Ideal versions (when found undressed, it is accredited to Ideal), all-compo, sleep eyes, OM with teeth, mohair wig, dressed and all-original **$700-800**

Author's note: The various bisque and composition Shirley Temple dolls average about $125-150 either nude or in original or near-original clothes. These are rare and scarce and Japanese made, and are found only in small sizes (under 10").

Vinyl and Plastic Shirley Temples 1957

12", Shirley. Original clothes **$85-100**

15", Shirley..................... **$95-115**

17", Shirley.................... **$125-150**

36", Shirley. The coveted 36" Shirley (made of plastic) made its debut on March 10, 1959, at Gimbels in New York, when Shirley Temple Black arrived in person to autograph the new Shirley Temple line for Ideal. More than 14,000 people crowded into the store to see Shirley Black and have her autograph their dolls. The number actually autographed was never recorded, but an authentic autograph would add around $2000 to the value of the doll **$800-1,500**

Vinyl and Plastic Shirley Temples 1972-1973

14½", Shirley. Hazel sleep eyes, OM with four teeth, rooted blond synthetic hair, flocked nylon dress, red velveteen vest, white plastic shoes, socks, swivel neck, jtd at the shoulders and the hips **$35-50**

16½", Shirley. Hazel sleep eyes, OCM, rooted blond synthetic hair, white nylon dress with red dots, red trim and bow, red shoes and white stockings **$25-30**

15
Effanbee Dolls

Since so many Effanbee dolls come into the hands of collectors and dealers, a special section is devoted to them and to their history.

The F & B doll dates to 1913 when Bernard E. Fleischaker and Hugo Baum decided to begin manufacturing dolls in their small New York store. The store opened in 1910 mainly as a retail outlet for toys. Early Effanbee dolls were rag and composition, although they also experimented with bisque. (Lenox, Inc. of Trenton, New Jersey. These rare heads were never marketed.)

There are too many F & B dolls to list all of them here, but these basic prices will aid in pricing similar dolls in various sizes from the same years. The yardstick for pricing is always quality, condition, degree of originality, and the doll's overall popularity. These dolls are in good condition and wear old or original clothes.

7", Bubs. All-compo, dark type, ptd features, black wig, jtd at shoulders and hips, c. 1920. This doll has a mld Indian costume beneath her Hawaiian grass skirt and lei **$65-85**

9", Girl with Bobbed Hair. All-compo, ptd eyes to the side, fully jointed body, c. 1926. Mark: "FB 23" (Patsy type) **$65-75**

10½", Baby Huggins. All-compo, stationary head, movable limbs, mld/ptd hair, ptd blue eyes, CM, crude old compo, c. 1913. Mark: "FB 1" **$85-125**

11", Baby Bright Eyes, Jr. Deeply modeled compo shoulder head, compo bent arms, sawdust-filled cloth body and legs, limbs jtd at shoulders and hips, ptd features, mld/ptd hair, c. 1915. Mark: "FB 1." (This doll is called the Happy Baby Grumpy) **$135-155**

11", Suzette. All-compo, ptd eyes to the side, CM, mohair wig, fully jointed body, c. 1939. Mark: "FB 42" **$85-95**

Skippy, 14", c. WW II, original costume,
$135-155.

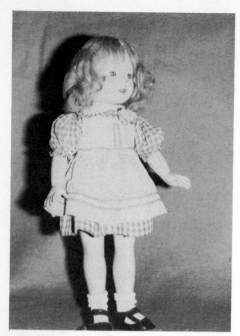

Anne Shirley, 17", marked "EFFANBEE ANNE SHIRLEY," Pat and Sunny Lupton collection, $200-250.

Baby Grumpy, marked "GRUMPKINS," $150.

12", Baby Grumpy. Compo shoulder head (mld lower on chest), compo limbs, sawdust-stuffed cloth body, ptd features, mld hair, c. 1912. (Some Grumpys of this period had sawdust-stuffed cloth legs and were marked "FB 1.") Mark: "FB 32" **$145-165**

12", Boy and Girl Candy Kids. All-vinyl, mld/ptd hair, blue sleep eyes, CM, fully jointed body, original red and white gingham outfits, sold as a pair, c. 1954 ...... **$70-90**

12", Portrait Doll. All-compo, swivel head, CM, blue sleep eyes, brown mohair wig, fully jointed body, dressed in original bridal outfit, c. 1940 .... **$65-85**

12", Sleeping Babies. Compo head and hands, cloth body, legs and arms, ptd hair, ptd features, these twins came with open and closed eyes, called Babyette and Babyet, original clothes, pair, c. 1943 ..... **$225-245**

13", Baby Dainty. Compo shoulder head and arms, CM, blue ptd eyes, mld hair, cloth body and legs (perhaps this doll set the style for future Patsy dolls and should be included in Patsy collections), c. 1912. Mark on doll reads: "FB 1" **$165-185**

13½", Candy Kid. All-compo, brown sleep eyes, mld brown ptd hair, CM, fully jointed body, c. 1946. Mark: "FB 22" **$95-125**

14", Baby Dainty. Compo shoulder head and limbs, blond mld hair, tin sleep eyes, cloth body, jtd at shoulders and hips, c. 1920. Mark: "FB 2" (Patsy forerunner) **$95-125**

14", Beautee-Skin Baby. Hard plastic head, latex rubber kapok-stuffed body, mld/ptd hair, CM, brown sleep eyes, fully jointed, c. 1945. Mark: "FB 29" **$35-55**

14", Skippy. Compo swivel head on compo shoulder plate, compo arms and legs, legs have black mld knee socks and black mld shoes, brown ptd hair, ptd features, original short pants, white skirt, neckerchief, cap, cloth body (the earlier versions chipped and cracked). Mark reads: "EFFANBEE SKIPPY C.P.L. Crosby" **$135-155**

14", Skippy. Dressed as a sailor (earlier 1935 versions dressed as sailor, soldier, baseball player, cowboy, fireman, aviator, or in typical Skippy clothes), c. 1942 . . . . **$135-155**

14", Skippy. With "magic" or "magnet" palms that held six items, c. 1940 . . . . . . **$225-245**

14", Suzanne. All-compo, CM, blue sleep eyes, mohair wig, fully jointed body, magnetic hands, original costume, c. 1940. Mark on doll reads: "FB 38" **$125-145**

15", Aunt Dinah, Baby Snowball, Uncle Moses. Black dolls, compo shoulder heads and arms, cloth-stuffed bodies and legs, ptd features, sold individually **$95-125**

15", Baby Bubbles. All-rubber, compo head, jtd at shoulders and hips, brown sleep eyes, OM with four teeth, mld/ptd hair, c. 1933. Mark: "FB 41" **$65-85**

15", Coquette. Compo shoulder head and arms, cloth body and legs, mld hair, ptd features. Mark: "FB 1." (This was one of the character dolls made in 1918; others were Lady Grumpy and Brother) **$165-225**

15", Harmonica Joe. Compo shoulder head and arms, cloth body and legs, ptd features, OM with tube connected to midsection, plays a harmonica, dressed in brown overalls, blue shirt, jockey cap, patent leather black shoes, socks, c. 1925 . . . . **$185**

15", Harmonica Joe. Black **$250-300**

15", Little Lady. Compo and rubber, blue or brown sleep eyes, CM, mohair wig, fully jointed body (lovely long fingers), original long dress and hat, parasol, c. 1940. Mark: "FB 31" **$165-185**

15", Pajama Baby, Bobby, Baby Dainty. Compo shoulder head and arms, OM, ptd features, mld hair, cloth body and limbs (this Baby Dainty is more the baby type with bent limbs; both babies are in baby dresses and have pacifiers in mouths; Bobby is dressed like a little baby boy), sold individually, c. 1913. Mark: "FB 1" **$165-185**

15", Skippy. Patsy's boyfriend, originally had a Patsy body, all-compo, blue ptd eyes to the side, blond mld hair, swivel head, jtd at shoulders and hips, original clothes, c. 1928.

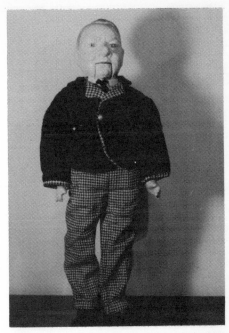

W.C. Fields Ventriloquist's Dummy, 20", original costume, $475-525.

Effanbee Clown, 14½", by V. Austin, ptd compo, original costume, $200.

Puggy, 12", all-original, $400-450.

Mark on doll reads: "FB 18" (head) and "FB 7" (body) **$125-145**

16", Betty Lee. Compo shoulder head and limbs, cloth body, blue sleep eyes, HHW, shoulder joints, stitched hips, c. 1924. Mark: "FB 32" (also came in 24") **$95-125**

16", Brother and Sister. Compo swivel heads and hands, CM, blue ptd eyes, cloth body and limbs, cotton yarn wig, original outfits, sold as a pair. Mark: "FB 29" **$250-300**

16", Soldier Boy. Compo shoulder head, cloth body and limbs, ptd hair and features, dressed as WW I doughboy (jumbo boy and girl look similar), c. 1918 . . . . **$145-185**

16", Sweetie Pie. Compo swivel head, tiny CM, blue or brown sleep eyes, caracul wig, mama voice box, compo bent limbs, c. 1939. Mark: "FB 29" **$125-145**

16½", Betty Brite. All-compo, sleep eyes, CM, caracul wig, jtd at shoulders and hips (this is a hard-to-find doll), c. 1933 . . . . **$145-165**

17", Mary Lee. Compo swivel head on shoulder plate with limbs, sleep eyes, OM, brown mohair wig, V-shaped cloth body, c. 1932. Mark: "FB 34" **$145-165**

17½", W.C. Fields. Compo shoulder head, hands and feet, ventriloquist doll with hinged mouth, ptd features, red nose, mld/ptd hair, ptd teeth, cloth body, original pants, coat, shirt, necktie and hat, c. 1929. Mark on doll reads: "FB 36" **$425-450**

18", Bubbles. Deep-set compo shoulder plate and limbs, mld hair, tin sleep eyes, OM, two teeth, dimples. Mark: "FB 3" **$125-165**

18", Honey. Hard plastic, blue sleep eyes, HHW (some have wigs of mohair or nylon), CM, fully jointed, original clothes and hat, c. 1950. Mark: "FB 29" **$85-95**

18", Little Lady. All-compo, swivel head, CM, brown sleep eyes, mohair wig, jtd at hips and shoulders. Mark: "FB 23" **$125-145**

18", Little Lady. All-compo, swivel head, blue sleep eyes, CM, cotton yarn wig, jtd at the shoulders and the hips, c. 1942. Mark: "FB 23" **$95-125**

18", Pat-O-Pat. Compo swivel head on plate, guantlet hands, CM, ptd features, doll claps hands when stomach is pressed (looks like the Bye-Lo), c. 1925. Mark: "FB 23" . . **$225-265**

18", Rosemary. Compo shoulder head and limbs, cloth body, sleep eyes, OM with four teeth. Mark: "FB 5" **$115-135**

19", Beautee-Skin Baby. Compo head, latex-rubber stuffed body, blue sleep eyes, CM, mld/ptd hair, fully jointed body, original romper, c. 1944. (This doll must be mint to command this price as most have darkened with age.) Mark: "FB 29" **$45-65**

19", Howdy Doody. **$125**

20", Baby Catherine. Compo head and limbs, cloth body, sleep or ptd eyes, mohair wig, OM with pacifier, c. 1918. Mark: "FB 1." (Also available in 12", 14", and 16") **$165-225**

20", Dy-Dee Baby. Rubber head, soft rubber body and limbs, sleep eyes, mld hair, OM for bottle, c. 1933. Mark on doll: "FB 35." (This doll was made for more than forty years in various sizes) **$95-125**

20"-22", Jumbo Infant. Compo head, arms and legs, cloth body, ptd features, mohair wig, OM with pacifier, c. 1918 . . . . **$165-225**

21", Baby Bright Eyes. All-compo, mld blond hair, CM, blue flirty eyes, fully jointed body, c. 1940. Mark: "FB 23" **$85-95**

21", Marilee. Negro, compo shoulder head, sleep eyes, suede body, black imitation caracul wig, OM, c. 1924. Mark: "FB 4" . . **$250-300**

22", Alice Lee. Compo shoulder head and limbs, cloth body, sleep eyes, HHW, c. 1924. Mark: "FB 32" (also 16") **$125-165**

22", Anne Shirley. Anne of Green Gables, all-compo, brown (sometimes green, blue, or hazel) sleep eyes, CM, HHW, fully jointed, large portrait hands, c. 1936. Mark: "FB 31" (also 9", 12", 15"; Anne Shirley dolls must have the Anne Shirley head to be a bona fide version, as other heads appeared on Anne Shirley bodies). **$165-185**

22", Heartbeat Doll. Compo head and limbs,

Skippy, 14", marked "c" (in circle) and "C.P.L. Crosby," c. WW II, original costume, $135-155.

221

cloth body, windup key under left arm distinguishes this rare doll (she must have her own stethoscope to be perfect), c. 1942. Mark: "FB 23" $200-250

22", Tommy Tucker. All-compo, brown flirty eyes, CM, caracul wig (some with HHW), fully jointed body (this doll is the Bright Eyes doll with hair), originally came with a stuffed kitty-kat, c. 1940. Mark: "FB 23" .. $95-125

23", Howdy Doody. Hard plastic head and hands, cloth body, sleep blue eyes, mld/ptd hair, OCM with teeth, original cowboy outfit and hat, c. 1947. Mark: "FB 29" .. $165-185

24", Mickey. Compo swivel head and hands, CM, blue or brown sleep eyes, mld hair or wig, cloth body and limbs, original red corduroy overalls, basque shirt, cap, c. 1939 (this doll was issued until 1949). Mark on doll reads: "FB 23" $125-145

24", Sugar Baby. Swivel head on compo shoulder plate, compo limbs, cloth body, mld hair, blue-green sleep eyes, CM, c. 1936. Mark: "FB 30" (another Sugar Baby has mark "FB 25") $145-165

25", Jumbo Infant. Compo shoulder head, ptd features, mld/ptd hair, cloth with sawdust-filled body and limbs, stitched fingers, c. 1915. Mark: "FB 1" $185-210

25", Red Cross Nurse. Compo shoulder head and arms, ptd features, cloth-stuffed body and legs, HHW, outfit, c. 1918. .... $125-165

26", Kali-Ko-Kate. All-cloth, hand-painted features, percale costume, c. 1933. Mark on doll reads: "FB 23"................ $65-85

27", Compo Shoulder Head and Limbs. Cloth body, OM with two teeth, gray tin sleep eyes, unpainted mld hair (this doll came without a wig). Mark: "FB 4" $135-185

27", Marilee. Compo shoulder head and limbs, cloth body, OM with four teeth, sleep eyes, HHW. Mark: "FB 4" $135-185

28", Anne Shirley. All-compo, blue sleep eyes, CM, HHW, fully jointed body, no mark (but she is still an authentic Anne Shirley), large hands $285-300

28", Lovums. Compo swivel head on shoulder plate, compo limbs, cloth body, sleep eyes, OM with four teeth, bent limbs, c. 1928. Mark: "FB 6" $145-165

29", Mae Starr. Compo shoulder plate and limbs, cloth body, sleep eyes, OM with four teeth, HHW, talking device in body with wax cylinder records, mint, original (including clothes), c. 1928. Mark: "FB 9" ... $300-350

16
The Effanbee
Patsy Line

The F & B Patsy doll became the most popular and most imitated doll in doll history. Similar Patsy types were manufactured prior to the doll's initial debut in 1927. A 1934 Patsy had a composition shoulder head, cloth body and limbs. Some Patsy collectors have refused to consider the 25" Patsy Ruth and the 28" Patsy Mae as genuine Patsys due to the fact that they have cloth bodies and are oversized. These dolls also wore human hair wigs, which added to the confusion, although standard Patsys wear wigs of mohair and human hair.

As late as the 1970s, a vinyl Patsy was reissued as a special edition doll for fervent Patsy collectors. The Shirley Temple doll conceived by Ideal in 1934 was also a widely imitated doll, but her popularity was short-lived. People soon grew weary of the dimpled and sweet Shirley Temple doll.

Every little girl of the 1930s will remember the Patsy Doll Club and Aunt Patsy who traveled all over America to greet her little admirers. The Patsy Doll Club had over 275,000 members. Aunt Patsy kept them posted on Patsy's happenings via the club's own newspaper, *The Patsytown News* and another little publication called *My Doll's Magazine*. These rare items are collected today the world over, as is the well-known Patsy book, *Patsy Ann—Her Happy Times* (by Mona Reed King, Rand McNally & Company).

The value of the Patsy doll has been overestimated, and I feel the prices here are more in keeping with her current worth. The countless Patsy look-alikes listed in another section are also worthy of collection. All dolls listed here are mint and in original clothes with original heart bracelets. If a doll is other than mint or original, it cannot command these prices.

5", Wee Patsy. All-compo, CM, blue ptd eyes to the side, brown ptd hair, mld/ptd black strap shoes and white socks, head in one with body (stationary), jtd at shoulders and hips, c. 1930. Mark: "FB 15" **$125-145**

8", Patsy Babyette. All-compo, CM, mld

Effanbee Patsy Junior, 12", $125-135.

brown hair, blue sleep eyes, jtd at shoulders and hips, c. 1927. Mark: "FB 39" (revised, 1940s; plastic reissue, 1950s) **$95-110**

8", Patsy Tinyette. All-compo, CM, blue ptd eyes, mld/ptd hair, jtd at shoulders and hips, c. 1933. Mark on doll reads: "FB 29" (head) and "FB 13" (body) **$95-110**

9½", Patsyette. All-compo, blue ptd eyes, brown ptd hair, CM, swivel head, jtd at shoulders and hips, bent right arm, c. 1931. Mark: "FB 11" **$95-110**

9½", Patsyette. Same Patsyette called the Colleen Moore Fairy Princess Doll. This beautifully dressed Patsyette came with a replica of Colleen Moore's famous miniature castle dollhouse **$400-450**

9½", Patsyette and Her Sewing Kit. Mint and all-original (other Patsyettes can be found in their original foreign costumes and are priced at **$95-100** each) **$200-250**

9½", Patsyette wins. These twins (boy and girl) came in a square flat suitcase with an assortment of clothes, hats, and shoes, c. 1931 (in 1932, Patsyettes had wigs) **$300-350**

10", Patsy Babykin. White version, all-compo, blue sleep eyes, CM, mld/ptd hair, swivel head, jtd at shoulders and hips, c. 1932. Mark: "FB 20" **$125-140**

10", Patsy Babykin. Black version, all-compo, black ptd eyes, CM, mld/ptd black hair with three black yarn braids, swivel head, jtd at shoulders and hips, c. 1932. Mark: "FB 20" (originally called Baby-Kins and marked "Patsy Baby") **$235-265**

11½", Patsykins. Patsy, Jr., all-compo, brown ptd eyes to the side, red ptd/mld hair, CM, swivel head, jtd at shoulders and hips, bent right arm, c. 1930. Mark: "FB 10". . **$95-110**

13½", Patsy. All-compo, swivel head, CM, ptd/mld hair, blue ptd eyes (some had sleep eyes), fully jointed body, no mark on the doll, marked box and all-original clothes, c. 1946-1949 . . . . **$55-65**

Author's note: In 1949, Patricia, Patsy Babykin, and Patsy Joan were given "magnetic" or "magic" hands. This rare feature adds $100 to the value of these dolls.

14", Patricia. All-compo, CM, green sleep eyes, red HHW, swivel head, jtd at shoulders and hips, c. 1932 (other Patricias had blue sleep eyes, brown eyes, brown wigs; Patricia came in six sizes with different faces). Mark: "FB 19" $125-145

14", Patsy. All-compo, CM, swivel head, mld/ptd hair and features, jtd at shoulders and hips, c. 1927. Mark: "FB 7" ... $95-110

14", Patsy. All-compo, CM, gray sleep eyes, brown HHW, swivel head, jtd at shoulders and hips, c. 1933. Mark: "FB 7" .. $125-140

17", Black Patsy Joan. No marks on doll, mark on box only, same characteristics as white version, box and all-original doll, c. 1946-1949 .... $75-85

17", Patsy Joan. All-compo, CM, mld/ptd hair, blue sleep eyes, mohair wig (some came without wigs), blue sleep eyes, fully jointed, no mark on doll, marked box and all-original clothes, c. 1946-1949............... $65-75

19", Patsy Ann. Patsy's big sister, all-compo, CM, blue tin sleep eyes, mld/ptd hair, jtd at shoulders and hips, c. 1929. Mark: "FB 40" (head) and "FB 8" (body) $145-160

19", Patsy Ann. All-compo, OM with four teeth, blue sleep eyes, blond caracul wig, dimpled chin, swivel head, jtd at shoulders and hips, c. 1933. Mark: "FB 8" $165-180

20", Patsy Joan. All-compo, CM, brown sleep eyes, mld/ptd hair, swivel head, jtd at shoulders and hips, bent right arm, c. 1930. Mark: "FB 16" $125-140

22", Lovums. This doll has a Patsy Lou unmarked compo head with unpainted hair on a Lovums shoulder plate, brown sleep eyes, CM, cloth body with cloth upper legs, compo arms and lower legs, c. 1928. Mark on shoulder plate: "FB 6" $100-125

22½", Patsy Lou. All-compo, blue-green sleep eyes, jtd at shoulders and hips, mld/ptd hair, c. 1929. Mark: "FB 43" $225-235

25", Patsy Ruth. Compo swivel head and limbs, CM, blue sleep eyes, cloth body, mohair wig, c. 1936. Mark: "FB 12" (head) and "FB 6" (body) $300-400

28", Patsy Mae. Compo swivel head and limbs, OM with four teeth, brown sleep eyes, HHW, swivel shoulder head, jtd at shoulders and hips, cloth kapok-stuffed body, c. 1934. Mark on doll reads: "FB 14" (head) and "FB 6" (body) $350-400

Late Patsys

These two late versions did not look like Patsy at all. They only used her name as a come-on. Nevertheless they are collected by Patsy collectors.

11", Patsy. All-vinyl, CM, sleep eyes, rooted Saran wig, fully jointed body, original rickrack-trimmed velveteen dress, tafetta panties, shoes and socks, wears a ribbon hair bow, c. 1959..................... $35-45

15", Patsy Ann. Rigisol vinyl, CM, sleep eyes, rooted Saran hair, fully jointed, original outfit, c. 1959. Mark: "FB 33" $52-53

Author's note: In 1936, colorless celluloid fingernails were added to Patsy, Patsy Joan, and Patsy Ann. This rare feature adds $100 to the value of these three dolls.

17
Paper Dolls

Movie Star Booklets

The most popular of the collectible paper doll sets continues to be those of the Hollywood movie stars, the most coveted being the glamorous early sets printed in 1930s. To command top dollar, a paper doll booklet must be perfect in every way and uncut. Paper dolls that have been cut and played with by children are still desirable. But again, to demand the most money the dolls must be intact (their ankles and wrists were easily broken) with complete wardrobes in good condition. The books listed in this section are all mint examples.

Carolyn Lee Cut-Out Dolls by Queen Holden, Whitman, 1943, Herron collection, $28.50.

1930s Booklets

All Aboard for Shut-Eye Town. AP65E, 1937.............................$36.50

All-Star Movie Cut-Outs 985. Whitman, 1934.............................. $38

Annette, Emilie, Marie, Cecile, Yvonne 1055. Whitman, 1936, individual books are sold separately......................... $37

Charlie McCarthy 995. Whitman, 1938. $36

The Dionne Quintuplets 998. Merrill, 1935.............................$37.50

The Dionne Quintuplets M3488. Merrill, 1935.............................$37.50

The Dionne Quintuplets. Dell, 1937.. $36.50

Jane Withers. Dell, 1938 .... $36

Jane Withers 977. Whitman, 1936 ..... $37

Jane Withers 996. Whitman, 1938 ..... $36

Movie Star Paper Dolls (Queen Holden) 900. Whitman, 1931 .... **$39.50**

Our Gang (Queen Holden) 900. Whitman, 1931 .... **$39.50**

Princess Paper Doll Book 2216. Saalfield, 1939 .... **$35.50**

Shirley Temple 1715. Saalfield, 1935. . . **$37.50**

Shirley Temple 1719. Saalfield, 1935. . . **$37.50**

Shirley Temple 1727. Saalfield, 1935. . . **$37.50**

Shirley Temple 1739. Saalfield, 1935. . . **$37.50**

Shirley Temple 1761. Saalfield, 1937. . . **$36.50**

Shirley Temple 1765. Saalfield, 1936. . . **$37**

Shirley Temple 1773. Saalfield, 1938. . . **$36**

Shirley Temple 1782. Saalfield, 1939. . . **$35.50**

Shirley Temple 2112. Saalfield, 1934. . . **$38**

Sonja Henie 3475. Merrill, 1939. . . . . **$35.50**

1940s Booklets

Alice Faye 4800. Merrill, 1941 . . . . . . **$29.50**

Ann Sothern 2438. Saalfield, 1943. . . **$28.50**

Ann Sothern 986. Whitman, 1944 . . . . . **$28**

Ava Gardner 965. Whitman, 1949 . . . **$25.50**

Baby Sandy 996. Whitman, 1940 . . . . . . **$30**

Baby Sandy 3426. Merrill, 1941 . . . . . **$29.50**

Bette Davis 4816. Merrill, 1942 . . . . **$29**

Betty Brewer 1016. Whitman, 1942 . . . . **$29**

Betty Field 332. Saalfield, 1943 . . . . . **$28.50**

Betty Grable 962. Whitman, 1946 . . . . . **$27**

Betty Grable 972. Whitman, 1942 . . . . . **$29**

Betty Grable 976. Whitman, 1943 . . . **$28.50**

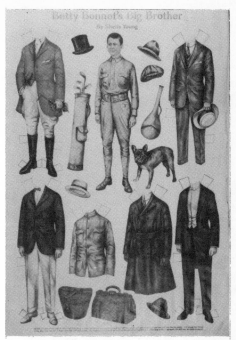

Betty Bonnet's Big Brother by Sheila Young, uncut and mint, Ladies Home Journal, *May, 1917, Herron collection, $25.*

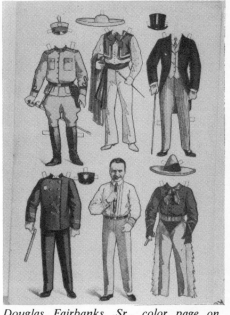

Douglas Fairbanks, Sr., color page on lightweight card, uncut, Herron collection, $25.

227

Betty Grable 976, front and back covers, Whitman, Herron collection, $28.50.

Betty Grable 989. Whitman, 1941 . . . **$29.50**

Bob Hope and Dorothy Lamour 976. Whitman, 1942 . . . . **$29**

Carmen Miranda 995. Whitman, 1942 . . **$29**

Carolyn Lee 984. Whitman, 1942 . . . . . . **$29**

Carolyn Lee 997. Whitman, 1943 . . . . **$28.50**

Chaplin and Goddard 2356. Saalfield, 1941 . . . . **$29.50**

Claudette Colbert 2451. Saalfield, 1943 . . . . **$28.50**

Claudette Colbert 2503. Saalfield, 1945 . . . . **$27.50**

Cora Sue Collins 1016. Whitman, 1942 . . . **$29**

Deanna Durbin 3480. Merrill, 1940 . . . . **$30**

Deanna Durbin 4804. Merrill, 1941 . . **$29.50**

Dinah Shore 977. Whitman, 1943 . . . **$28.50**

Dionne Quints 3488. Merrill, 1940 . . . . **$30**

Elizabeth Taylor 968. Whitman, 1949 . . **$25.50**

Errol Flynn (Sea Hawk) 967. Whitman, 1940 . . . . **$30**

Fanny Brice 991. Whitman, 1940 . . . . . . **$30**

Four Mothers and Their Babies (Lane Sisters, Gale Page) 968. Whitman, 1941 . . . . . **$29.50**

Gene Tierney 992. Whitman, 1947 . . . **$26.50**

Glenn Miller and Marion Hutton L1041. Lowe, 1942 . . . . **$29**

Gloria Jean 156. Saalfield, 1940 . . . . **$30**

Gloria Jean 1664. Saalfield, 1941 . . . . **$29.50**

Gloria Jean 1666. Saalfield, 1941 . . . . **$29.50**

Gone with the Wind 3404. Merrill, 1940 . . . **$30**

Gone with the Wind 3405. Merrill, 1940 . . . **$30**

Greer Garson 4848. Merrill, 1944 . . . . . **$28**

Hedy Lamarr 3482. Merrill, 1942 ..... **$29**

Hollywood Personalities L1049. Lowe, 1941 .... **$29.50**

Hour of Charm 1505. Saalfield, 1943. . . **$28.50**

Jane Withers 986. Whitman, 1941 . . . **$29.50**

Jane Withers 989. Whitman, 1940 ..... **$30**

Jeanette MacDonald 3460. Merrill, 1941 .... **$29.50**

Jeanette MacDonald 3461. Merrill, 1941 .... **$29.50**

Joan Carroll 2426. Saalfield, 1942 ..... **$29**

Judy Garland 980. Whitman, 1941 . . **$29.50**

Judy Garland 996. Whitman, 1945 . . **$27.50**

Judy Garland 999. Whitman, 1940 .... **$30**

King of Swing and Queen of Song (Benny Goodman and Peggy Lee) L1040. Lowe, 1942 .... **$29**

Lana Turner 964. Whitman, 1947 . . . **$26.50**

Lana Turner 975. Whitman, 1945 . . . **$27.50**

Lana Turner 988. Whitman, 1942 ..... **$29**

Let's Play House with the Dionne Quintuplets 3500. Merrill, 1940, one booklet for each child, booklets sold individually **$30**

Linda Darnell and Tyrone Power 3438. 1941 .... **$29.50**

Lucille Ball 2475. Saalfield, 1944 ...... **$28**

Margaret O'Brien 963. Whitman, 1946. . . **$27**

Margaret O'Brien 964. Whitman, 1946. . . **$27**

Margaret O'Brien 970. Whitman, 1944. . . **$28**

Mary Martin 1539. Saalfield, 1942 .... **$29**

Mary Martin 2492. Saalfield, 1944 .... **$28**

Movie Starlets 991. Whitman, 1942.... **$29**

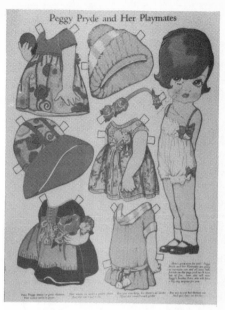

Peggy Pryde and Her Playmates, uncut, mint, Pictorial Review, *1926, Herron collection, $25.*

Boots and Her Buddies, Saalfield, 1943, Herron collection, $28.50.

229

Dolly Dingle's Little Friend Peggy, Pictorial Review, *May 1920, Herron collection.*

Quiz Kids 2430. Saalfield, 1942 .... **$29**

Rita Hayworth 1529. Saalfield, 1948... **$26**

Rita Hayworth 3478. Merrill, 1942 .... **$29**

Roy Rogers 995. Whitman, 1948 ...... **$26**

Shirley Temple 1787. Saalfield, 1940... **$30**

Shirley Temple 2425. Saalfield, 1942... **$29**

Sonja Henie 3418. Merrill, 1941..... **$29.50**

Sonja Henie 3492. Merrill, 1940....... **$30**

Virginia Weidler 1016. Whitman, 1942. .. **$29**

˒ Ziegfeld Girl 3466. Merrill, 1941 .... **$29.50**

1950s Booklets

Ann Blyth 2550. Merrill, 1953 ...... **$18.50**

Ann Sothern 4415. Saalfield, 1959... **$15.50**

Annette 1958. Whitman, 1956 .... **$17**

Annette 2083. Whitman, 1958 .... **$16**

Annie Oakley 1960. Whitman, 1956 ... **$17**

Annie Oakley 2043. Whitman, 1954 ... **$18**

Annie Oakley 2056. Whitman, 1955, with Tagg and Lofty **$17.50**

Arlene Dahl 1587. Saalfield, 1953 ... **$18.50**

Arlene Dahl 4311. Saalfield, 1953 ... **$18.50**

Ava Gardner 2108. Whitman, 1953 .. **$18.50**

Barbara Britton 4318. Saalfield, 1954 .. **$18**

Barbara Britton 5190. Saalfield, 1954 .. **$18**

Betty Grable 1558. Merrill, 1951 .... **$19.50**

Betty Grable 2552. Merrill, 1953 .... **$18.50**

Betty Hutton & Her Girls 2099. Whitman, 1951 .... **$19.50**

Bob Cummings Fashion Models 2732. Bonnie Brooks, 1958 .... **$16**

Carmen Miranda 1558. Saalfield, 1952. .. **$19**

Coronation Paper Dolls and Color Book 4450. Saalfield, 1953.............. **$18.50**

Cyd Charisse 2084. Whitman, 1956.... **$17**

Darlene (Gillespie). Aldon Industries, 1958............................... **$16**

Davy Crockett 1943. Whitman, 1955... **$17.50**

Debbie Reynolds. Dell, 1953. .... **$18.50**

Debbie Reynolds 1178. Whitman, 1953. .... **$18.50**

Debbie Reynolds 1955. Whitman, 1955........................... **$17.50**

Debbie Reynolds 1955. Whitman, 1957........................... **$16.50**

Debra Paget. Dell, 1958 .... **$16**

Diana Lynn 2611. Saalfield, 1955 ... **$17.50**

Dinah Shore 1963. Whitman, 1958 .... **$16**

Dinah Shore 2042. Whitman, 1954 .... **$18**

Dinah Shore 2060. Whitman, 1956 .... **$17**

Dinah Shore/George Montgomery 1970. Whitman, 1959 .... **$15.50**

Doris Day 1179. Whitman, 1954 ...... **$18**

Doris Day 1952. Whitman, 1955 .... **$17.50**

Doris Day 1952. Whitman, 1956 ...... **$17**

Doris Day 1977. Whitman, 1957 .... **$16.50**

Doris Day 2103. Whitman, 1952 ...... **$19**

Ed "Kookie" Byrnes 2085. Whitman, 1959 .... **$15.50**

Elaine Stewart. Dell, 1954 .... **$18**

Elaine Stewart 2048. Whitman, 1955. .. **$17.50**

Elizabeth Taylor 1177. Whitman, 1953. **$18.50**

Elizabeth Taylor 1193. Whitman, 1952 .. **$19**

Elizabeth Taylor 1951. Whitman, 1955. **$17.50**

Elizabeth Taylor 2057. Whitman, 1956 .. **$17**

Elizabeth Taylor 2057. Whitman, 1957. **$16.50**

Elizabeth Taylor 2112. Whitman, 1954.. **$18**

Emmett Kelley (Punch-Outs)........ **$15.50**

Esther Williams 1563. Merrill, 1950 .... **$20**

Esther Williams 2553. Merrill, 1953 . **$18.50**

Eve Arden 2746. Saalfield, 1956....... **$17**

Eve Arden 4310. Saalfield, 1953..... **$18.50**

Evelyn Rudie 4446. Saalfield, 1958 .... **$16**

Evelyn Rudie 4475. Saalfield, 1958 .... **$16**

Faye Emerson 1557. Saalfield, 1952 ... **$19**

Gale Storm 2061. Whitman, 1958 ..... **$16**

Gale Storm 2089. Whitman, 1959 ... **$15.50**

Gene Autry at Melody Ranch 1184. Whitman, 1951........................... **$19.50**

Gene Autry's Melody Ranch 990. Whitman, 1950............................. **$20**

Gigi Perreau 2605. Saalfield, 1951 ... **$19.50**

Gisele MacKenzie 4421. Saalfield, 1957........................... **$16.50**

Gisele MacKenzie 4475. Saalfield, 1958 . **$16**

Grace Kelly 2049. Whitman, 1955 ... **$17.50**

Grace Kelly 2609. Whitman, 1956 ..... **$17**

Hedy Lamarr 2600. Saalfield, 1951 .. **$19.50**

Honeymooners 2560. Lowe, 1956 ..... **$17**

Hopalong Cassidy 2198. Whitman, 1951........................... **$19.50**

Hopalong Cassidy 2198. Whitman, 1951........................... **$19.50**

Jane Powell 1171. Whitman, 1952..... **$19**

Jane Powell 1171. Whitman, 1953... **$18.50**

Jane Powell 1185. Whitman, 1951... **$19.50**

Jane Powell 2055. Whitman, 1955... **$17.50**

Jane Powell 2085. Whitman, 1957... **$16.50**

Jane Russell 2651. Saalfield, 1955 ... **$17.50**

Janet Leigh 2554. Merrill, 1953 ..... **$18.50**

Janet Lennon 1956. Whitman, 1959........................... **$15.50**

Janet Lennon 1964. Whitman, 1958..... **$16**

Joan Caulfield 2725. Saalfield, 1953 . **$18.50**

Joanne Woodward 4441. Saalfield, 1958............................. **$16**

Judy Holliday 1591. Saalfield, 1954 ... **$18**

Julie Andrews 4474. Saalfield, 1958 ... **$16**

June Allyson 970. Whitman, 1950 ..... **$20**

June Allyson 1173. Whitman, 1953 .. **$18.50**

June Allyson 1956. Whitman, 1955 .. **$17.50**

June Allyson 2089. Whitman, 1957 .. **$16.50**

June and Stu Erwin 1592. Saalfield, 1954............................. **$18**

Kim Novak 4408. Saalfield, 1957.... **$16.50**

Kim Novak 4429. Saalfield, 1958...... **$16**

Laraine Day 2731. Saalfield, 1953 ... **$18.50**

Lassie 1965. Whitman, 1959 .... **$15.50**

Lennon Sisters 1979. Whitman, 1958 .. **$16**

Lennon Sisters 1991. Whitman, 1959........................... **$15.50**

Linda Darnell 1584. Saalfield, 1953.. **$18.50**

Linda (Hughes) 1957. Whitman, 1957........................... **$16.50**

Loretta Young 4352. Saalfield, 1956 ... **$17**

Lucille Ball and Desi Arnaz 2101. Whitman, 1953........................... **$18.50**

Lucille Ball and Desi Arnaz with Little Ricky 2116. Whitman, 1953 .... **$18.50**

Marge and Gower Champion 1966. Whitman, 1959........................... **$15.50**

Marilyn Monroe 4323. Saalfield, 1954 .. **$18**

Martha Hyer 4423. Saalfield, 1958 .... **$16**

Mary Hartline 1175. Whitman, 1953.. **$18.50**

Mary Hartline 2044. Whitman, 1955.. **$17.50**

Mary Hartline 2104. Whitman, 1952... **$19**

Mary Martin 2601. Saalfield, 1952 .... **$19**

McGuire Sisters 1938. Whitman, 1959........................... **$15.50**

MGM Starlets 2060. Whitman, 1951 . **$19.50**

Mouseketeer Cut-Outs 1974. Whitman, 1957........................... **$16.50**

My Little Margie 2737. Whitman, 1954 . **$18**

Natalie Wood 1962. Whitman, 1957 .. **$16.50**

Natalie Wood 2086. Whitman, 1958 ... **$16**

Oklahoma 438. Golden Press, 1956.... **$17**

Oklahoma 1954. Whitman, 1956 ...... **$17**

Ozzie & Harriet with David & Ricky 4319. Saalfield, 1954 .... **$18**

Pat Boone, 1966. Whitman, 1959.... **$15.50**

Pat Crowley 2055. Whitman, 1955 .. **$17.50**

Patience and Prudence 1807. Abbot, 1959........................... **$15.50**

Patti Page 2406. Lowe, 1957........ **$16.50**

Patti Page 2488. Lowe, 1958......... **$16**

Pier Angeli. Dell, 1955............ **$17.50**

Piper Laurie 2551. Merrill, 1953 .... **$18.50**

Polly Bergen 4442. Saalfield, 1958..... **$16**

Rhonda Fleming 5191. Saalfield, 1954 .. **$18**

Ricky Nelson 2081. Whitman, 1959.. **$15.50**

Rock Hudson 2087. Whitman, 1957 .. **$16.50**

Rosemary Clooney 1256. Lowe **$16**

Rosemary Clooney 2487. Lowe, 1958 .. **$16**

Roy Rogers and Dale Evans 998. Whitman, 1950............................. **$20**

Roy Rogers and Dale Evans 1172. Whitman, 1952 .... **$19**

Roy Rogers and Dale Evans 1186. Whitman, 1950............................. **$20**

Roy Rogers and Dale Evans 1950. Whitman, 1954 .... **$18**

Roy Rogers and Dale Evans 1950. Whitman, 1957 .... **$16.50**

Roy Rogers and Dale Evans 2118. Whitman, 1953 .... **$18.50**

Sandra Dee 4413. Saalfield, 1959.... **$15.50**

Shari Lewis 4447. Saalfield, 1958.... **$15.50**

Sheree North 4420. Saalfield, 1957 .. **$16.50**

Shirley Temple 300. Gabriel **$16**

Shirley Temple 303. Gabriel **$16**

Shirley Temple 4420. Saalfield, 1959 . **$15.50**

Shirley Temple 4440. Saalfield **$16**

Shirley Temple Playkit 6032. Saalfield, 1958 .... **$16**

Spanky and Darla 2759. Saalfield, 1957 .... **$16.50**

Story Princess (Alene Dalton) 1727. Saalfield, 1957 .... **$16.50**

Vera Miles 2086. Whitman, 1957.... **$16.50**

Virginia Mayo 4422. Saalfield, 957 .. **$16.50**

1960s Booklets

Angela Cartwright 4101. Transogram Toy Co., 1961 .... **$9.50**

Annette 1953. Whitman, 1964 .... **$8**

Annette 1956. Whitman, 1952 .... **$9**

Annette 1971. Whitman, 1960 .... **$10**

Annette 4621. Whitman, 1962 .... **$9**

Annette in Hawaii 1969. Whitman, 1961 .... **$9.50**

Beatles 1938. Whitman, 1964 .... **$8**

Beverly Hillbillies 1949. Whitman, 1964 .... **$8.50**

Beverly Hillbillies 1955. Whitman, 1964 .. **$8**

Bewitched 144. Magic Wand, 1965 ... **$7.50**

Blondie 4434. Saalfield, 1968 .... **$8**

Brenda Lee 2785. Lowe, 1961........ **$9.50**

Brenda Lee 4360. Merry Mfg., 1964 .... **$8**

Buffy 1985. Whitman, 1968............ **$6**

Carol Heiss Color & Cut-Out 1133. Whitman, 1961 .... **$9.50**

Carol Heiss 1964. Whitman, 1961 .... **$9.50**

Carol Lynley 2089. Saalfield, 1960 .... **$10**

Caroline (Kennedy) 109. Magic Wand . **$9.50**

Cleopatra 1000. Blaise, 1963 .... **$8.50**

Connie Francis 1956. Whitman, 1963 .. **$8.50**

Connie Stevens 4614. Whitman, 1961 .. **$9.50**

Cynthia Pepper 1919A. Watkins/Strathmore, 1963 .... **$8.50**

Debbie Reynolds 1948. Whitman, 1962 .. **$9**

Debbie Reynolds 1956. Whitman, 1960 . **$10**

Dennis the Menace (Jay North) 1991. Whitman, 1960 .... **$10**

Dennis the Menace 1996. Whitman, 1960 .... **$10**

Donna Reed 2743. Saalfield, 1961.... **$9.50**

Donna Reed 6403. Merry Mfg., 1964 ... **$8**

Dorothy Provine 1964. Whitman, 1962 .. **$9**

Dr. Kildare 2740. Lowe, 1962.......... **$9**

Elly May 1819. Watkins/Strathmore, 1963 .... **$8.50**

Family Affair 4767. Whitman, 1968 .... **$6**

Fess Parker 4356. ArtCraft, 1964....... **$8**

Finian's Rainbow 1336. Saalfield, 1968 .. **$6**

First Lady (Jacqueline Kennedy) 204. Magic Wand, 1963 .... **$8.50**

Flying Nun 5131. Saalfield, 1968 .... **$6**

Gidget (Sally Field) 601. Standard Toy Craft, 1965 .... **$7.50**

Gina Gillespie 1347. Saalfield, 1962 ..... **$9**

Ginny Tiu 2089. Whitman, 1962 .... **$9**

Green Acres 1979. Whitman, 1967 .... **$6.50**

Green Acres 4773. Whitman, 1968 ...... **$6**

Happiest Millionaire 4487. Saalfield, 1967 .... **$6.50**

Hayley Mills 1955. Whitman, 1965 ... **$7.50**

Hayley Mills 1960. Whitman, 1964 ..... **$8**

Hootenanny 4440. Saalfield, 1964 ...... **$8**

Janet Lennon 1948. Whitman, 1961 .. **$9.50**

Janet Lennon 4613. Whitman, 1962 .... **$9**

Judy Doll (Miss Teenage America) 4439. Saalfield, 1964 .... **$8**

Karen 1357. Saalfield, 1965 .... **$7.50**

Lassie (Robert Bray) 1926. Whitman, 1966 .... **$7**

Laugh-In 1325. Saalfield, 1969 .... **$5.50**

Lennon Sisters 1995. Whitman, 1963 .. **$8.50**

Lucy 1963. Whitman, 1964 .... **$8**

Lucy 4610. Whitman, 1963 .... **$8.50**

Lucy & Her TV Family 1991. Whitman, 1963 .... **$8.50**

Mark Antony 1001. Blaise, 1963 ..... **$8.50**

Mary Poppins GF238. Golden Press, 1964 .... **$8**

Mary Poppins 1982. Whitman, 1964 .... **$8**

Miss World (Ann Sidney) 1820-6. Watkins/Strathmore, 1965 .... **$7.50**

Mod Fashion (Jane Fonda) 1369. Saalfield, 1966 .... **$7**

Molly Bee 2091. Whitman, 1962 .... **$9**

Monkees. YWP/London, 1966 .... **$7**

Mouseketeers 1974. Whitman, 1963 .. **$8.50**

Munsters 1959. Whitman, 1966 .... **$7**

My Fair Lady 401. Standard Toy Craft **$7.50**

My Fair Lady 2960-2. Ottenheimer, 1965 .... **$7.50**

My Fair Lady 2961-0. Ottenheimer, 1965 .... **$7.50**

My Fair Lady 5860-2. Ottenheimer, 1965 .... **$7.50**

National Velvet 1948. Whitman, 1962 ... **$9**

Nurses 1975. Whitman, 1963 .... **$8.50**

Patty Duke 1991. Whitman, 1964 ...... **$8**

Patty Duke 1991. Whitman, 1965 .... **$7.50**

Patty Duke 4441. Milton Bradley, 1963 .... **$8.50**

Peggy Lee 370. Treasure Books, 1961 .... **$9.50**

Pepe & the Senoritas (Cantinflas) 4408. Saalfield, 1961 .... **$9.50**

Petticoat Junction 1954. Whitman, 1964 . **$8**

Pollyanna (Hayley Mills) GF163. Golden Press, 1960 .... **$8**

Shari Lewis 6043. Saalfield, 1962 .... **$9**

Shirley Temple 301. Gabriel, 1961 .... **$9.50**

Tabatha (Bewitched) 115. Magic Wand, 1966 .... **$7**

Tammy Marihugh 715. Saalfield, 1961 . **$9.50**

Tarzan (Ron Ely) 1933. Whitman, 1967 .... **$6.50**

That Girl (Marlo Thomas) 6066. Saalfield, 1967 .... **$6.50**

Tuesday Weld 5112. Whitman, 1960 ... **$10**

Twiggy 1999. Whitman, 1967 .... **$6.50**

White House 4475. ArtCraft, 1969 ... **$5.50**

Wonderful World of the Brothers Grimm. Saalfield, 1963 .... **$8.50**

Zorro (Guy Williams) 3D, Aldon Industries **$7**

1970s Booklets

Brady Bunch 4787. Whitman, 1972 ..... **$4**

Buffy and Jody 4767. Whitman, 1970 .. **$5.50**

Curiosity Shop 4343. ArtCraft, 1971 .. **$4.50**

Dodie 5115. ArtCraft, 1971 .... **$4.50**

HeeHaw (Jeannine Riley) 5139. ArtCraft, 1971 .... **$4.50**

Julia 5140. ArtCraft, 1971 .... **$4.50**

Julia 6055. Saalfield, 1970 .... **$5**

Lost Horizon 5112. ArtCraft, 1973 ... **$3.50**

Nanny and the Professor 5114. ArtCraft, 1970-1971 .... **$4-5**

Partridge Family 5137. ArtCraft, 1971 . **$4.50**

Susan Dey 4218. ArtCraft, 1972 .... **$4**

Tricia Paper Doll 1248. Saalfield, 1970 ... **$5**

Additional Celebrity Cutouts

Amos and Andy. Pepsodent Co., 1930 .... **$7.50**

Clark Gable & Jimmy Steward Movie Star Paper Dolls. Series, 1935 .... **$5 each**

Early Movie Star Sets. Saalfield, 1915-1920. A forerunner of their 1930s sets. Charlie Chaplin, Mary Miles Minter, "Fatty" Arbuckle .... **$10 each**

Elizabeth's Coronation Gown. *The American Weekly Magazine,* March 15, 1953, in full color **$7.50**

Hollywood Dollies, Inc. Series of miniature movie star paper dolls in full color on card in glassene envelope, 1925 .... **$3.50 each**

Movie and Muny Opera Dressographs. 1932-1933 .... **$7.50 each**

Movie Star Cut-Outs. Writing tablet covers, oversized heads, 1930s .... **$10 each**

Percy Reeves' Jumbo Movy Dols. 1920 .... **$12.50 each**

Percy Reeves' Movy-Dols. Magazine sheets from *Photoplay,* 1919 .... **$10 each**

Screen Life Movie Magazine's "Star Dolls." 1941 .... **$10 each**

The Dionne Quintuplet Set. Mint, uncut, Boston Post NEA Service, Inc., May 1935 .... **$10 each**

The Ladies' World "Movie" Dolls. Full-color set includes Mary Pickford, Marie Doro, Mae Murray, 1916-1918 .... **$15 each**

The Milwaukee Journal Movie Star Paper Doll Series. 1935-1936 .... **$5 each**

Author's note: Paper dolls dated 1974 bring $3; 1975, $2.50; 1976, $2.00; 1977, $1.50; 1978, $1; 1979, $0.50; 1980, $0.25. In general, paper dolls devaluate in price until they, too, earn a certain amount of "age" prestige.

The Woman's Home Companion Movie Children Paper Dolls. This set includes Baby Peggy, Jackie Coogan, Our Gang, 1925 .... **$12.50 each**

Who Are They? Movie Star Series. *The Delineater.* Set includes Doug Fairbanks, Mary Pickford, Francis X. Bushman, 1971 .... **$15 each**

Jenny Lind (boxed set). Swedish singer, 3⅞, c. 1850s .... **$200 complete**

Marie Taglioni (boxed set). French ballet dancer, 4", c. 1840s .... **$200 complete**

Marie Taglioni (boxed set). French ballet dancer, 5⅜", c. 1840s .... **$200 complete**

Jenny Lind (boxed set). Swedish singer, 7", c. 1850s. (There is a rumor that there is a thprd set which would also run in this price range if complete) .... **$200 complete**

Fanny Elssler (boxed set). Viennese dancer, 9⅛", c. 1840s .... **$400 complete**

Lucile Grahn (boxed set). Early British dancer, 9⅛", c. 1840s .... **$500 complete**

Marie Taglioni (boxed set). French ballet dancer, 9⅛", c. 1840s .... **$200 complete**

Old Standards

Alice in Wonderland (Charlotte Henry) 993. Whitman, 1933 .... **$38.50**

Alice in Wonderland Stand-Ups 964. Saalfield, 1934 .... **$38**

Blondie 963. Whitman, 1949 .... **$22.50**

Blondie 967. Whitman, 1947 .... **$26.50**

Blondie 967. Whitman, 1948 .... **$26**

Blondie 974. Whitman, 1950 .... **$20**

Blondie 975. Whitman, 1943 .... **$28.50**

Blondie 981. Whitman, 1944 .... **$28**

Blondie 982. Whitman, 1940 .... **$30**

Blondie 987. Whitman, 1945 .... **$27.50**

Blondie 993. Whitman, 1945 .... **$27.50**

Blondie 1174. Whitman, 1953 ...... **$18.50**

Blondie 1191. Whitman, 1949 ...... **$25.50**

Blondie 1191. Whitman, 1952 .... **$19**

Blondie 2054. Whitman, 1955 ...... **$17.50**

Blondie in the Movies 979. Whitman, 1941 .... **$29.50**

Blondie Introducing Cookie 996. Whitman, 1941 .... **$29.50**

Bonnie Braids 1559. Saalfield, 1951 .. **$19.50**

Boots and Her Buddies 330. Saalfield, 1943 .... **$28.50**

Brenda Starr 4438. Saalfield, 1964 ...... **$8**

Bringing Up Father 110. Hingees, 1944 . **$28**

Buster Brown & Tige. J. Ottomann Litho Co., c. early 1900s **$50**

Daisy Mae and Lil' Abner 1549. Saalfield, 1951 .... **$19.50**

Daisy Mae with Lil' Abner 280. Saalfield, 1942 .... **$29**

Flapper Fanny 9547. Whitman, 1938 .. **$36**

Fritzi Ritz 1259. Lowe, 1942 .... **$29**

Jane Arden 2408. Saafield, 1942 ...... **$29**

Lil' Abner and Daisy Mae 215. Saalfield, 1941 .... **$29.50**

Little Orphan Annie 299. Saalfield, 1943 .... **$28.50**

Little Orphan Annie & Mickey 938. Whitman, 1931 .... **$39.50**

Popeye 980. Whitman, 1937 .... **$36.50**

Prince Valiant & Princess Aleta 1601. Saalfield, 1954 .... **$18**

Sapphire (Terry & the Pirates) 907. Reuben H. Lilja............................... **$19**

Smokey Stover 108. Hingees, 1944 .... **$28**

Terry & the Pirates 105. Hingees, 1944 .. **$28**

Tillie the Toiler 997. Whitman, 1942... **$29**

Winnie Winkle and Her Paris Costumes D115. Gabriel, 1932 .... **$39**

Early Characters from Films, Radio, and Storybooks

Annie Laurie L1030. Lowe, 1941 .... **$29.50**

Baby Sparkle Plenty 5160. Saalfield, 1948............................... **$26**

Bonnie Braids 1559. Saalfield, 1951 .. **$19.50**

Fantasia Cut-Out Book 950. Whitman, 1940............................... **$30**

Ferdinand the Bull 925. Whitman, 1938 . **$36**

Kewpie kin 1313. Saalfield, 1967...... **$6.50**

Kewpies with Ragsy & Ritzy 969. Whitman, 1932............................... **$39**

Little Women L1030. Lowe, 1941 ... **$29.50**

Little Women 994. Whitman, 1934 .... **$38**

Lone Ranger and Silver 965. Whitman, 1940............................... **$30**

Pinocchio 6879. Whitman, 1939..... **$35.50**

Raggedy Ann & Raggedy Andy 946. Whitman, 1935........................ **$37.50**

Raggedy Ann & Raggedy Andy 2754. Saalfield, 1957 .... **$16.50**

Snow White & the Seven Dwarfs 970. Whitman, 1938 .... **$36**

Snow White & the Seven Dwarfs 2185. Whitman, 1938 .... **$36**

Three Little Pigs 989. Whitman, 1933............................... **$38.50**

Winnie the Pooh/Christopher Robin 947. Whitman, 1935 .... **$37.50**

Miscellaneous Cutout Sets

A Friend Paper Doll. Boucher Associates, 1967............................... **$6.50**

Angel 2755. Saalfield, 1957 .... **$16.50**

Archie's Girls 2764. Lowe, 1964 .... **$8**

Betsy McCall 1360. Saalfield, 1965 and 1968............................... **$7.50**

Betsy McCall 1969. Whitman, 1971... **$4.50**

Howdy Doody Puppet Show 2111. Whitman, 1952............................... **$19**

Juliet Jones 1351. Saalfield, 1964....... **$8**

Little Audrey 125. Gabriel, 1960 ...... **$10**

Little Lulu 1970. Whitman, 1971 ..... **$4.50**

Little Lulu 1999. Whitman, 1960 ...... **$10**

Nancy 1971. Whitman, 1971 .... **$4.50**

Pebbles and Bam Bam 1983. Whitman, 1964................................. **$8**

Sweetie Pie 2482. Lowe, 1958......... **$16**

Trixie 3920. Lowe, 1961 .... **$9.50**

Walter Lantz Cartoon Stars 1344. Saalfield, 1963............................... **$8.50**

Famous Faces Cutouts and Others

Activated Famous Actress Paper Dolls. Lillian Russell, Ada Rehan, jtd at shoulders and hips, each undressed, c. 1890. Watch for reproductions of these dolls!...... **$25 each**

Art Supplement to the *Boston Sunday Globe.* Celebrities of the day, c. 1895..... **$20 each**

Art Supplement to the *New York Sunday Telegram.* Stage star set, c. 1895 .. **$20 each**

Art Supplement to the *Philadelphia Inquirer.* Paper dolls depict international theatrical personages, c. 1895 .... **$20 each**

Bradley's Tru-Life Paper Dolls. Boxed set, twelve paper dolls, easel standards, eight sheets of brown paper patterns for each doll, paper, glazed, tweeds, tissues, complete, c. 1914............................. **$100**

Colonial Williamsburg Paper Dolls. Six paper dolls with costumes, c. 1939 .... **$35 set**

Comic Strip Paper Dolls. Boots, Blondie, Jane Arden, Dixie Dugan, Flash Gordon, Dale Arden, Mopsy Modes, Tillie the Toiler, Brenda Starr, Stella Clinker, Sofie Hoofer, Winnie Winkle, pre-historic cut-outs (these cutouts usually appeared in the Sunday comic strips either in full color or black and white), c. 1930-1950 ($5-10 each, if uncut).. **$3-5 each**

Dennison's Dolls and Dresses. Boxed set, jtd paper dolls, patterns, tissue, c. 1890s... **$50**

Dolls Who are Men of Mark. c. 1894, sold separately .... **$20 each**

Elsie Dinsmore. The Candyline Co., one paper doll, four costumes, c. 1918 ... **$12.50**

Famous Queens Set. Includes Martha Washington, Queen Victoria, Queen Louise, Marie Antoinette, their elaborate wardrobes on sheets, c. 1894 .... **$30 each**

Forbes Doll. *Boston Sunday Globe,* 1895, tinted on card, head with long tab for insertion in costume slots................ **$25 each**

Frank Leslie's Ladies' Magazine Paper Doll. 1866, rare .... **$135 complete**

Godey Children. First magazine paper dolls in color, rare, November 1859.. **$150 complete**

Grace Drayton's Dolly Dingle Paper Doll Series. *Pictorial Review,* pre-1920, **$25-30** (1920-1930, **$15-20;** early 1930s, **$12.50-17.50**), pages must be uncut, in good condi-

tion, and complete. (*Pictorial Review* with paper doll page intact, **$35.** This price also applies to other magazines with paper doll pages.) Cut Dolly Dingle with costume, **$5-10** complete, depending on the number of original costumes included **$20-25**

Little Colonel Doll Book. L. C. Page & Co., 1910, represents characters and costumes from the books by Annie Fellows Johnson, nine dolls and costumes...... **$75 complete**

Little Folks Magazine Paper Dolls from Famous Paintings. Blue Boy, Baby Stuart, c. 1916 .... **$12.50 each**

M.C. & K's Family of Seven Dolls. Lithographed head-and-shoulder dolls, double-cut "standing" costumes, complete, c. 1895 .... **$65 set**

McLoughlin XXXX Coffee Famous Queens Set. Set includes Martha Washington, Mary Queen of Scots, Queen Elizabeth.. **$20 each**

Mr. & Mrs. Tom Thumb Set. McLoughlin Brothers, N.Y., c. 1875 .... **$65 each**

Olde Deerfield Dolls (Little Captives of 1704). Dolls lithographed in color by a six-tone process. Each doll and costume printed on separate sheet, folder holds the sheets, also includes 3" x 4" double slip case which contains six tiny booklets titled with the name of the child whose story it tells. Stories written by Mrs. Hyde, very rare, must be complete, Mrs. Hyde of Deerfield, c. 1919...... **$300**

Palmer Cox Brownies Cut-Outs. Lion Coffee, 1898....................... **$12.50 each**

Polly's Paper Playmates. Betty Bonnet, Peggy Perkins, Betty Bobbs Family, Polly Pratt, Margery May, uncut .... **$25 each**

Prima Donnas as Christmas Dolls. *New York Sunday Herald,* opera personages of the time, Melba, Emma Eames, c. 1894 .... **$20 each**

Raphael Tuck's Favorite Faces Series of Dressing Dolls. Set depicts nine stage stars, elaborate wardrobes, c. 1890s ..... **$50 each**

Sheila Young's Lettie Lane Paper Doll Series. Cut paper dolls with complete costumes (choice set), October 1980-December 1911 (mint uncut sheets, **$25-35**) **$10-15**

238

Stage Folk as Children's Dolls. c. 1895 .. **$20**

Supplement to the *Boston Sunday Herald* Paper Dolls. Blond 10½" lady doll (March 24, 1895) in corset and four-ruffle petticoat, brunette 10½" lady doll (June 16, 1895) in same pose. Thirty-eight costumes were published (on Sundays) over a period of time for these two lovely ladies, costumes were interchangeable, gorgeous set ..... **$125 set**

The House of Hapsburg. Embossed Royal Family set, Kaiser Wilhelm of Germany, Prinz Eitel Friedrich, Kronprinz Friedrich Wilhelm, plus furniture, towns .... **$25 each**

The House of Windsor. Royal Family set, includes Queen Alexandra, as well as King Edward .... **$30 each**

Theda Bara Paper Doll. Osborn/Woods-Serendipity 11, 1916 .... **$25**

Miscellaneous Tuck Sets

Paperdolls for Little Girls. Serene Sybil, Sweet Sybil, Lovely Lily, Gentle Gladys, Playful Polly, boxed sets, usually one lovely doll and four costumes and hats, c. 1901-1910 .... **$50 complete**

Paper Toys for Little Boys. Action figures of children at play, paper soldiers, boys with animals, boys and girls on horseback, c. 1893-1901 .... **$20 each**

Author's note: Paper doll pages appeared in many early American magazines including *Ladies Home Journal, Good Housekeeping, Woman's Home Companion, Delineator, McCall's, Pictorial Review, Our Young Folks,* and *The Housekeeper.* Uncut paper doll pages from these magazines average $35-20 each page, $35 for a magazine with a mint paper doll.

Meet the Author

R. Lane Herron is such an internationally recognized authority on dolls that he needs no introduction. His hundreds of widely quoted articles written for every major antiques publication in this country and abroad, plus his excellent book, *Much Ado About Dolls,* have firmly established his expert reputation in the doll-collecting field. Herron is also a skilled dollmaker who has created beautiful portrait dolls of many famous people.

Born in San Francisco and the son of an antiques fancier, his early interest in antique dolls was stimulated at a time in life when most children are merely playing with toys, not wondering where they came from or who made them. From his high school days to the present time, Herron has been a real student of antique dolls. His formidable knowledge can be termed truly encyclopedic.

A souvenir booklet, comprised solely of Herron's articles on the subject of celebrity dolls, will be presented to members attending the national convention of the United Federation of Doll Clubs in Sacramento, California, in May of 1982.